MW01288932

To Rebecca

Karl C. Adams

Wake of the Wind Dancer

From Sea to Shining Sea,
By Paddle and Shoe

KARL ADAMS

iUniverse, Inc.
New York   Bloomington

iUniverse books may be ordered through booksellers or by contacting:

iUniverse
1663 Liberty Drive
Bloomington, IN 47403
www.iuniverse.com
1-800-Authors (1-800-288-4677)

Because of the dynamic nature of the Internet, any Web addresses or links contained in this book may have changed since publication and may no longer be valid. The views expressed in this work are solely those of the author and do not necessarily reflect the views of the publisher, and the publisher hereby disclaims any responsibility for them.

ISBN: 978-1-4401-6077-6 (sc)
ISBN: 978-1-4401-6076-9 (ebook)
ISBN: 978-1-4401-6075-2 (hc)

Printed in the United States of America

iUniverse rev. date: 9/15/2009

TABLE OF CONTENTS

CHAPTER 1
PLANNING

The Wake of The Wind Dancer
By Karl Adams

When I was launched into this world I brought with me certain characteristics: a passion for adventure, a desire to see what was over the horizon, and a love of travel by water. A car or motorboat couldn't take me where I wanted to go, but a paddle, a sail, and a strong pair of legs could take me anywhere in the world.

In my youth, whenever I was unable to participate in an adventure of my own, I would resort to reading books of the early explorers. I would have liked to have lived in that era. The migration of humans was the greatest adventure of all times. Early man drifted out of Africa and went north across Europe and Asia until they came to Northeast Siberia. Then, twenty to forty thousand years ago, they crossed over into what is now North America. After early man reached what is now Alaska, they started moving south and east. How long it took them to reach Florida, I have not been able to learn, but the Seminole Native Americans were there to greet the first Europeans.

In 1513, Ponce de Leon landed on the east coast of what is now Florida. Thinking he was exploring another island, he sailed around the tip of Florida to the west coast. His exploration of Florida was cut short by a Seminole arrow. Spain's next two candidates for the conquest of North America were Narváez and Núñez Cabeza de Vaca. In 1528, they landed on the west coast of Florida and moved north. After eight years, only Vaca and three others still survived. That set the stage for Desoto. In 1539, Hernando de Soto landed on the north coast of Florida near what is now Tallahassee. Once on shore he moved inland and looped around west to the Mississippi River, fighting Native Americans all the way. Hernando de Soto was the first European to reach the river. Unfortunately, he contracted a fever and died. His body was deposited in the Mississippi... Europe's first contribution to its pollution.

Things remained static for a few years while the whole eastern seaboard filled up with Europeans. Then the new Americans got into the act. Captain Robert Gray sailed around the horn of South America and up the west coast to where he found a mighty river. In May 1792, he sailed his vessel the *Columbia Rediviva* across the bar and named the river the Columbia after his ship. He anchored near Tongue Point, explored up river about thirty miles, and then left.

When George Vancouver learned of Gray's discovery, he dispatched his escort vessel the *Catham* with Lieutenant Broughton in command. He anchored near a sand island on the backside of what is now Cape Disappointment. He took a group of his men and two rowboats and rowed one hundred miles up the river. Then, from 1803 to 1805, Lewis and Clark made their epic journey: the Voyage of Discovery. This made the connection linking the Atlantic southeast with the Pacific Northwest. Thus, it took the Europeans 282 years to make the journey across the continent.

Reading about this history as a kid fired my imagination. I started daydreaming about a journey following those early explorers with a single trek from sea to shining sea. In the years which followed my youth, I spent twenty-three years in the military; I participated in three wars, visited three oceans and sixteen of earth's major seas, and explored the byways and waterways of over thirty countries.

In 1985, I retired from my job at a water treatment plant. My wife, Ruth, and I readied our boat, the *Sea Venture*, a thirty-eight-foot cutter rigged sloop, for a trip north to Alaska from Portland, Oregon. When we reached a point a little north of Victoria, Canada, I discovered the engine wouldn't start. I had to put about and sail back to Port Townsend, Washington, to make repairs. By the time I had the repairs completed, the summer was gone and so was my bank account. I was forced to sail back home and find part-time work to pump up my cruising fund.

I found a job in a yuppie parking lot guarding prestigious cars belonging to the members of the Willamette Athletic Club. The club lies a block from the Willamette River. So, while I was working, I would gaze at the river and dream of all the places it could take me. This experience awakened in me my old childhood fantasy of a journey across America by boat. Since Ruth was working full time, I was left with time on my hands.

On my off-duty time, I would go to the library and research the route from Oregon to Florida. I studied what would be of interest on a trip of that nature; geology, weather patterns, reptiles, and insects. Anything I could think of a person

3

would encounter on this journey. Was I planning on doing this adventure myself? No, I had a family and thought it would be inconceivable that I would ever to able to do this trek. I was simply feeding my fantasy with facts. I had estimated the distance to be about 5,500 miles, plus or minus one hundred. How long it would take would depend on how fast a person could paddle.

At that time I was going back and forth to work using my old, two-man, folding kayak that I had carried all over the world. Ruth and I lived on board our sailboat. In the morning, I would step off the boat, get into the kayak, and paddle down river. When I would get within a half mile of the club, I would go ashore, put two wheels under the boat, pull it up to the club, and park it by the bike rack. I figured a person could use the same system on a trip across America.

What I wanted to know at this point was how long the trip would take. You would think a person who had paddled a boat for over thirty years would know how fast he could paddle, but I didn't. I used my boat to explore. Speed was not a concern. My attitude was: if you enjoyed what you were doing, why hurry? This journey wouldn't be a race, but for logistic purposes, a person would need to know how long it would take.

During my library research, I had consulted back issues of *National Geographic* and *Outside* magazine, looking for articles of similar journeys. In one article I read, a man stated that he averaged twenty miles a day on a trip he had taken from Alaska to Washington state using the inside passage. That was a nice round figure, but could it be done going against the current of the Columbia River? I decided to find out.

My boat, the *Sea Venture*, was moored at the Waverly Yacht Club about a quarter of a mile above the Sellwood Bridge on the Willamette River. From there down to the Columbia River was seventeen miles. Up the river another twenty-five miles was Roster Rock State Park. This made the total distance forty-three miles. That, I thought, would be a good test run. Early one

4

Saturday morning, I loaded my camping gear in my old folding Klepper kayak and headed down river. By midday, I reached the lower end of Hayden Island. I stopped for lunch and then resumed my test. By late afternoon, I reached a group of islands known as the Sand, Lemon, and Government Islands located above Portland.

Between the Lemon and the Sand Islands there was a narrow channel used as a popular anchoring place for the yachting group affectionately called "beer can alley."

As I paddled thru this channel, I came across a sailboat stranded on a sand bar. I paddled over to the boat and suggested to the skipper that he give me his anchor. I paddled up the river with his anchor to deeper water and dropped it there, which made it possible for him to kedge off. Once he was free I continued on and camped overnight on the lower end of Government Island. The next morning, I got an early start and paddled over to the town of Washougal, Washington. At the Parkers Landing Marina, I used their phone and called Ruth to come and pick me up at my final destination of Rooster Rock State Park.

I arrived at the park about two PM. A short time later, Ruth arrived. Before I packed the boat up, we made a tour of the local nude beach. My own attitude about nudity was quite liberal. If people wanted to go nude, it was fine with me. If a person doesn't like to see nudes, don't look. For me it's a matter of comfort. If I'm warm, I take clothes off. If I'm cold, I put clothes on. I wear shoes on deck because kicking a chain plate can be painful. I also wear shorts because I don't want anything to get hung up in the rigging.

After the tour, we packed up the kayak and returned to Portland. My test was complete. I had made the forty-three-mile trip in less than two days, proving a twenty-mile-a-day average was feasible. Dividing the 5,500 miles by twenty it would require 279 days to cross from Oregon to Florida. When planning a trip of this magnitude, it would be foolish to think a person could do it immediately. I estimated a person could carry fourteen days of food supplies; therefore, a person would have to stop every two weeks to replenish supplies. Also, there would be laying over for repairs, storms, and sightseeing. It seemed prudent to add another ninety days, which would make the journey one year long.

Having resolved that question, I moved on to the next. The most difficult part of the quest would be the trek over the mountains. That was the most difficult part for Lewis and Clark. I anticipated it would be the same for anyone else using only the power of their own body. The minimum weight of boat, food, water, and equipment would be about two hundred pounds. The elevation of Lewiston, Idaho, is 738 feet. At the top of the Lolo Pass in the Bitterroot Mountains, it is 5,233 feet. McDonald Pass in the Rocky Mountains is 6,330 feet. Could a man pull that weight up those steep slopes?

Before I continued this fantasy further, I needed to find out. There was no other way except to go look, so I rented a car and drove to Lewiston. I drove long the US Highway 12, if you could call it that. I pulled off the road and watched the traffic. I drove all the way to the Missouri River, twenty miles north of Helena, Montana, and picked a possible launch site from the Missouri River. I returned to Portland a depressed and disillusioned man. I could see no way a man could pull a seventeen-foot kayak over that route and survive.

It was not the steepness of the mountains which was the problem; it was the condition of the road and the traffic. US Highway 12 was a narrow, crooked, two-lane road, heavily trafficked with eighteen-wheel tractor-trailer rigs carrying logs, wheat, and petroleum products. I pulled off the road and watched their action. They zipped along the road at sixty miles an hour. On one side of the highway, a rock cliff came right down to the side of the road. On the other side of the highway, there was a guardrail, the Clear Water and Locksa rivers below. There was no shoulder much of the way. To try to pull a kayak over that route would be suicidal. I had been accused of living on the edge, but suicidal I was not.

It was my practice to arrive at work two hours early. This gave me enough time to do a workout, ten minutes in the hot tub, and a shower before going on duty. It happened that another gentleman would join me in the hot tub. Charles Hoar was the owner and CEO of an engineering firm. He was the kind of guy who loved to solve other people's problems. In fact, he made you feel like you were doing him a favor by letting him help you. In our hot tub session after I returned from my mountain reconnaissance mission, I told him there was no way a person could walk pulling a kayak and survive. I explained the peril posed by those monstrous trucks hurtling down the road at sixty miles an hour. Over the year I worked at the club, we often talked about my project and he took an active interest in it. "Karl," he said, "I have friends in Lewiston. Let me consult with them and see if we can't enhance your chances of survival." I was dubious, but willing to let him try.

Two weeks later Charley appeared at our conference room (the hot tub) with a smile on his face. "Karl," he declared, "I have the answer you're looking for on how to make the mountain crossing."

"How?" I asked.

"Simple," he replied, "you talk to the drivers. Tell them where you are and ask them for mercy."

I looked at him as though he had gone daft. He explained that his friend Buzz in Lewiston had gone to a truck stop and talked to the drivers. He found out they all monitored channel nineteen on their CB radios. If a person had a CB radio with that particular crystal, they could talk to the drivers when they were far enough away and avoid an accident. While not completely eliminating the possibility, it did reduce it to an acceptable limit. I remembered a long held belief I had: "If you don't have the knowledge or the intelligence to handle something, it pays to have friends who do".

When I finished the hot tub session, showered, and prepared to take my position in the parking lot, Charley called me over to his locker. He pulled out two CB radios and presented them to me. He had gone to Radio Shack and had the needed crystals installed.

"Charley," I exclaimed, "I haven't decided to do this trip yet."

"Yes, you have. You're just delaying the decision as long as you can to keep from making the commitment. I believe you would have tried it even without the radios."

I admitted I had tumbled the idea in my head. Now I had concluded it could be done, but I still had two problems to face and neither would be easy: telling Ruth about what I was going to do and buying another kayak.

All along when Ruth and I were discussing this project, I assured her I was just researching the possibility. She was skeptical and let me know in no uncertain terms that she was against it. There had been a couple of times in our marriage when the "D" word had been mentioned in connection with my boat purchases. On those occasions, Ruth told me we were married until death do us part. That gave me only two options: suicide or murder. Neither of those was acceptable. I could not imagine my life without Ruth. She had been my only friend and companion for over twenty-five years. On the other hand, I had lived with the dream of this trek across America for over fifty years. Now that I had convinced myself it could be done, could I just walk away from it? With me, dreams die hard. If I came to the end of my life without making the attempt, I would hate myself.

I decided to throw caution to the wind. I would make the trip and hope I could pick up the pieces and put our marriage back together when it was over. I told Ruth my decision and my stock immediately dropped to an all-time low. Ruth didn't immediately issue an ultimatum, but I knew I was in deep trouble. I decided not to mention my need for a new kayak.

The old Klepper kayak I drug all over the world was in no condition to make the trip. Its oak frame was brittle and warped. The hull was tattered and torn. I needed a hard-shell, fiberglass ocean touring kayak.

I went to a canoe and kayak shop a few blocks from where I worked in Portland, named the Ebb and Flow. They had what I was looking for, the *Wind Dancer*. The cost was $1,200. Now that was a problem. How could I raise the money? In our negotiation on the family budget it was proclaimed I could not spend any more than $200 in any one month on my boats, equipment, and travel. To save enough money to pay for this craft would take me six months. It was now September and my target date for the journey was on or about the first of April. I wanted to get the boat as early as possible to get acquainted with it. Did I go to Ruth and ask for a variance? No way. I needed another strategy.

As far as I knew, Ruth only had two weaknesses: gambling and me. For years she had asked me to take her to Reno, Nevada, to gamble. My plan was to split my pocket money, giving half to Ruth, and throw my fate to the winds of chance with the other half. Did I know what I was doing? Yes. All my life I lived with the laws of probability. Whatever I wanted to do, I would study it and try to reduce the chance of failure to its lowest common denominator, and then leave it to my own wit and reflexes. Now I was relying on the whims of lady luck. It was something I didn't like doing. The chances that I could win enough to buy the boat were virtually nil.

Ruth and I arranged with Reno Airlines for one of their weekend package deals, a red-eye special. On a late Friday evening we made our flight. When we arrived in Reno, we went directly to the casino. By ten o'clock, we began to play. All day long I moved from table to table playing black jack, craps, roulette, and even poker. As the day wore on, my fortune waxed and waned. At eleven o'clock, I was suffering from excessive liquid due to the free drinks supplied by the casino.

Ruth was playing the slots. I found her and explained where I was going.

The rest room was located on the second floor mezzanine. When I walked out, I came face to face with three slot machines lined up along the railing overlooking the main floor below. The center one featured three clowns, various bars, and an assortment of fruit. If three one-dollar tokens were deposited, it had a grand jackpot of $1,200. Just what I needed!

I reached in my pocket and counted my tokens. I had six one-dollar tokens left. Two bad pulls on the handle and the *Wind Dancer* would hit a reef. Nothing ventured, nothing gained, as the old saying went. I dropped three tokens into the slot and pulled the handle. The wheels whirred—clang, clang, clang—and then they come to stop. Six tokens dropped into the tray. Two cherries had appeared in the window.

Now I had nine tokens representing three pulls. I dropped three more into the machine and pulled the handle. Again, the wheels spun, came to a stop, and six more tokens dropped into the tray. This machine played with me. It paid just enough to keep me playing without giving me enough to do anything with. But what the hell, I was still in the game.

I picked up three tokens, dropped them into the slot, and pulled the handle. This time all hell broke loose. Bells rang, lights flashed, sirens sounded, and the machine started kicking out tokens like an avalanche. I grabbed an empty plastic bucket someone had abandoned and scooped them up as fast as I could before they fell to the floor.

The impossible had happened: I had hit the three clowns. Half the jackpot was paid out by the machine the other half would be paid by the cashier. By the time I had the tokens collected, the floor manager had arrived. He verified the jackpot, took a token, and pulled the three clowns off the machine then led me to the cashier. They counted the take and gave me twelve one hundred dollar bills. They asked me if I wanted to play more.

I explained to them I was quitting gambling forever. I was not cut out to be a gambler.

I found Ruth in a state of panic. I had been gone for over an hour and she was about to call the casino security when I showed up and explained what had happened. My gambling was over. I wanted her to win, too, so I staked her with a hundred dollars from my winnings. That lasted about a half hour before it was gone. I added another hundred. I still had enough to purchase the *Wind Dancer*.

Lady luck smiled on her. Ruth started winning big time. She played a bank of six one-dollar slots, moving from machine to machine as fast as she could pull the handles. Every time she hit a jackpot, the floor manager would give her a bottle of champagne. Soon, she had champagne sitting all around. She gave spectators a few of the bottles. I followed her around with a bucket and gathered her winnings. At one point she had over a thousand dollars. Her winning streak didn't last long. Her fortune shrunk to six hundred and she decided to quit while she was still ahead. I was happy. We were both physically and emotionally exhausted. It was two am on Sunday morning and our plane was scheduled to leave eight hours later.

When we flew back to Portland, Ruth had her six hundred dollars and a case of champagne. I had the wherewithal to buy my kayak. With the euphoria of winning, my stock rose slightly with Ruth, but it quickly dropped back down when I came home two days later with the *Wind Dancer*. The atmosphere aboard the *Sea Venture* stabilized with icy acceptance. Ruth realized nothing was going to stop me from making the journey.

It was now October 1986. I had gone to work for the club in October 1985. All the elements were in place for the trip, but there was a lot of fine-tuning to be done. My target date for launch was March 28, 1987, just six months away. The ideal time for me to reach buoy #7, the point where I intended to begin my trek, was at seven AM, the low slack tide that day. Each item I carried with me needed to be checked for practicality, size, and weight because the storage area in the *Wind Dancer* was limited. I didn't want anything left out where it would likely come loose and go adrift.

I started out with the equipment I already had. The set of wheels I used to pull the old kayak would fit in the back compartment in front of the rudder. The two-man tent shoved up into the forepeak. In the forward compartment there was enough space to fit fourteen half-gallon-sized Ziploc bags, each filled with one day's ration of food. Next task was the cockpit. Between my legs I placed a sixteen-inch square dishpan, six inches deep, which carried my camp stove, a quart size bottle of propane, a loaf of bread, a squeeze bottle of jam and another of margarine, a jar of peanut butter, and various hardware. I would need to fix my snacks while paddling. Behind my seat I could fit four half-gallon plastic bottles of water and a water purification device I picked up at a Norm Thompson store. That was a precaution in case I ran out of potable water. A woman doctor, who was a member of the club, put together a medical kit for me. Since I would be my own support team, I would have to be my own physician. At the age of sixty, I didn't have any aches, pains, or afflictions, but I wanted to be prepared just in case. The medical kit was placed behind the seat. A machete fit under the seat. I intended to use this if I needed to chop myself loose from an entanglement. It could also be used if a wild animal attacked me. I wouldn't take a firearm.

After checking the loading of the cockpit, I moved to the aft compartment where I carried my extra clothing, sleeping bag, air mattress, and a spare propane bottle. One of the items of clothing I had was a one-eighth-inch neoprene shortie wet suit. The wet suit would enhance my chances of survival in icy water by about ten minutes. I would carry two sets of clothing. Each item was folded, placed in a plastic Ziploc bag, and further packed in a waterproof stuff sack. This made a roll about eight inches in diameter. My air mattress was called a Thermo-Rest.

It rolled up tight and fit in a stuff sack about six inches in diameter and twenty-four inches long.

My sleeping bag was an expensive item. I got it from the Eddie Bauer store. It had a goose down filling and a silver metallic liner, rated to a keep person warm down to a temperature of forty degrees. I knew it would get colder than that going over the mountains and I would have to wear a pair of thermal underwear as well. The sleeping bag, packed in its stuff sack, was about the size of a two-liter water bottle. Every item I was going to take with me was measured, weighed, and fitted into the kayak just like a weight master on an airliner would do.

Balancing the cargo fore, aft, port, and starboard, I wanted the *Wind Dancer* to sit perfectly flat when I paddled. The *Wind Dancer* weighed 50 pounds, my equipment weighed 150 pounds, and I weighed 185 pounds. That meant I would have to move 385 pounds a distance of over five thousand miles using the power of my own body. Could I do it? I was convinced I could.

Another important person came forward and volunteered to help me on my journey: Rick Runckel, vice-president of a water sport manufacturing company named the Barracuda Sportswear. They designed and manufactured sunglasses and swimming and surfing goggles. Since I paddled my boat to and from work nearly every day, he often gave me equipment to test for him. When he learned of my plans, he pledged me the cost of a month's ration of food and gave me some of his equipment. He also told me he would call each city's chamber of commerce where I would stop for supplies, and see if he could arrange a place for me to stay. The most important item he gave me was his toll-free phone number. This allowed me to call anywhere outside Oregon and tell him where I was. He was to be the only one to know of my whereabouts within a one-hundred-mile range.

The time passed quickly. People who learned what I intended to do had various reactions. One young fellow brought his girlfriend to the parking lot to meet me. When she learned what I was doing, she reached into her purse, pulled out her business card, and invited me to visit her for free. I found that very interesting until I looked at the card. She was a psychiatrist.

I went to Trisha, the Willamette Country Club manager, and told her I was quitting. She asked me why. I told her about my planned trip. She said she had already heard about it and was waiting for me to tell her. She said they would give me a year's leave of absence, and that my job would be waiting for me when I got back. I hadn't expected so much from her, and with the excitement of the day, I gave her a hug. They put up a large USA map in the club and Rick kept them informed of my progress.

Wind Dancer

A 17'ft. Ocean touring kayak

CHAPTER 2
THE COLUMBIA RIVER 1987

Before dawn Wind dancer was made ready

Saturday, March 28

I met the Coast Guard station commander on the beach at
Fort Canby State Park in Washington at six o'clock. I hadn't
slept well the night before. I wasn't bothered by anxiety, but
rather by thoughts of all the men that had gone before me on
their own journeys of discovery. The first explorers, according

to anthropologists, were nomads from Siberia who crossed a land bridge during the last ice age. They made their way down the west coast by land and boat. Then they spread out over the continent. In my fantasies, I could see myself as the reincarnation of the first human to paddle on the rivers in that area.

I remembered reading that the first non-native to view the mouth of the Columbia River was the Spanish captain Bruno Heceta in 1775. He believed it was a river or strait, but because his men were sick, he didn't try to cross the bar, but continued sailing north.

In 1788, Captain John Meares sailed along the coast looking for the river that Captain Heceta had reported, but Captain Meares never found it. Out of his disappointment, he named the point Cape Disappointment. The next adventurer was the British Captain George Vancouver. In early 1791, Captain Vancouver looked for a river that was reported to be there. When he observed the turbulent water at the point that Captain Mears had described, Captain Vancouver concluded there was no river and sailed on to what is now Vancouver Island. Then, on May 11, 1792, Captain Gray sailed his ship the *Columbia Rediviva* up the river and remained for trading with the Native Americans for nine days.

I sympathized with those early sea captains who crossed the Columbia bar. At high slack tide, the Columbia bar could be like a mellow millpond. However, with a westerly wind and an ebb tide, the Columbia bar was a living hell. It was called the "Grave Yard of the Pacific" for good reasons. It is the most dangerous bar in the Pacific. Over one hundred ships had gone down there. The day before, a Coast Guard officer told me I was insane to cross the bar in a fifty-pound, seventeen-foot kayak.

I wondered if those early explorers would understand why I needed to attempt the dangerous task.

I wished I had been born in their time. Somehow, I had been misplaced in time.

A few years ago, I crossed the bar under rough conditions in my ten-ton, thirty-eight-foot cutter-rigged sloop the *Sea Venture*. It nearly cost me my wife. When I got back to Astoria, Ruth said to me, "Karl, take me back to Portland. I don't want to see you or that damn boat again." If I had stuck the *Sea Venture* where she told me to, I would have been very uncomfortable. I had to wine and dine her in the finest restaurants in Astoria for several days before things got back to normal.

There was a small group of people on hand who witnessed the start of my journey across America: Ruth, a couple of newspaper reporters, a television crew, and a few members of the Coast Guard and their commander. The weather had moderated, but it was still a little choppy, though not something I couldn't handle. The Coast Guard commander still didn't like the idea of me taking a kayak out. Nevertheless, he gave me permission to go. He said he would send the forty-one-foot Coast Guard cutter out to follow me just in case something happened.

I was dressed for the occasion. I had on my wet suit, a pair of nylon pants, polypropylene socks, wading boots, a waterproof paddler's jacket, and topped it off with a life vest and my cap. The spray skirt hung down over my front and rear like an oversized loincloth. The torso sleeve was pulled up under my arms. The rain jacket fit over the top of it sealing me off from the weather or water in the event of my capsizing. I was ready to go.

I waved good-bye to everyone and kissed Ruth. That poor woman made the mistake of marrying the last Neanderthal.

I picked up the grab handle on the *Wind Dancer* and headed for the surf. Her keel cut a line in the sand pointing to the open sea. The time was seven AM. That gave me half an hour to reach the buoy before the tide started coming in. I waded into the surf until the boat floated free. I stepped into the cockpit and gave a push that sent the kayak out through the incoming waves. The bow caught a wave and tossed it up into my face. It hit like a cold slap. I took a few quick strokes to get through the surf and then paused, took the large sponge that I carried and dried the water that came in, and then fastened down the spray skirt to keep anymore water out. I picked up a coarse parallel to the north jetty and paddled, singing an old song.

> Oh! My father was the keeper of the Eddystone light.
> He slept with a mermaid one fine night.
> And from that union there came three.
> A porpoise, a porpy, and me.
> Oh, ho, oh, the wind blows free.
> Oh, for the life on the open sea.

The open sea? In a seventeen-foot boat? No wonder the Coast Guard officer thought I was insane. I had paddled for about fifteen minutes when I heard the grumbling of a large diesel engine. I turned and looked back. The Coast Guard vessel was coming up behind me, just idling along. I continued my stroke. When I was about two hundred yards from the buoy, a curious thing happened. There was a flock of cormorants that had been flying around me in a V formation. When they passed in front of my boat, a huge California gray whale rose up just fifty feet in front of me, and seemed to be guiding the way forward. The Coast Guard crew let out a cheer.

I continued paddling toward the buoy with the whale in front of me and the Coast Guard behind me. I followed the whale as it passed to the right and turned around the buoy. The Coast Guard vessel chose to go to the left and waited until I was safely headed back across the bar.

After I picked up my easterly heading, the whale breached, lifted high in the air, and at the same time lifted his right flipper as if in a salute. When he hit the water, he disappeared as suddenly as he had arrived. Again the crew on the boat cheered.

I'm not a religious person. I don't believe in miracles. Logic told me that neither the cormorants nor the whale knew what

I was doing. Nevertheless, a wave of elation washed over me. The "Gods" of the deep had blessed my journey and I was on my way. That seemed to set the tone for the entire trek. Over the next few months, there would be many incidents that I could not explain. There were two forces at work: one which tried to keep me from succeeding and the other one that helped to keep me going.

The Coast Guard cutter gunned its engines and headed back to base. I was left bobbing like a peanut shell on the Columbia bar. The only sounds were the calls of the sea birds: terns, gulls, the Common Merganser, a few puffins, the Western Grebes, and the cormorants. The surface of the water shimmered with a mist of tiny fish breaking the surface. When they jumped, the birds fed on them. The ocean swells were rolling in from the northwest about five feet high. When they came, they lifted me up which allowed me to pick up speed as I surfed down their face. I had to be careful that they didn't turn me sideways or I'd flip over.

I picked up my stroke and headed for the city of Astoria on the Oregon side of the river. It wasn't long before I saw the Astoria Bridge spanning the Columbia River between Oregon and Washington; my destination for that day. Rick had arranged for Ruth and me to stay at the Thunder Bird Hotel near the south end of the bridge. Once I was inside the two jetties the water smoothed out except for a small chop kicked up by a light northeast wind. That didn't bother me much because I was being pushed along by the incoming tide. The *Wind Dancer* cut through the water like a wetted knife.

Since Ruth was to meet me at Astoria, I elected to cross the bar without the added weight of a load of equipment and food. I was concerned about that because with 150 pounds of gear in the boat, the changes of doing an Eskimo roll was a real possibility. I had executed that maneuver empty, but never loaded. If a roll was going to happen, that would have been the likely spot.

On the right side of the river, just past the town of Warrenton, was Bakers Bay. That was where Captain James Baker had his trading schooner *Jenny* anchored when Lieutenant Broughton came aboard. It was also where Lewis and Clark landed when they moved from the Washington side of the river to the Oregon side to establish their winter camp at what is now Fort Clatsop.

I reached the west marina at Astoria at one o'clock, just six hours after I began. Ruth was there with the camera to take my picture as I came in. I pulled the *Wind Dancer* up to the dock and out of the way of the rest of the boats. I passed a chain through an eye in the back of the kayak then around a piling and locked it. I didn't want the kayak to go missing during the night. Ruth and I walked around town that afternoon. Our conversation was strained. She was angry that I would make the journey against her wishes. I could sympathize with her; she deserved better.

There are those men that are docile creatures that are easy for a woman to train to do their bidding. But unfortunately, I was not one of them. Once I programmed myself to do a certain thing there was no force in the universe that could stop me. My daughter, Debbie, and her daughter came down from Portland to meet Ruth and me in Astoria so that we could all have dinner together. Ruth and I retired early for the night. I had a lot of work to do the next day.

Sunday, March 29

Ruth and I had breakfast together and then I loaded the boat. It took time to carry all the gear down to the kayak, but the actual loading went quickly. I knew where every item needed to be stored. Once it was all on board, I slid the boat off the dock into the water and checked its trim. I estimated it would take me five days to reach Portland. I slipped into my spray skirt, pulled my rain jacket over the top of it, and then put my life vest on. I kissed Ruth good-bye and told her I would see her in five days.

I would try to be there at five o'clock. Ruth walked up the ramp without looking back. Things were still frosty between us.

It was ten o'clock when I cleared the marina and pointed the bow upriver. A light rain fell and a northeast breeze was bucking me, but the tide was coming in and I got a lift from that. I hadn't paddled long when I crossed under the Astoria Bridge then past the East Basin Marina. From there, the main shipping channel swung to the north through small sand islands. The estuary was quite wide at that point because the Army Corps of Engineers had dredged the channel over to the Washington side.

I stayed close to the Oregon side, paddling with a steady stroke passing Tongue Point. It was there that Captain Robert Gray anchored his boat in May 1792 to do his trading. I wove around a mired bunch of islands and stayed as close to the shore as I could in order to protect myself from the wind and the waves. Some of the islands were nothing more than tidal mud flats. Others were covered with heavy vegetation with a great deal of wildlife. Along with the usual sea birds, there were heavy concentrations of mallards and geese, while overhead I saw the American Bald Eagle and the osprey.

I ate my noon meal by nosing my kayak onto an exposed beach to keep from being blown down river. In the meantime, the tide had changed so I now bucked both the tide and the wind. I was deep inside of a location that contained over one hundred islands linked together with areas of tall reeds and marsh, which made an almost impenetrable maze.

While I wasn't lost, neither did I know exactly where I was. I had hoped to be in the vicinity of Cathlamet by that time, but I could see I wasn't going to make it. I began to suffer from an acute case of anxiety. The vegetation on the islands was so dense that there was no place to camp. It was late afternoon and the light was fading. Then, out of the gloom, a houseboat appeared. A houseboat...out here in the middle of a swamp? Not likely, I thought, but it was.

I paddled up to it. It had a large deck on the down river end of it. There were "No Trespassing Government Property" signs posted in various locations around the houseboat. I assumed it was a research building. Since I was a retired military man, I authorized myself to use it as a campsite. I pulled the *Wind Dancer* up on the deck and proceeded to pitch my tent. In order to fix it fast to the deck, I had to wedge the pins into cracks in the planks. Like the nomads of the desert, I now had my tent up.

I returned to my boat and took my air mattress, sleeping bag, dish pan, water jug, and food packet, and placed them in my tent then replaced the storage compartment and cockpit covers. With that done, I had a more immediate concern. I was cold and soaking wet both from the rain and perspiration. I warmed some river water with my propane stove, poured it into my dish pan with a little liquid Dawn, and gave myself a sponge bath to wash the perspiration off. I dried myself off and slipped into my lounging pajamas (a fleece-lined sweat shirt and pants) and a pair of warm socks. That stopped the chills.

With that accomplished, I dried my rain jacket and wetsuit as best as I could and spread them in the corner of the tent to air out. Then I had one other item that needed to be taken care of—my black, silk long underwear. I had worn them under my wet suit and they were soaked. Again, I turned to my liquid Dawn dish soap. I used it for everything: clothes, dishes, body, and shampoo. I should have written a commercial for them.

After the wash and rinse, I rolled the underwear in a towel and twisted them to get as much moisture out as I could. Normally, on my long distant treks, I stopped early enough so that there was a little sunlight left which allowed me to hang them over a tree limb to let the sun and breeze quickly dry the silk. But, since it was wet and cold, I knew that they wouldn't dry out even in the tent. I had a special technique for drying them in that weather condition.

I took off my lounging pajamas, slipped on my wet underwear and crawled into the sleeping bag. The down that insulated the bag kept the heat of my body in while the metallic silver lining reflected the heat back. In a matter of minutes the fabric was warm. I knew that in a couple of hours my underwear would be dry. I learned that trick in my war years in North Korea. I had been told that I liked to torture myself, but that just wasn't true. I had a high tolerance for heat, cold, hunger, and pain; therefore, I didn't suffer like some people.

With the laundry done, I turned to my dinner. In a packet that I had taken out earlier was freeze-dried beef stroganoff. I liked the freeze-dried food because of its ease of preparation. All I had to do was pour boiling water into the pouch, stir it with a spoon, let it sit for a few minutes, then eat it out of the pouch with the same spoon. After I finished eating, I placed the pouch back into the bag to be carried out of my camping area so that I could dispose of it later in a trashcan. For vegetables, I had an assortment of carrots, celery sticks, and radishes. For fruit, I carried with me four each of bananas, apples, and oranges. The first four days I would eat the bananas because they would be the first to go bad. After that I would alternate between the oranges and apples.

After dinner, I prepared for breakfast. That required making milk. In the Ziploc bag I had included a one-quart packet of powdered milk. To mix it I used Ruth's Tupperware gravy maker, which I borrowed for the trip. I poured in the powdered milk and filled it to the fourteen ounces line with water. With the mixing wheel on top, I shook it vigorously for about thirty seconds. Then I poured it into a quart-size plastic container and added a four-ounce can of evaporated milk. That added richness and flavor.

That task out of the way, I propped myself up on one elbow in my sleeping bag and made a few notations in a spiral notebook that I used for my journal. I had my headlamp on to shine light on to the page. My journal was a simple affair. Just the date, location, and a few notes to use as a memory reminder when I got back home and showed my slide program. When I was done, I switched off the light, laid my head on my folded life jacket, and prepared myself for sleep.

Outside the wild life was creating a din of noise. I could hear aquatic animals, ducks, and geese making a racket. I reflected back over my life as a wanderer. Years ago, Tennessee Ernie Ford sang a song called "The Flight of the Wild Goose" and Harry Bellefonte sang "Looks Like I'll Never Stop My Wondering." Other men like me were not bound to a chunk of earth. With that thought, I fell asleep.

Monday, March 30

I awoke at five am and broke out my battery-powered electric razor and shaved in the dark by feel while I was in my sleeping bag. I was loath to leave its warmth. My breakfast drink was orange flavored Tang. Next, I ate some mucilage using some of the milk that I had mixed the night before, and made a cup of coffee using hot water and freeze-dried coffee. After breakfast, I mixed up my midmorning snack: a shake made from chocolate instant breakfast mix. I tried to have something every two hours because my body was like an old fashioned steam engine. Everything that I put into it was burned up in two hours.

I broke camp, loaded everything up, and slid the *Wind Dancer* into the water. The first paddle stroke of the day hit the water at seven AM. It was difficult for me to find my way through the tangle of trees and bushes. There were hundreds of small islands with many blind channels. I observed white tailed deer on some of the islands and I saw a lot of Great Blue Herons as they stood on tree stumps.

By paddling slowly, I got so close to them that I saw the color of their eyes and the shape of their irises. When I got too close, they flexed their knees in nervousness and then flew off a short distance, landed and looked back to see what I would do.

I often saw small sticks floating in the water, peeled completely clean of their bark. That was evidence of beaver in the area. I was startled by one of the beaver when it slapped its tail on the surface of the water to warn others that I was in the area. There were heavy concentrations of vegetation, such as fir, oak, willow, and alder on the islands and the riverbanks.

Since I left Tongue Point the day before, I had seen no evidence of human habitation except for the houseboat that I camped on the night before. I continued probing the blind channels. Finally at about nine o'clock, I broke out of what I called the Columbia bayous and emerged into the main channel, which skirted a high bluff area on the Washington shore. It then swung to the south toward Oregon. I had joined the main channel just below Puget Island. Lieutenant Broughton named the island in honor of Lieutenant Peter Puget, an officer aboard Captain Vancouver's ship the *Discovery*. The main shipping channel went south. I choose to take the narrower and shallower channel up the north side for two reasons. One, it was shorter, and two, there was a small town named Cathlamet located on the Washington side where I wanted to stop.

I paddled up under a bridge and tied my boat to a log raft which was anchored to the shore. All up and down the river there were many abandoned, rotting log rafts along the riverbanks. They created a terrible eyesore. I'd often been tempted to take a bolt cutter and let them loose to force the government to clean them up. However, I knew if I did I might be caught and hung from the yardarm.

Cathlamet only had about a thousand inhabitants. I had two carrying nets in my gear that I put water jugs into and proceeded to the nearest restaurant. It was my intent to replenish my water supply and have a second breakfast. At ten o'clock, I arrived at a restaurant and ordered pancakes and eggs. While I was there, a man recognized me from the television coverage that I received and called the local newspaper. Before I could finish my meal, a reporter showed up. He followed me back to the boat and interviewed me along the way then took my picture as I left the log raft and continued up the river.

All along the riverbank there were two types of blackberries, the native Oregon and the Asian variety. I could tell the difference when I looked at the leaves. The Oregon blackberries had small loosely clustered leaves and rather spindly stems, while the Asian variety had large, dense clusters of leaves and larger sturdier stems. The Asian variety was not present when Lieutenant Broughton and Lewis and Clark traveled that route. The vines clung to the stones the ships carried as ballast, floated free, and then rooted and thrived in the mild climate of the northwest. The seeds were spread by the birds that ate the fruit. The plant spread to areas over a large portion of the west coast. In some locations, they crowded out some of the native plants.

After I pulled away from the log raft, I crossed over to the island and kept as close as I could. The shore impeded the flow of the water and made it easier for me to paddle. Once I reached the head of the island, I maneuvered around the wing dam that protected the island from erosion. Unfortunately, once I passed the wing dam, I received the full brunt of the river's current. Again, I crossed over to get as close to the Washington shore as I could. A combination of the shallow water and the shore caused little back eddies that gave my kayak a lift.

I hadn't been bothered by the river traffic since I left Tongue Point. Now that I was in the main shipping channel, I had to be very watchful. The big ships were not the problem. They stuck to the navigation channel and their wake rolled like a ground swell and the *Wind Dancer* just rode over the top of it. The deep draft pleasure boats were the problem. They often came so close to me that I couldn't turn into their wake fast enough and their swells would break over the top of me.

I traveled along Grimm's Island. It was originally named Baker's Island after an officer on the *Discovery*, the same man that Mount Baker was named after. The shoreline showed signs of cultivation as I paddled further up the river. There were small farms, parks, and fishing areas. The fishing areas caused me some problems. The bank fisherman cast their lines out into the river as far as they could, which forced me out further into the channel where I had to buck the full force of the current. That slowed me down, but I thought, "What the hell, they have a right to do their thing as much as I have to do mine."

I continued up the river. Since I had a rather heavy second breakfast of bacon, eggs, and pancakes at Cathlamet, I had my snack while I sat in the kayak. I just nosed into the bank so I wouldn't drift downstream while I ate. Normally, I would have gotten out and stretched my legs, but after my snack, I just paddled on. It had been a pleasant day and I made good time in spite of the delays. On the downside, my camera quit working. It got wet, even though I had been very careful. I decided that when I got back to Portland I'd switch to an underwater camera. I wouldn't be able to take close up pictures of wild life, but it would be better than nothing.

At seven PM, I pulled the *Wind Dancer* up on a sandy beach of Lord Island far enough so I didn't have to worry about it floating off during the night. As an added precaution, I took the painter and tied it off to a tree to make damn sure it didn't go adrift. Lord Island was just across the river from Longview, Washington. I made camp and had dinner while watching the sun set in soft colors of pink, yellow, and orange.

Tuesday, March 31

The previous night was very noisy. Aside from the ducks and the geese, I endured a constant racket of the Longview police department's sirens. They seemed to be the most active police force in the nation. My boisterous neighbors, the geese, woke me up at five am. I blamed the geese, but really it was my built-in alarm clock that woke me up at the same time every morning. I fixed my morning meal, broke camp and at 6:30 am, I launched the kayak. I picked up the stroke and after a short

27

while I passed under the Longview Bridge. After I paddled for about two more hours, I reached the Rainier Marina. I tied up at the dock, loaded up the two empty water bottles, and walked uptown. I made the pit stop for three reasons: to stretch my legs, replenish my water supply, and get a good meal that I didn't have to cook. It also made my food supply last longer and kept me from losing too much weight.

After my second breakfast, I made my way back to the *Wind Dancer* and resumed my journey. At noon, I pulled up on a bank for my midday meal. The area I chose appeared to be a park. There were a group of fishermen with their families about fifty yards downstream from where I landed. While I did my stretching exercises, two children appeared. They asked me questions about my boat and what I was doing. I told them my story.

I learned over the years that friendship with children could open many doors. That time was no exception. Soon the children scampered off to their parents, who in turn invited me to have lunch with them. They recognized me from the *Oregonian* newspaper article. Cathy Appel and Mike Timmins gave me some dried fish, which I appreciated very much. I thanked them for their friendliness, and got back on the water.

In two hours I reached to the Trojan Nuclear Power Plant located on the Oregon side of the river. Here the width of the river narrowed which caused the water to run swifter and made it impossible for me to make any progress on that side. Once again, I switched sides to the Washington shore to take advantage of the eddy currents. Above the bottleneck, I moved into an area of flat water where I picked up my stroke. I wanted to make my next overnight stop in St. Helens, Oregon. But to make it, I couldn't waste anymore time.

I passed the Port of Kalama on the Washington side. The small river port had grain elevators which loaded ships bound for Asian markets. I paddled up the river and angled over to the Oregon side past the towns of Goble, Deer Island, and Columbia

City. To get to St. Helens, I maneuvered between some small islands. At five pm, I sighted Sand Island, located just across a narrow channel of the Columbia River, directly across from the city hall of St. Helens. I landed at the small city park which had a floating dock and a ramp that went up to the town. As I paddled up to the dock, I noticed there was enough space under the ramp for me to maneuver, which allowed me to land on the inside of the dock out of the current.

Tied up to the dock was a thirty-foot black schooner. Two sailors sat on the dock, playing cards, eating peanuts, and passing a jug of wine between them. When I stepped out of the *Wind Dancer* and stretched, one of the sailors passed me the jug and said, "Here, have a pull and help yourself to the peanuts. You just won me a buck." "How did I do that?" I asked. "When we saw you paddle up my partner bet that you would come up on the outside to the dock. I bet you would go underneath and come to the inside. So, I won." I accepted the jug, took a drink, and a handful of peanuts. Then I pulled off my spray skirt, folded up my life jacket to sit on, and spent the rest of the afternoon swapping lies with the two sailors and drinking their wine.

I had a very pleasant evening. When the jug was empty, the two sailors gave me the rest of their peanuts, gathered up their gear, got on their boat, and headed back to the marina. I finished the peanuts and ate some of the dried fish that I was given earlier in the day. I was in no mood to do my whole camping routine, so I pitched my tent on the dock, climbed into my sleeping bag, and went to sleep as I listened to the call of the wild goose. I was sure of one thing: there was no danger that the Canadian goose would become extinct on the Columbia River.

Wednesday, April 1

I slept pretty well that night in spite of the geese. Maybe it was the wine. I woke up early as usual, broke camp, and was under way at seven am. I had only paddled a few minutes when

29

I came to a twenty-mile long island named Sauvie Island. It sat between the Columbia River and the Multnomah Channel. It's one of the most fertile farmlands in Oregon. When Lieutenant Broughton camped there on his journey up river, he was met by a group of Native Americans dressed in war paint and equipped to wage war. He was nervous about their intent, but they proved to be friendly. He named that portion of the island Warrior Point. Today it's called Warrior Rock.

Since leaving Astoria, I had paddled faster than I anticipated. I was now only about twenty miles from Portland. All things being equal, I expected to arrive at Hayden Island late that afternoon; an entire day ahead of schedule, which created a problem. I told everyone that they could expect me to arrive the next day at about five. Now it looked like I would to be there early. Rick had arranged for Ruth and I to stay overnight at the Thunder Bird Hotel on Hayden Island. Half way up the island there was a marina tucked back into a tiny cove. I decided to pull in there and make some phone calls. I hoped to make other arrangements. I had traveled along the east side of the island for an hour. In the summertime there was usually some pretty nice scenery about that time of day. It was a nude beach. The local farmers hated it. They tried to get laws passed outlawing it, but they didn't succeed. My attitude was: if you don't like it, don't look.

I arrived at the marina at noon, had my lunch, and then made some phone calls. I wasn't able to reach anyone, so I went on. When I reached the lower end of Hayden Island, I camped for the night. I decided that the next day I would hang around camp and tend my gear, then make my entrance at the appointed time. In four days, I had paddled over a hundred miles against the Columbia River current; not bad for an old man of sixty. I pulled a muscle in my right arm as I patted myself on the back.

Thursday, April 2

The past two days had been nice with a little breeze. The night before was clear and the stars were bright. The morning looked like another promising day. I wasn't pressed for time to do anything so I just took it easy. I fixed my breakfast and brewed a cup of coffee. Once the sun was well up, I took down my tent and hung it over a tree limb to dry. There had been a heavy dew the night before. I emptied all of my gear out of the boat and spread it on the ground trap to air out. Next, I warmed some water and washed my boat. With that accomplished, I rolled out my sleeping pad in the warm sun and watched as the seagulls slowly circled over head. Once I had all my equipment tidied up, I repacked the *Wind Dancer*. By that time it was about four o'clock, my destination for the day was only about a mile away. I decided to just dink along and be a few minutes late just to get them anxious.

As I was paddling up to the floating dock in front of the Red Lion Hotel, I saw a few people waving to me. I paddled up and tossed the painter to someone on the dock. They steadied the boat while I extracted myself from the cockpit. There was a lot of laughing, hugging, kissing, and shaking of hands. You would have thought I'd finished the entire trip instead of just the first hundred miles.

Ruth, Rick, and all of my friends from the club were there. There was even a representative from Mayor Bud Clark with a note to warn me about the winds around Iron Mountain in the Columbia Gorge. While we stood there, the Channel 8 news crew came in a motorboat they had rented to meet me on the river. But because I had camped on the island the night before, they missed me. We all went up to the Red Lion Hotel's dining room for dinner. The restaurant manager, Heather, presented me with a poppy seed cake. She found out it was my favorite. After dinner, everyone dispersed and Ruth and I were left alone. We went to our room. Instead of my usual camping routine that night, I enjoyed a hot shower and a comfortable bed, but I missed the song of the wild goose.

Friday, April 3

Ruth had to be at work at seven AM, so we had to be up early. We had our breakfast and made plans for her to bring additional supplies to Hood River. I told her to be sure and bring my underwater camera. That meant that between Portland and Hood River I wasn't able to take pictures. Ruth left for work and I carried the supplies that I needed. Then I went to the snack bar and waited for the Channel 8 news team. At the dock, they wired me for sound. I slid the *Wind Dancer* off the dock and headed up the river while they motored along beside me for their interview. That took about a half an hour, after which time they took their equipment off me and headed back to the dock. I kept to the south side of the river.

I was paddling opposite Government Island when I saw my oldest son Bob hailing me. He worked for the phone company as an installer and was out on a job when he saw me on the river. We chatted for a few minutes. Bob promised to take good care of his mother as we said our good-byes.

It was along this section of the river that Lieutenant Broughton first saw a great snowy mountain and named it Mount Hood after Lord Hood of Britain. On the south side of the river was Troutdale, Oregon. On the north side was the Washington community of Camas. The day was rather gloomy. A northeast wind was blowing and a light rain fell. I tucked my head down and paddled. A couple of miles above Camas were two small towns known as Washougal and Point Lawton Creek. Lieutenant Broughton named the area Point Vancouver on October 30, 1792. That was as far east as he went. He claimed the area in the name of England and returned to the mouth of the river. Lewis and Clark were the first white men to travel that part of the river from that section on toward Idaho.

For the next one hundred miles, I passed through the Columbia Gorge. The gorge was cut through the Cascade Mountains thousands of years ago by a massive flood and several smaller ones that originated near Missoula, Montana. I sat there in my kayak and wondered if any Native Americans had witnessed that sight. I tried to think how it would feel to look up and see that massive wave come toward me. The beauty of that area is hard to describe. With high mountains on either side of the river, some areas of the hillsides are heavily wooded while others contain basalt cliffs with magnificent cascading waterfalls.

The river's edge is covered with cottonwood tree, fir, pine, and willows. The river itself is dotted with many islands, and also covered with trees and populated with ducks and geese. The scent of the newly opened leaves filled the air with a spicy sent so I didn't mind the rain that fell. In spite of the delays that morning—the headwind and paddling against the river current—I made good time. I covered about thirty miles. I intended to camp at Rooster Rock State Park, but it was early so I pushed on. I paddled for an hour more before I found a sheltered flat spot under a large tree on the riverbank on the Oregon side and camped for the night. I ran through my standard camping procedure.

Saturday, April 4

My first stroke hit the water at 6:30 am. I had a good reason for my early start. Ahead I faced the locks at Bonneville Dam. I didn't know what problems would face me. As I passed by an island, a floatplane dropped out of the sky and landed close by. It taxied up to me. The occupants said that they had seen the news the night before and wanted to add their support for my journey. I asked them how far it was up to the locks. When they told me it was about ten minutes away I thought, "Yeah, right. Ten minutes away at one hundred fifty miles an hour." When I got closer to the locks, the river got narrower and the current got faster. I passed by Beacon Rock, the largest monolith on the west coast. Lewis and Clark named it when they came through there in 1805. I tried to get past it on the Oregon side, but no luck. The current brought me to a dead stop. A tugboat came by, blew its horn, and the crew waved. They cheered as I struggled. I could see that I hadn't made any headway so I angled over to the Washington side to once again hitchhike the eddies to get through the narrow channel. Even above the restriction and close to the bank I had to paddle hard to make it up to the locks. My progress was slowed and it took me nearly an hour to reach the holding area to enter the locks.

Once I got there, I was faced with another problem: how to notify the lockmaster of my arrival and get the instructions to enter the locks. There was a rope at the end of the locks that was pulled to activate the speaker system to communicate with the lockmaster. The pull rope was designed for larger boats that allowed the crew to reach it from their deck. Since I sat right at the waterline, the pull rope was four feet above my head. I landed on the rocks below the lock wall, climbed up, pulled the rope, and explained to the lockmaster my situation. They informed me a tugboat was due to lock through. Commercial traffic had the right of way. I could lock through with them if the skipper gave his permission. They called the skipper and he said it would be alright. It would take them two hours to arrive.

That was fine with me. I prepared my noon meal up in the lockmaster's lounge and they furnished me with free coffee. I had a comfortable meal and a pleasant chat with the two lockmasters. The time passed quickly. When the tug arrived, the skipper had me tie the *Wind Dancer* to the port side. The lockmaster started the pumps and brought the tug up to the rivers level. While on the tug, the skipper warned me about the winds in the gorge. He said even the big tugs had to tie up when the wind was strong.

Above the Bonneville Locks, the landscape underwent a gradual change to rolling hills topped with ancient lava flows. The town of Hood River that I paddled toward is famous for their fruit orchards of apples, pears, and cherries. The fruit is shipped all over the world. Above Hood River is another change to the landscape; this time to semi-arid. The Cascade Mountain Range divides the state between east and west. In the west, it's fairly wet with dense forests and farmland; while in the east, it's dry with wheat, cattle, and sheep farms. Over a thousand years ago a massive landslide blocked the flow of the river creating a huge dam that the Native Americans called the Bridge of the Gods. Eventually, the river cut through the natural dam and made a series of waterfalls. I continued up river. Late in the afternoon I pulled over to the riverbank on the Washington side and camped for the night. For the next day, I planned to stay overnight in Hood River. That would be the last time I'd see Ruth until I reached Lewiston, Idaho.

Sunday, April 5

I broke camp at my usual early morning time. I had not paddled long when the wind picked up. I maneuvered to the Oregon side of the river. There was a series of clumps of dead trees that stuck above the water. They were the remnants of the forest that was there before the dam was built. I took advantage of these trees and used them as a windbreak. They blocked the formation of the waves, which made it easier to paddle, but they also proved to be a hazard. The trees were anywhere from one to two feet in diameter and several feet high, and the wind caused them to thrash back and forth. If they caught my kayak between them they would crack the hull like a nutshell in a nutcracker. The wind blew from the northeast but it wasn't anything that I couldn't handle.

After I paddled for about three hours, I saw Hood River in the distance. It was about one o'clock. In spite of the delays caused by the wind and the current, I made faster time than I thought I would. As I made my approach to the Hood River Marina, I heard the sound of a car horn. I looked toward the sound and saw Ruth as she stood on the sea wall and pointed to the entrance to the marina.

I pulled into the marina behind the nineteenth century Danish schooner *Sarah*. Ruth came down to the dock and helped me lift the kayak up onto the dock. Then we checked into the Nendels Motor Inn for the night.

Monday, April 6

When morning came, we had breakfast together. Ruth had to leave immediately to go back to her job. I carried the supplies that she brought, which included my little underwater camera. Now, once again, I could take pictures of the landscape as I traveled through. I was in a hurry to get started. I wanted to clear the locks at the Dalles before dark. I reached the locks at four o'clock. That time I was able to reach the pull rope for the speaker system from the cockpit of my kayak. The dock masters ushered me in and let me float free. There were no other boats with me.

Today was the first time I locked through by myself and I must admit I was a little nervous. My little craft was dwarfed by the size of the cavity that I found myself in. The gates closed behind me and the pumps brought water in. It swirled around me. I kept the boat in the center of the basin without a problem. Once I reached the upper level, the gates opened on the upriver end and I sallied forth. The whole process took about half an hour. I had been lifted about fifty feet from where I started.

Next on the agenda was to find another campsite. I paddled and kept close to the Washington shore. When the sun was low on the horizon behind me, I looked for a place to camp. Unable to find a good site, I finally settled for a rocky shelf just above the high water line. I had to wedge the tent pins between the rocks to get the tent to stay. I pulled the *Wind Dancer* up on the rocks as high as I could and then took the added precaution of tying the painter around a large bolder. It was lucky I did, because in the middle of the night, I heard the waves move the boat around on the rocks and I had to get up and move it and myself higher.

Tuesday, April 7

At first light, I was on the move again. I paddled along the north shore with the idea I would be more protected from the wind there. However, the sky was clear and the surface of the lake was like a mirror so there seemed to be no need for the precaution. Around ten o'clock, I began to feel small puffs of wind. These were the signs I was told to watch for. I looked for a place to land, but there was none.

For as far as I could see, there were either sheer rock cliffs or big boulder riprap to protect the railroad. I decided to try the Oregon side. Maybe I would have better luck over there and find a beach or cove where I could land. No such luck. The Oregon shore was the same as the Washington shore. It was all well and good for people to tell me to get off the river when the wind picked up, but where? That was the question.

By then I was really getting hammered. As far as I could tell, the wind had risen to about fifty knots. I could no longer make any forward progress. The wind forced me backward and the waves broke with five-foot white caps. When the waves hit me broadside, I had to lean into them, reach through, and pull the paddle toward the boat as hard as I could. I paddled the kayak into the wave and allow it to break over the top of me.

The waves forced me ever closer to the rock wall. As the waves hit the riprap, they shot twenty-five to thirty feet into the air. Between the waves and the wall was a twenty-five foot wide area of tormented water. It was clear I was caught between a rock and a hard place; if you could call a wave a hard place.

Several times I got that sickish feeling that I would broach. Each time I saved myself with a quick brace. I could tell that at any minute I would go for a swim, get bashed against the rocks, or both. It was inevitable. I decided to make a controlled exit as best as I could onto the rocks. Good luck! I waited until a wave rebounded and slowed the incoming one. I made my dash to the rocks, swung the kayak parallel, and proceeded to disembark. My version of Murphy's Law states, "That which can happen will happen, and if the situation can change it will get worse."

Well, that might not have been "the" law right then, but it was close…and things did get worse. As I popped the spray skirt loose, it caught shortly on the lip of the cockpit, which slowed my exit for a fraction of a second. The incoming wave slammed into the side of my boat just as I got one foot on the rocks. I braced my legs to cushion the impact. As the hydraulics of the waves hit the rocks, they lifted the boat above the riprap and rolled the kayak upside down, spilling me out on the rocks. I jerked my legs back to keep the *Wind Dancer* from landing on my legs. The kayak hit on its top, and before I could grab it, it rolled back into the river and was swept out past the tortured water area. The kayak and all my equipment floated thirty feet out in the river and I was on shore.

"Is that where my journey ends?" I thought. Hell, no! I plunged into the river and swam out to where my boat floated upside down. I turned the boat right side up, gathered what equipment I found on the surface, put them into the cockpit and then found my paddles which were afloat nearby.

The cockpit was full of water but the kayak was not in danger of sinking because the storage compartments were sealed, which gave it positive flotation. Another thought crossed my mind at that point. The young lady that sold me the wet suit said that it would extend my life expectancy by ten minutes from hypothermia. I figured I had that long to get the kayak back on shore. I took my paddles in my left hand, clamped the painter in my teeth, scissor kicked with my feet, and swam back to the riprap as I drug the kayak behind me.

Once I got back to the wall, I crawled up backward. Each time a wave would come in, I used its lift to get the kayak up and pulled it further onto the rocks. Once on top of the rocks, I emptied the water out which made it easier to handle. I cringed because I knew that each time I dragged the boat across the rocks I damaged the bottom, but I had to pull it far enough that I could get it past the spray area before I could dry it out.

While I was in the water, I had no memory of being cold, but with the wind I figured the chill factor had to be near freezing. I got my bag of dry clothes out. My first task was to dry my waterproof paddlers jacket so that I could use it for a windbreaker. No water got into the stuff sack even though there was about a gallon of water in the compartment. I had been wrong when I thought that the seals were watertight. I stripped down until I was completely nude.

The wind whistled about my body. My skin turned blue and even my goose bumps had goose bumps. I began to shake uncontrollably and my teeth chattered like a Spanish flamenco dancer's castanets. I toweled myself dry and put on dry clothes. By the time I got that done, my paddler's jacket was dried by the wind. I pulled on a navy watch cap. Shortly the shakes stopped and the castanets were silent. Then I turned my attention back to the *Wind Dancer*.

I emptied everything out on the ground and inspected the kayak for damage. There were some gouges in the top, and the bottom was scraped, but it was only cosmetic damage. I was surprised because the poor craft really got hammered. Empty, it was now light enough to be carried up to the railroad. There was a narrow dirt road beside the track. I put the wheels under the *Wind Dancer*, then made several trips back to the rocks, and carried all my gear to the boat and reloaded it all into the cockpit to balance the load over the wheels.

Before I left the area, I went back to where I pulled the boat in to see if I could find some of the equipment that was missing.

The next day I would have to declare a layover day to inventory and see what needed to be replaced. I picked up the grab handle and started down the road singing a song.

On a summer day in the month of May,
A burly bum came stridden. Down a shady lane,
Near the sugar cane just a look'en for a liven.
He hummed a song as he strolled along
Of a land of milk and honey,
Where a bum can stay for many a day,
And not need any money.

Why did I sing? I sang because I was happy to be alive. I had just had my first bout with the Grim Reaper and was victorious. He had stalked me all of my life, and each time he appeared, I had been able to beat him. He knew, and so did I, that someday he'd take me out, but not that day.

Oh! The buzzin' of the bees in the cigarette trees,
A soda water fountain, the blue birds sing
Around the lemonade springs,
On the Big Rock Candy Mountain.

I was raised by my maternal grandfather in a small gold mining community in northern Nevada during the Great Depression. Everyone in those days dreamed of the Big Rock Candy Mountain. It was unfortunate that the youth of today does not have a meaningful song to sing. About an hour down the road, I met a pickup truck with three men in it. They were railroad maintenance workers. They stopped and kidded me about pulling the boat down the railroad when I should have been out on the river. I told them that an hour ago I had been out there and the river kicked me off and threw me up on the rocks. I explained what happened. We all had a good laugh. I was told I was lucky to be alive. I disputed that. If I had been lucky I wouldn't have been battered by elements in the first place. Again, we laughed.

It was strange how a short space of time could change things from a grim life threatening situation to one of humor. The men told me that Arlington was about nine miles down the road. I tucked my head down to protect my face from the wind. It tore at me and blew sand. It was two pm. If I had nine miles to go, I should reach my destination at about five o'clock. I walked, and rolled into Arlington at 4:30 pm, a little ahead of schedule. That was just fine with me.

In the excitement of my river experience, I neglected to eat my midday meal and snacks. My stomach thought that my throat was cut. A couple of hamburgers and a mug of hot coffee would fix that. I headed for the restaurant I saw up ahead, pulled into a parking place, and went inside and placed my order.

The waitress had watched me approach through the window. When I sat down she asked me if I was the fellow that was paddling across the continent. I admitted that I was. She wanted to know if I had just come off the river. Again I explained what happened. She shook her head and walked off to wait on other customers. She told the story to them and they came over to hear me talk about my experience. Soon the story had spread throughout the community. Several people came to meet me and invited me to dinner and drinks later that evening. It was a very friendly town.

After I had eaten, I was directed to a camping site across the street at a park. I found a sheltered area out of the wind and pitched my tent. I already had my bath for the day so all I did was lay out my sleeping gear and returned to my newfound friends. They had waited for me and we celebrated my victory over the Grim Reaper.

Later on, the local newspaper reporter joined us. Apparently an Oregon State Trooper had reported that a wind surfer had floundered in the river. I told her it was not a wind surfer. "That was me in the creek and the breeze blew me up on the rocks," I said. "Creek!" she exclaimed. "That is the mighty Columbia River and that was no breeze. That was the worst wind storm we've had this year." "Yes," I replied, "I believe you."

Everyone laughed hilariously. We shared camaraderie, food, drink, songs, and adventures—both theirs and mine. Could there be a better way of life? Not for me there wasn't. I returned to my tent feeling a warm glow.

Wednesday, April 8

I awoke late and went to breakfast. The sun was shining and the breeze was blowing, but nothing like it had the day before. When I returned to my campsite, I stripped everything out of the boat, inspected it, and made a note of everything that was missing. I draped my life jacket and wet suit over the tent to dry. Everything was still soaking wet so I laid all of my equipment on a picnic table to air out. That accomplished, I rechecked the *Wind Dancer* for damage. When I checked the day before, I couldn't believe there wasn't more damage than I found. After the beating it took, I expected it to be a basket case.

The damage seemed to be just minor scratches but nothing deep enough to go through the jell coat. It was still structurally sound. I gathered up my dirty clothes and took them with me to the restaurant. I got directions to the laundromat and to the sporting goods store. In my inventory that morning, I noticed that several items of equipment were missing. Most I could replace there. The missing items were my river charts, the water jugs, my journal, batteries for my CB radio, and my camera. My underwater camera was now under water. It was the one thing I wouldn't be able to replace. A new camera just wasn't in the budget.

After my midday meal, I drifted uptown with my clothes. While they were washing, I went across the street to a stationary store for the notebook and then on to the sporting goods store.

I was able to replace everything except the river charts. Not to worry; I picked up my clothes and went to a gas station and purchased a Washington state road map that had the campsites marked on it. It wasn't as good as my lost charts, but it was better than nothing.

After these tasks were completed, I returned to my tent and turned my gear over. One of the gentlemen at last evening's get-together was the manager of the motel next door to the restaurant. He told me that if I went over to the motel before they made up the rooms, I could take hot shower. I am absolutely shameless. If someone offers me a kindness, I take advantage of it. After all, a hot shower beat the hell out of a cold dip in the river.

With the shower out of the way, I went back to the restaurant, got a cup of hot coffee, and settled down in a booth to write about the last two days in my new journal. I was lucky. When I had met Ruth in Hood River, I had removed my notes up to that day and gave them to her to take back to the *Sea Venture* for me. Therefore, I had only lost one day of notes. Now all I had to rewrite were last two days. After bringing the journal up to date, I wrote Ruth and my friends back at the club a letter explaining what happened. I asked Ruth to see if she could find another camera for me and bring it and some new equipment to Lewiston, Idaho, where we planned to meet next.

After the letter was written, I returned to the park and checked my gear. Things were drying nicely. I took my sleeping pad into a sunny spot and lay down for a little nap. I believed that would be my last rest until I reached Lewiston, which was about three hundred miles away. After my nap, I carried the boat down to the dock located in a small cove right there in the park. I sat it down and proceeded to carry my equipment to the boat and repack like I had before. I left my tent, pad, and sleeping bag where they were to be packed in the morning.

Arlington Chamber of Commerce
Arlington, Oregon

Newly aquired friends at Arlington

When evening shadows began to fall, I returned to my favorite place to eat. It was cheaper for me to eat at the restaurant than it was for me to replace my food. The whole village treated me like a local hero. Someone got an advertisement of the city and several of people signed it and put their address on it and asked me to write to them when I finished my journey. My day of rest was just about over. I wanted to be on my way at first light. My adventure on the Arlington rocks cost me a few expensive items—a pair of boots and my camera—along with one day. All in all, I felt pretty good about the whole affair. Score one for Captain Karl over the Grim Reaper.

Thursday, April 9

All good things must end. I got up early, packed my tent and sleeping gear, and went to breakfast. A few of my friends came down to say good-bye and see me off. At seven am, I was once again on the move. It was a nice day with only a slight breeze blowing. I made good time.

The landscape was much different than it was before Hood River. On the west side of the Cascade Mountains, the trees were starting to leaf out and the air was spicy from their aroma; the grass had not started to grow yet, leaving the hills brown and barren. Their tops were covered with lava and sharp cliffs, evidence of volcanic upheavals from millions of years ago.

I ate my snacks in the cockpit of the *Wind Dancer,* anxious to go as far as I could that day. Late in the afternoon, I camped near Crow's Butte, Washington. I found a flat spot next to a rocky outcropping that offered a little protection from the wind. It took me two hours to go through my complete camping routine. But, that is part of the life of a nomad. I slid into my sleeping bag. The wind was shaking my tent a little but I soon fell asleep.

Friday, April 10

Morning came; I broke camp, packed my gear, and continued my journey up river. I was far enough above the impoundment that islands began appearing. I passed by an island that was named Goose Island, for the number of geese on it, by Lewis and Clark in October 1805. I could see why. There were still hundreds of geese on the island. After I paddled for about an hour, the wind started to build again from the northeast. I stayed close to the Washington shore. The waves were choppy but manageable.

About ten o'clock, the wind became so strong that I could no longer make headway. I elected to put the wheels under *Wind Dancer* and go by land. There was a road near the shore a little east of Paterson, Washington. As I walked along, a group of young people came up the road in a car. They were shouting and laughing. They must have been high on pot because one of the young ladies had her torso pushed through the front window and waived both of her hands. But that wasn't the only thing that waived; she was topless.

At two o'clock I had to make a decision. I was approaching the I-82 freeway. I found a sheltered spot where I could make some measurements on my road map. I figured out that if I went back on the river, it would be forty-five miles to the mouth of the Snake River and would take me two days. If I could get on the river, which at that time I couldn't, the wind would be too high. If I went on to the freeway, it was about twenty-five miles to Kennewick, and I could make it in one day. Kennewick got the call. I picked up the grab handle of my kayak and continued to march. I had solved one problem and created another. As I approached the entrance to I-82, it was posted, "Motor Vehicles Only, No Hitchhiking." While I wasn't hitchhiking, I also wasn't motorized. What were the odds that I would get away with it? I was about to find out.

I walked up the on-ramp and entered the freeway. I walked a short distance and there was a truck weighing station. Parked at the station was a Washington State patrol car. I headed straight for it. If I was going to have a problem, I'd hit it head on. As I approached the policeman, he got out of his car and waited for me. I introduced myself and told him what I wanted to do and why.

"Are you going to Florida in that?" he asked. "You've got to be kidding." "No, I'm not," I told him. I pulled out one of the news articles and let him read it. He told me I was insane. I replied that he was not the first to reach that conclusion. He told me to go ahead and stay on the shoulder and he would tell the other patrols what I was doing. He didn't think anyone would bother me. With a chuckle and a shake of his head, he got into his patrol car and drove off.

I thought to myself, "If I can keep people laughing all the way to Florida, I am going to be alright." I continued marching down the freeway pulling the kayak behind me. Three more hours down the road, I pulled off the freeway into a construction site and camped for the night.

Saturday, April 11

When the sun peaked over the horizon, I was on the move again. If my distance estimates were right, I was about ten miles from Kennewick and the Columbia River. That would place me a little above the Snake River. I was looking forward to getting there. I had pulled the boat over thirty miles and my feet were blistered. The police had not bothered me. In fact, I had not seen one since the weight station. In three more hours, I would be home free.

All along the way I kept expecting someone to give me a hard time. Sometimes that happens because my lifestyle is so much different from others that they fail to understand what I am doing. I decided to camp early so I could make my entrance into Kennewick the next morning; that would give me time to pick up some needed supplies before I launched into the Columbia River to reach the mouth of the Snake River. There weren't very many supply points on the Snake.

Sunday, April 12

I got under way early, and at 1:30 in the afternoon, I rolled into the outskirts of Kennewick. I changed from the shoulder of the freeway to a sidewalk alongside a street leading to the river. I didn't know exactly how to get to the river from there, but I knew that if I kept walking northeast I would reach it. As I continued walking, I came to a fried chicken restaurant. All of a sudden, I was overtaken by an urge for some fried chicken, French fries, and a root beer float. Since I had a habit of catering to my own desires, I parked my kayak in the parking lot and went in for lunch.

Afterward, I returned to my boat and continued on my journey. I had not gone very far when I noticed that the kayak had gotten suddenly hard to pull. Investigating it, I discovered that the right tire on the carriage had gone flat. Have you ever heard of having a flat tire on a kayak? Well, it can happen. Not to worry; I had a tire patch kit in my repair kit. I got the patch kit out, took the tire off, and prepared to patch it. Then I discovered that the new tube of cement which had never been opened had solidified. No cement, no patch.

I took one of my spare propane bottles, lifted up the carriage, and propped it up with the bottle. I carried the wheel back to a gas station to have it repaired. The gas station attendant told me modern cars didn't have tubes so he couldn't help me. He directed me to a variety store to get a new kit. After purchasing the kit, I returned to the gas station and made my repairs. Perseverance pays off. Then back to the kayak I went.

I was in the act of replacing the wheel when a young man arose out of the tall grass by the sidewalk with a camera. He was a newspaper photographer. He told me that he saw my kayak and knew there was a story in it. I told him my story. He wanted to take some pictures of me pulling the kayak on its carriage. I complied. After he took his pictures, he gave me directions on how to reach the river. He was from the *Tri-City Herald.*

After he gave me the directions, he told me he was going back to his paper and sending a reporter to write the story. I proceeded toward the river using the instructions he gave me. I had gone about a half mile when a car came up behind me and blew its horn. The person in the car motioned me to stop. It was the reporter. As we stood there besides the road talking, I kept looking across a hedge at a motel. It kept beckoning to me. I was tired, my feet hurt, and I could see that I was not going to make the Snake River that day.

After the interview, I walked around the corner into the parking lot and approached the manager's office. I inquired about a room. The manager explained to me that the motel had special rate for truck drivers. I told her that I was trucking a kayak across America and I could use their special rate of nine dollars. It was granted; a cost that was within my budget. The manager, Mickey Turin, took me to my room. She told me that I shouldn't leave my kayak outside because by morning it would be gone. I asked her what she would suggest. "Bring it inside," she said. Now that was going to take some engineering. How do you get a seventeen-foot kayak into a twelve-foot square room? Very carefully; where there is a will, there is a way. I took everything out of the kayak and piled it in a corner, then took the wheels off. The manager's husband came, and we turned the kayak up on edge and angled it across the bed diagonally. I slept curled up around the bow of the *Wind Dancer.*

Monday, April 13

I had breakfast in my room from my food stores. Then Mickey's husband came and we maneuvered the boat out of the room. When I checked out, I joked with Mickey; I told her I would bet her that I was the first man to stay at her motel that slept with a kayak. She laughed and told me I was right. Off I went heading for the marina. Just as I got there, damned if

I didn't have another flat tire. That time I took it off and went
to a Michelin tire dealer. They fixed the tire for no charge.
The morning newspaper was out and there was my story. As I
walked along the street, people stopped and chatted. I launched
in the Columbia River at eleven o'clock. It felt good to be back
on the water again. My feet burned like they were on fire. Not
to worry; at noon I approached the mouth of the Snake River.
If my calculations were right, I had traveled 325 miles.

Chapter 3
The Snake River

The Snake River

Washington, State

Monday, April 13

I turned into the river and picked up the stroke. From Kennewick to the Snake, I paddled with the current. Once again I was paddling up stream. I was making better time than I expected and I was not really pushing myself. I stopped for lunch in the South Bank State Park at Burbank. I was back on the water at 12:30, and determined to get as far up the river as I could.

I locked through the Ice Harbor Dam at four o'clock and immediately started looking for a campsite. Soon, I came upon Charbonneau State Park; a beautiful park with full camping facilities: tap water, toilets, and showers. When I inquired about the price, I was told it was $8.50 a night. I replied that I didn't want to buy the place; I just wanted to rent one hundred square feet for one night. I only paid nine dollars the night before for a motel room. The lady called the Bureau of Land Management (BLM) park ranger for a special rate. I was denied a special rate but told that I could paddle farther up the river and camp on the riverbank for free, which was alright with me.

I went back to the *Wind Dancer* and resumed paddling. I had no sooner cleared the marina when I observed two ladies clambering down the rocks toward the river, shouting and waving to me. "Now what?", I asked myself. I paddled over to see what they wanted. It was the park supervisor and her daughter. The daughter had overheard the phone conversation and objected to me going farther up river to camp. She convinced her mother that I should camp on their front lawn. I told them that I was content to go up river, but they insisted, so that is what I did. That was a very friendly gesture for Holly and her mother, Linda Nutt, to have made.

Tuesday, April 14

The next morning I carried my tent and equipment back to the marina where I left my boat. I got under way, back up the river at 7:30, and then stopped for breakfast later in the morning. The weather was good for two days. After breakfast, I paddled for another two hours and stopped for my midday meal. I did some stretching exercises and rested a bit. I could see that I was traveling much faster than I thought I would and needed to slow down some or I would be in Lewiston days before the time specified for Ruth to meet me. I didn't want to spend too much time waiting for her because it would be too expensive. After a while, I continued on my way. At about 2:30, the wind increased in velocity and in another hour the kayak become hard to control. The *Wind Dancer* was aptly named because it certainly did dance in the wind. Within two hours, I reached the Wind Dust State Park. That park was aptly named as well. The camp attendant, Jim Campbell, allowed me to pitch my tent in the lee of the restroom and he invited me to dinner. He lived in a trailer house on the campground. I spent the evening with him, and we told each other about our adventures.

Wednesday, April 15

This day was a real loser. The wind blew so hard that I didn't even try to paddle. I hung out in Jim's trailer and we continued our storytelling time. I was thankful for his kindnesses. One story he told me, I really appreciated. He told me that one night on a drive home, he stopped to watch some rattlesnakes cross the road. Two of them reached up and struck at his headlights. If it had been me, I wouldn't have stopped to watch snakes. I would have been long gone. Before I returned to my tent, Jim gave me a map of the Snake River system showing the dams, campsites, and parks. That was a good replacement for my lost river charts. After hearing about the snakes, you can believe that I made damn sure that my tent was securely zipped up that night.

Thursday, April 16

When morning came, I had breakfast with Jim then got back on the river. Along the way I came upon a group of BLM workers who were setting wooden tripods about eight feet tall with platforms on top, which they supplied with sticks and reeds hoping to encourage Sand Hill Cranes to nest. I stopped and chatted with them awhile. Again, I was warned about rattlesnakes. One of the biologists with them had been bitten twice that morning by one. Luckily, he wore a very heavy pair of canvas leggings for protection. Before I left, they gave me one of their snakebite kits. I didn't tell them that I had no faith in the kits figuring if worst came to worst, I would use it. Maybe it would help.

I locked through the lower Monumental Dam. Here on the Snake River, the lockmasters were stricter than they were on the Columbia. They made sure that I tied up to a cleat before they started their pumps to raise me up to the next level. I used my painter. I tied it into a figure eight on a small cleat just forward of the cockpit, then ran it over to the floating cleat on the basin wall, then tied it off with a clove hitch.

That was very windy country, especially that time of year, but I managed. I nosed the kayak into the bank and had my midmorning snack sitting in the cockpit. Then I got out and stretched my legs. After my fifteen-minute break, I continued for another two hours. I elected to stop at the Lyons Ferry Marina for lunch. I had a hamburger and filled my water jugs. This made my camping routine easier in the evening. When I returned to the river, I pushed on.

The landscape on either side of the river remained about the same. It consisted of barren rolling hills as far as the eye could see. I reached the Texas Rapids Campsite at five that evening and set up camp. There were two motor homes in the camping area. I introduced myself and chatted with the campers a few minutes. One of the couples invited me to come for breakfast in the morning.

I borrowed a hammer to set my tent pins because the ground was so hard that I couldn't get them to penetrate, and I couldn't find a rock to pound them in. I finished my evening meal and was in the act of hanging up my wet underwear on the fence in front of my tent when the sun winked out and I felt a cold chill on the back of my neck. When I turned and looked back over my shoulder where the sun had been a minute before, I saw a big black cloud sliding down the hillside at an in creditable speed straight for the campsite.

I grabbed my underwear off the fence, dove into my tent, whirled around to zip up the rain fly and then the main tent. I fell back on to my sleeping pad. Within seconds the wind hit. It smashed my tent completely flat bending the fiberglass rods nearly double. Why they didn't shatter I can't explain. I rolled over on my back and grasped the rods with both hands and stuck my feet up in the air bracing them as best I could. I laid there for fifteen minutes with both arms and legs stuck up in the air like the little dog Snoopy in the comic strip *Peanuts*, expecting any minute to be swept into the river while the wind tore at my tent. After the initial blast, the wind slacked off a bit but all night long it raged about my tent. There was no sleep for me that night.

When morning came, the tent was still in one piece, which surprised me. It was not the best tent in the world; I had only paid thirty-four dollars for it.

Friday, April 17

I was lucky that Ellen and Gene had invited me to breakfast. With the heavy winds that still blew, it would have been impossible for me to have started my little propane stove to fix my coffee. In fact, I used their kitchen table to bring my notes up to date. After breakfast I chatted with them awhile, but I didn't want to be a nuisance, so I drifted over to visit with my other neighbor. They also had invited me over the night before. The two of them were citizen band radio enthusiasts, which gave me an idea. My radio got wet when I went for my swim down at Arlington. I dried it off the best I could and checked the batteries. The radio appeared to be in working order but I had no way to test it. I told the gentleman what happened. He had a good laugh at my story. He suggested that I walk a couple hundred yards up the hillside and we would test it. I was hoping he would say that. The radio checked out fine. In a few days, I would need it. The radio check was worth the gale. The day passed quickly and I returned to my tent to endure the shaking and rattling of the tent rods.

Saturday, April 18

I arose at the break of day and got on the water immediately. The wind had dropped to an acceptable level. I paddled steadily all morning and locked through the Little Goose Dam. I made it as far as the willow landing when I was again stopped by the high winds. I don't remember reading in the Lewis and Clark journals that they had to fight these winds. But they came through here in the late summer. Maybe it was calmer then.

Sunday, April 19

I broke camp and got under way. The wind had dropped to a whisper. It was a beautiful day and the *Wind Dancer* sliced through the water like a whetted knife. It was a real pleasure not to have to fight the wind. It was like my grandfather told me, "You have to taste the bitter before you can really enjoy the sweet." This was about as sweet as you could get.

I locked through the Lower Granite Dam without a problem. The lockmasters knew I was coming. The lockmasters at little Goose Dam had told them that I was on my way the day before. I reached Blyten Landing at about five pm. I had made good time having covered over thirty miles. I still had plenty of daylight to pitch my tent and do my camping routine. I was in a very relaxed mood. The campsite was deserted. It was too early in the year to attract a lot of campers, therefore I had the whole campsite to myself. I decided my next campsite would be Chief Timothy State Park, only twelve miles away.

Monday, April 20

I got off to a very lazy start. Again, it was a beautiful day with no wind. All things being normal, I would only have about a three-hour paddle. I could afford to just dink along. I watched for birds and other wildlife. I saw a small animal that I couldn't identify. It looked like a ferret or a weasel except it had coal black fur. That was the kind of traveling I liked to do; to go leisurely along and sort of smell the roses. This style of traveling was a real pleasure.

I arrived at Chief Timothy State Park at about one that afternoon. It was a beautiful park with cut grass and full camping facilities. It also had a camping fee of six dollars a night. Since I was on a low-budget journey, I worked a deal with the park ranger. For four hours of policing the trash, I could camp free. I didn't mind doing this because it gave me something to do after I set up camp.

While I wandered around picking up the trash, I visited with the other campers. There were more people here than the park I had camped at the night before. After my rubbish detail, I returned to my tent and fixed a cup of hot chocolate and a peanut and jam sandwich. I was sitting with my back up against a tree when a big motor home pulled into a campsite right in front of me. The motor home was a forty-foot Silver Bullet. He backed on to a concrete slab then he got out of his rig and hooked up a water hose, a sewage line, and an electrical cord. His next operation was to take the leveling jacks and level the rig. After that was done, he retreated inside.

I sat there in front of my tent sipping my mug of hot chocolate when I heard a weird whirring noise. A satellite dish arose out of the top of that great silver can.

I had to smile. I had him pictured sitting inside sipping his mint julep and watching TV. I couldn't help but contrast his camping with mine. Was I envious? No, not at all. I could not imagine me herding that bucket of bolts over a highway. That would be more frightening to me than fighting a gale. And he would never be able to see the things that I saw. Then again maybe he didn't want to; to each his own.

I called Rick in Portland. He gave me the names and telephone numbers of the people who wanted to talk to me in

Lewiston, Idaho. A newspaper reporter wanted to take some pictures of me taking off from the dock in the morning. At that point I was only eight miles from Lewiston and five days ahead of schedule. I wasn't looking forward to sitting around for five days cooling my heels, waiting for time to pass. Both my wife and youngest son worked, so they couldn't come until the weekend. So, I just dosed in the afternoon sun.

Tuesday, April 21

When I got everything packed into the kayak, I called the newspapers, channel 3 TV station, and the city managers that Rick told me to call. Bob Hudson, the editor of the *Valley American News* wanted me to wait for him. He wanted to take some pictures of me leaving the park. We had a nice chat before I took off. I got the *Wind Dancer* under way at 10:30. Again, I just dinked along killing time and enjoying what was to be my last paddle for two to three weeks.

I arrived at the Army Corps of Engineers' marina in Clarkston, Washington, close to one o'clock. It was only an eight-mile paddle. Gene Hagenson, the local channel 3 news director, met me. He filmed my arrival. Rick had arranged a complimentary stay at the Nendels Motor Inn in Clarkston. So, I put my kayak on wheels and pulled it up the hill a short distance to the motel. I chained it to a tree in front of the motel and checked in.

I recounted my adventures up to that point. I had had one upset—two days of portaging due to high winds. I had been battered by high winds for six days and passed through seven sets of locks. My longest portage on foot was forty miles from Patterson to Kennewick, Washington. My longest days paddling were over thirty miles, which I accomplished on two occasions. I had traveled 465 miles in twenty-six days. Not bad for an old man over sixty years old.

Now the long march would begin. Lewiston, Idaho, was just across the river. I would cross over tomorrow.

CHAPTER 4
THE LONG MARCH

The long haul

Three hundred fifty miles from the Snake River to the Missouri River

Wednesday, April 22

After breakfast I moved the *Wind Dancer* across the river to the Lewiston side. That is where the Clear Water River joins the Snake River. I would like to have continued paddling up the

Clear Water, but it was much too swift. Any time that I could not make at least twenty miles a day by kayak, I put the wheels on and walked. On Lewis and Clark's journey, they used horses to carry their equipment over the mountains. It was my plan to pull my kayak walking wherever I couldn't paddle. I wanted to make the entire journey from the Pacific Ocean to the Atlantic Ocean using nothing but the power of my own body.

I had lunch at the Kiwanis Club after moving the kayak. They had invited me to be their guest speaker. That was a very interesting experience. I had never been a speaker before. They wanted to know all about my journey and why I was doing it. After I completed my talk, I went back to the motel and checked out. Charley, my friend at the Willamette Athletic Club, told me to visit with Buzz and Pat Manning. Buzz was the person that gave Charley the information about the CB radio that made it possible to talk to the truck drivers. When I called Buzz and Pat they ask me to stay with them until Saturday. That was when Ruth and Mike would arrive. It was very kind of them and it helped me out a lot.

Thursday, April 23

Buzz loaned me his car because he lived a little way out of town and I needed to run some errands. First I went to the Idaho State Police and told them I was going to be on Highway 12 for the next two weeks. Then I went on to the truck stop and posted a notice to the drivers that I would be on the road for that length of time. While I was there, a truck driver pulled in with his rig and I asked him to check out if he could receive my radio signal. It checked out fine. He laughed when I told him what I was doing and told me that I was out of my mind.

My next stop was at an Army Surplus store where I bought some webbing to make a chest harness. The rope had cut into my shoulder on my last portage. This time I would be pulling the kayak for over three hundred miles and I wanted it to be as comfortable as possible. The Army Surplus store shopkeeper sent me to a boat shop to get the harness made. The guy designed the harness and sewed it for me for free. When he asked what it was for he called his wife—who was a weather reporter for the local weather watch—and she put my journey in her report for the next day.

To say that I was a little worried about the trip over the mountains would be an understatement. It scared the living hell out of me. Even with all the precautions I had taken, I felt that my chances for getting over the mountains were next to zero. The Idaho Highway Department had posted a notice for bicycles to stay off the highway and here I was taking a seventeen-foot kayak on it against the flow of traffic. That was really giving the Grim Reaper a clear shot at me. From the boat shop I went to a shoe store and bought two pairs of silk socks. I was told that silk socks under my heavy socks would protect my feet from blisters. With my shopping out of the way I returned to the house.

The rest of the afternoon I washed my kayak and inspected it for damage. It was in remarkably good condition considering what it had gone through. When I completed the inspection I removed the rudder and packed it away. On my shopping spree I had picked up some pieces of old tires and a bicycle flag. I duct taped the pieces of tires to the bow and stern of the kayak to protect it in case the kayak got away from me while being pulled up and down the mountains. The bicycle flag I taped to the bow to increase its visibility. About that time I heard a call to come to dinner. The rest of the evening I spent visiting with the Manning family. My stay in Lewiston was far different than I had expected. I thought that I would be cooling my heels on the bank of the Clear Water River with nothing to do but wait. Instead, I was spending my time with the most friendly and helpful people that I could imagine.

Friday, April 24

The Lewiston Tribune interviewed me this morning. That was a most fortunate occurrence. After the interview, I spent the rest of the afternoon reading the history of Idaho. In the evening, the Manning's had a going away dinner for me. The plan for the next day was to go to the Austin Spring Festival for breakfast.

Saturday, April 25

After our breakfast at the Austin Spring Festival, we paid a visit to the Elks Lodge. Many of the members wished me well for the continuation of my journey. There was no way that people could have treated me better. Afterwards, Buzz helped me move the kayak to the Holiday Inn. I got a room for the night for Ruth and myself and one for my youngest son, Mike.

Ruth and Mike arrived late in the afternoon bringing me the needed supplies for my trip over the mountains. The Willamette Athletic Club members had taken up a collection and with it, Ruth had purchased a new Canon underwater camera for me. Also, she had gone to the Ebb and Flow Kayak and Canoe Shop and borrowed two wheels with solid rubber tires which I had asked her to do. I didn't want to repeat the experience I had with the flat tires on the long haul over the mountains. The solid tires solved that problem alright, but they created another. The wheels were larger in diameter than the old ones. They rubbed on the bottom of the kayak. I found a dead tree limb about two inches in diameter and I cut two sections with my machete that were two-feet long, and duct taped them across the frame—I never travel far without duct tape. The wheels rolled free after that. Mike helped me load the equipment into the kayak and we made everything ready to take off the following morning.

About the myth that absence makes the heart grows fonder— not true. Ruth was still angry, but I was still determined to keep on going. I had hoped that when she saw that I could make it, her mood would soften. But that wasn't the case. I wouldn't see her again until the end of the trek.

Sunday, April 26

We had breakfast at a nearby restaurant. Afterwards, Ruth and Mike took off back to Portland. I walked back to the motel, tied off the painter with a figure eight to the cleat in front of the cockpit, slipped into the shoulder harness, picked up the grab handle, and headed up the road to the Lolo Pass.

Oh! Oh! The songs of the prophets are hardy and bold
And quite unaccustomed of fear.
But the most reckless of life and limb
Was Abdul Bulbul Emir.

This song was a classic from the Ottoman era between a Turk and Ivan Skavinsky Skvar, a Cossack. They may have been unaccustomed to fear, but they never faced an eighteen-wheel truck roaring at them at one hundred kilometers an hour.

I hadn't been on the road very long when I heard a truck down shifting as it came into a curve ahead of me. I whipped the radio up to my lips and sang out, "Trucker! Trucker! This is a red kayak in the westbound lane. I hear you approaching me. There is no shoulder. Watch for me." Instantly I got a reply, "Red kayak, I hear you." Then I got the question, "What the hell are you doing out here on the road with a kayak?"

I had two minutes to tell him my story before my radio broke up. From that point on a truck passed me about every fifteen minutes. After a few days, every truck driver plying that road knew what I was doing. They passed on my location to each other and watched for me. Not only was the radio a life-saving device, it was a means of entertainment. At each passing, I would have a two-minute friendly chat. Those truck drivers were a great bunch of guys.

I made it to mileage marker twenty-four and camped on the bank of the Clear Water River. I wondered if Lewis and Clark had camped there. All along that area of the road there were markers that read that this was the "Lewis and Clark trail." After going through my camping routine, I had to filter two gallons of river water for drinking. But I used half a gallon to back flush my filter so that I only gained one and a half gallons. That would barely get me through the day. My next task was to tend to my feet. The silk liners for my socks didn't stop my feet from blistering.

Monday, April 27

My march continued. Just outside of the town Orofino, a lady met me. She had read the story the *Lewiston Tribune* printed about me. She wanted the Orofino newspaper to take a picture and print a story for their town. I told her that I was going to stop in town for the night. Off she raced. Soon she came back with a gift certificate for the Ponderosa Motel. When I got to the motel, I met the mayor of Orofino, Ray Clay. I was guest of the town for the night. While in town I went to a drug store and purchased several sheets of moleskin to bandage my blisters. By then my feet were blistered big time. I had never had problems like that before. I guessed that pulling the kayak must have put extra stress on my feet. I was still making better than twenty miles a day.

Tuesday, April 28

As I was getting ready to take off, a news reporter showed up to take my picture with the owner of the local sporting goods store, who was the husband of the lady that had presented the gift certificate to me. I was rather amused. The owner of the sporting goods store had to show the reporter how to operate the camera. Merrily I rolled along. Well, maybe not so merrily. My feet burned like fire. I wouldn't make a good firewalker.

The weather was unseasonably warm. The temperature was eighty-five degrees. I was drinking water like it was going out of style, pulling that kayak along at a steady three miles an hour. I soon ran out of water even though I had filled my water jugs before I left Orofino. It was lucky that I came upon some people who allowed me to fill my jugs at their home; otherwise, I would have had to go to the river and filter more water. That would have killed an hour of my marching time.

The river canyon was very beautiful. The mountains sloped down to the cliffs along the side of the roadbed and on the other side of the road was the river. Occasionally, I saw a kayaker and fishermen in drift boats. There was little traffic on the road except for the trucks. I had lost my fear of them. They gave me a lot of pleasure.

I went as far as the town of Kamiah and camped beside a bridge over the Clear Water River. Between the town of Kamiah and Syringa lies the Nez Perce National Historic Park. It was along there that I saw a mound—perhaps a hundred yards in diameter and fifty yards high, as measured by my calibrated eyeball—shaped like a heart. According to a roadside sign, that mound was the heart of a monster. The sign said that according to a Nez Perce legend there had been a monster that roamed the earth devouring all the animals and people. The monster was tricked into swallowing the coyote whole, along with his knife. While he was inside the monster, he cut its heart out and let all the animals and people out. From the blood that was sprinkled on the ground sprang the first Nez Perce Native Americans.

I have great respect and sympathy for the Nez Perce tribe. Without their help, Lewis and Clark would not have survived this part of their journey. Lewis and Clark had promised the tribe that the white man would not take their land. But they did. Every treaty that was made with them was broken. And when they revolted and fled the reservation, the army chased them down killing many of them, and forced the survivors back on their reservation.

A little further down the road there was a lava formation in the shape of an arch. There was a road sign that described the formation. It was called the battle of the ant and the yellow jacket. The Great Spirit had become tired of the ant and yellow jackets constantly fighting and turned them into stone. I found the legends of the native people very interesting. Someday I will go back and learn more about them.

Before I went to sleep, I had to attend to my feet. They were very badly blistered and the little toe on my right foot had become infected and had turned black. I thought I might have to cut it off. Instead, I sterilized a pair of surgical scissors the good doctor gave me from the athletic club and cut away all the infected flesh. Next, I rubbed some Neosporin into the wound and bandaged it.

Wednesday, April 29

I put in a miserable night. I didn't put my foot into the sleeping bag because I couldn't stand the pressure on my toe, but my foot got cold. Before I started my morning routine, I inspected my toe. It was red and was quite painful. "Not to worry," I thought. It would feel better when it quit hurting. I changed the bandage, put on my marching shoes, and continued my trek. The sooner I reached the Missouri River, the quicker I would get off my feet.

I walked about two hours when I met a very interesting man. As I came around a corner I looked ahead and saw this gentleman standing beside the road. This didn't surprise me, because on several occasions when people had gone to the roadside to get their mail and saw me dragging the *Wind Dancer* along, they looked at me with obvious wonder.

"Hello, Karl. I've been waiting for you," he said when I got about ten feet from him.

"How do you know my name and when I was coming?" I asked.

He said that he had read the article in the Lewiston newspaper that quoted me saying I'd average twenty miles a day. So, he figured I would be coming by that day. He had also asked his neighbor, who lived down the road apiece, to call him when I came by his place. So, there he was waiting for me. He told me that he admired my lifestyle. He too was a world wanderer and had many adventures. His name was Don McComb. He owned a small ranch that he named the Ranch by the River. He asked me to come up to his house for a cup of coffee and lunch. I accepted his invitation. But instead of having coffee, I asked for some cold water. The temperature was over eighty and hauling that kayak up the road was hard work. It seemed that every pore in my body was leaking water out like a sieve.

Don was the author of a book entitled *The Trails and Tales of Northern Idaho*. I bought one of his books. He wanted to give it to me, but I insisted on buying it. Not far from his ranch he had found his own personal paradise—a lake tucked back in the mountains so rugged you couldn't reach it with a packhorse; you had to backpack into it. He showed me a picture of it. He invited me to come back when my journey was over to show me where it was. He said that after he retired he turned his ranch into a hummingbird sanctuary. His back yard was full of hummingbird feeders and wild flowers. The hummingbirds numbered into the hundreds. The little guys were flitting about in wild abandonment.

Sitting there on his back porch, drinking ice tea, eating lunch, and listening to his stories was a real pleasure. We sat there and chatted for over two hours. I added his name to the ones that I would send postcards to as I continued my journey. (I intended to go back when I came home. Unfortunately, Don died of a heart attack before I could get back. I have often wondered if I could find his paradise lake on my own.)

Don's ranch was near a small community named Syringa. It was named after the Idaho state flower. After leaving Don's ranch, I continued on my way. I camped that night near a small store for free. It seemed that any friend of Don McComb was a friend of the storeowner. There was a whole different way of life here in the woods. People go out of their way to help. My feet were still sore, but I still made over twenty miles a day.

Thursday, April 30

I camped that night in the corner of a truck stop. After I broke camp, I went into the truck stop restaurant. As I was sitting there eating, a gentleman walked up to my table and asked me if I was the guy kayaking across America. I told him I was. He said the he was one of the truck drivers that I had talked to on several occasions. He had seen my kayak out front as he was driving by and stopped in to meet me. He introduced himself and said, "Karl, you have more balls than any man that I have ever met." I guessed that was a truck driver macho expression for courage. We talked for a few minutes. As he got up to leave, he picked up my meal ticket and said, "Your breakfast is on me." He shook my hand and left.

I woke up that morning with the sound of rain on my tent, which was both good and bad. While the rain beating on a person is a little depressing, it does lower the body temperature and it was still hot. The availability of water was limited, so I had to rely on processing the river water in evenings and in the mornings. That meant it took me a little longer to prepare my campsites at night and a little longer to get started. According to my research on that stretch of the road, there were no settlements or stores for the next seventy-five miles.

Road side camping

On the long haul I camped beside the road

Often farmers driving trucks stopped and asked if they could haul the kayak to Missoula. They laughed when I told them that I intended to go to Florida using only the power of my own body. They shook my hand and wished me well. Except for my two-minute conservations with the friendly truck drivers, I didn't have much contact with people.

Friday, May 1

I camped this day on the bank of the Lochsa River at mileage marker 143. Day by day I was getting closer to I-75, which was the Lolo Pass. It was now two days away. My feet were sore but I pressed on. I used all my film which meant that I couldn't take any more pictures until I reached Missoula, Montana.

It has been raining for the last three days, but it didn't slow me down and it had not dampened my spirits. When you live like I do, you just adapt to the weather as it comes. I camped on the bank of the Locksa River that night. According to the Lewis and Clark journals, they made a stop on a river to make dug-out canoes, but I hadn't been able to find out exactly where that was. Whether it was on the Clear Water River or the Locksa River, I didn't know. This was my last stop on the Locksa. From here on, I would be moving inland, away from the river toward the Lolo Pass.

Saturday, May 2

I made it to the Locksa Lodge at the base of the Lolo Pass. I rented a little log hut because I didn't want to bother setting up camp and then have to tear it down in the morning. It was a rustic affair and looked like a cabin built in the eighteen hundreds. Inside was warm, with a small pot bellied stove and pieces of wood and kindling to build a fire. I appreciated that, as it was quite cold outside. The cabin had a washbasin and a bucket of water; no running water. But it was better than my tent. It was quite comfortable.

When I started at Lewiston, the elevation was 738 feet. The slope of the land following the river was rather gradual. I estimated that I had gained about 500 feet, which meant that this area more than 1,200 feet high. The elevation of the Lolo Pass is 5,235 feet. That meant that I would make a gain of over 4,000 feet the next day. People had estimated that it would take me two days to clear the summit. I hoped to make it in one. So I needed to make an early start the next morning. I ate my evening meal at the main lodge. On the morrow I would assault the Bitterroot Mountain's Lolo Pass.

While I was at dinner, several people came by to talk to me about my journey. They were fascinated by the idea that I was making the entire journey using nothing but the power of my own body. I was told that a couple weeks ago a man came by who was using a wagon and a mule to make a journey. They didn't know how far he was going. The owner of the resort told me that it was about fourteen miles to the summit

After my evening meal, I returned to my cabin. I had set the fire before I left so now the little stove was glowing rosy red and the room was warm. I made my notes in my log, banked the fire for the night, and retired.

Sunday, May 3

I arose early, had breakfast at the lodge, filled my water jugs, and got under way. There was a heavy coat of frost covering the *Wind Dancer*, testifying to the cold night.

The slope of the road after leaving the lodge was rather mild. Over the first eight miles, I probably gained 500 feet. I walked that distance in about three hours. Then came the hard part: the road exceeded a 6 percent grade. From where I was standing, the road looked straight up. The next six miles would not be fun. I leaned into the harness and pulled. Pulling the two hundred pounds of kayak and gear on the flat was not bad, but this was shear torture for my back, legs, and feet.

I didn't get very far on the first pull—only a couple of hundred feet—and I had to stop and rest. I had the feeling this was going to be a long day. Then I devised a strategy. Alongside the road were a series of posts that I estimated to be a hundred yards apart. I fixed my eyes on the next post and determined to make that goal before my next rest. Once I reached that post, I continued until I had walked the length of the kayak. That insured that if I couldn't make my goal, I wouldn't feel that I had failed. I was able to do that.

However, another problem manifested itself. When I had walked on a level road, I became accustomed to the pain in my feet and I was mentally able to dismiss it. I couldn't do that now. At every rest post the pain subsided. But when I leaned into my harness for the next pull, the pain intensified and I didn't get used to it again until I reached my next rest stop. I got so I hated to stop. But I just didn't have the energy to go on.

From the very outset of my journey I knew that this mountain was going to be my greatest challenge. It certainly didn't let me down. While it was a little on the grim side, it did have its up side. I had my cheering section: the truck drivers. The ones that came up behind me cheered me on. When they would meet the ones coming toward me, they would notify them what I was doing. They all gave me a blast on their air horns and the thumbs-up sign as they passed by.

There had been some doubt that I would make this mountain. I would be damned if I was going to show anyone my weakness. I was going to get that kayak over that hill if I had to do it on my hands and knees. At two pm, I arrived at the summit—seven hours after leaving the Locksa Lodge. Not bad for an old duffer. I would celebrate my sixty-first birthday in a couple of days. I was congratulating myself on my successful assent of the mountains. But that was short-lived.

All the time I was going up the hill, I had promised myself an overnight stay at a luxury hotel that I had pictured in my mind was at the top. But when I arrived and looked around, there was nothing. There were a few buildings, one had a lighted bulb on the outside, but they were all locked and there was not a soul around. I stood there utterly bankrupt, both mentally and physically.

I was unable to even think. I didn't want to camp on top of the mountain. The night before, the temperature was below freezing at the base of the mountain. I was now 4,000 feet higher. I figured that the temperature would drop three to four degrees for each one thousand feet of altitude. My sleeping bag was only comfortable to a temperature of forty degrees. Even with wearing two sets of long handle underwear, I was going to freeze my ass off. This was definitely not my day.

I stood there trying to decide what to do when I heard the sound of a motorcycle.

The biker pulled up about ten feet from where I stood, stopped his bike, shut off the engine, and sat there looking at me. He wasn't much bigger than me and I would say he was between forty-five and fifty years old. I thought he was a tourist motoring through.

As he continued to gaze at me, I could see the question on his mind, but he didn't say anything. I broke the silence. I said I was hoping to get a room for the night but it didn't look like anything was open.

"No," he replied. "There is nothing up here, not even in the summer time."

"Oh, you're a local then?" I responded.

"Yes," he told me. He owned the store at Lolo Creek and often rode his bike up there to admire the beauty of the place and get away from the store. He introduced himself. His name was Bill Bartlet. That opened the way for me to introduce myself and to tell him about my program. Rather than tell him a long story, I handed him the news article the *Lewiston Tribune* had written. The reporter did a good job with the story. The biker read the story and was really impressed. He hadn't heard of anyone doing it before. I told him that as far as I knew, no one ever had. I told him my misgivings spending the night up there. He said the Lolo hot springs were about seven miles further down the road. There had been a resort there but it had gone bankrupt. There was no one there except the caretaker. He said he was sure that the caretakers would let me camp there over night because they were real nice people.

Bill cranked up his bike and off he roared in true Jedi style. I called him the Jedi, in reference to the movie *Star Wars*, because he appeared out of nowhere.

A rock cliff nearby had a trickle of water coming off of it from melting snow. I ran it through my filter and refilled my jugs. On the way up, I had depleted my water supply. With that done, I harnessed up and with a song I headed down the mountainside. The way down was a mirror image of the way up. Both sides were forested. The road was a little better on the Montana side and the shoulder was wider. I wasn't hanging out in the traffic as I was before. The friendly truck drivers were still watching out for me. They were happy that I had made it. They knew about my struggle from the drivers who had passed me going up. They admitted that they thought I wouldn't make it. They told me that I was a gutsy old man. I indicated to them that among my friends I was well known to have more guts than brains. That brought a laugh over the radio.

Going down the pass was nearly as hard as going up. First I turned the kayak around and tried to let it pull me down. I found it too hard to control. Then I turned it around, tucked the bow under my arm, and leaned back, bracing it, and let it push me down the road. That was better, but it was far from easy.

I had been under way about an hour when I heard the unmistakable sound of an approaching motorcycle. Bill was back with good news. He had talked to the caretakers of the resort and I was welcomed to camp there. He had also gone on to his store and made up a care package of fresh food for my evening meal. He further told me that his store was a little over twenty miles past the Lolo Hot Springs Resort. He had a pickup truck with a camper on it and I could spend the night there tomorrow.

My mood made a dramatic swing from self-pity to optimism and well-being. I had a good camping spot assured and a place to stay the next day. And all things being normal, I would be in Missoula the following day to celebrate my sixty-first birthday. I didn't think that things could have gotten better than that, but they would. Bill took off again back to his store and I continued my trek. An hour passed since I had first met Bill on the mountaintop. It was three o'clock and I had about five more miles to go to get to the resort. I estimated that I would arrive there between five and six that evening. I would have plenty of time to set up camp before night fell.

I continued to march. I arrived 5:30 pm. I had cleared the Lolo Pass and traveled twenty-one miles in ten and a half hours, pulling a kayak and two hundred pounds of gear. I was "Captain Karl, the Invincible". How could I have had doubted myself? I nearly broke my arm patting myself on the back.

When I pulled into the parking area, the caretakers weren't there. Bill had told me that they likely wouldn't be. They had to go into town. I had started to setup camp when the caretakers arrived and stopped me. They told me it was going to get cold that night and they wanted me to sleep inside. They opened up a room in the resort. The resort was warmed by the thermal springs underneath it. That had been the spot of one of Lewis and Clark's campsites on their journey linking the Columbia and the Mississippi rivers in 1806.

The caretaker's names were Don and Becky Compton. They were very friendly folk. They lived in a trailer house on the premises and invited me to sit down and visit with them. After we had visited a while, they suggested that I go to my kayak and get my towel and swim suit. They were going to open one of the hot pools so we would go for a swim. I was a little dubious of that, thinking about my poor blistered feet. I didn't know if I could stand the hot water but I decided to try it.

I sat on the edge of the pool and tried to screw up my courage. Finally, I bit the bullet and plunged both feet into the hot water. It burned like crazy for a minute then it actually felt good. I slipped into the pool and went for a swim. It felt heavenly. We swam for a while. Don and Becky returned to their trailer to fix their dinner. They told me to finish my swim and then come over for a visit. I showered off, put on some clean clothes, and went over to their trailer.

While we were swimming, I told Don about the gift of food that Bill had given me. When they got out of the pool, Bill went to my kayak and picked up the food and Becky fixed it for me. After dinner Don had some work to do and Becky went to her kitchen, leaving me alone in their living room sitting in an easy chair; well, not quite alone.

They had a three-year-old son; a bright eyed little boy who was very friendly. He wasn't afraid of me even though I was a stranger. He got his favorite book and brought it to me. He wanted me to read to him. He climbed up on my lap, placed his head on my chest, and I began to read.

With a laugh Becky came in and picked him up to put him to bed. Both of us had fallen asleep.

I sheepishly excused myself, said good night to them both, and went to the room they had opened for me. I had rolled out my sleeping pad and bag on the warm concrete floor. Becky had given me one of the resorts pillows so I would not have to use my rolled up life jacket. Before I went to sleep, I made a few notes in my log. It was clear to me that this was going to be one of the highlights of my whole journey if not "the" highlight.

That day had been a real roller coaster. I had gone through everything imaginable, both physically and mentally: self-doubt, anger, pain, frustration, exhaustion, triumph, disappointment, and then kindness and warmth from a caring family.

Was this a five-star hotel? No! Would I trade this for a five-star hotel? No! For me that was as good as it could get. I lay down and drifted off to sleep; perfectly content, though I wished Ruth wasn't angry with me.

Monday, May 4

When I awoke in the morning, I loaded my gear. Becky called me for breakfast. After breakfast I said good-bye. They gave me their address and asked me to send them a postcard when I reached Miami. I promised I would. Then I gave the little boy a hug and hit the road. I wished that I had film so I could take a picture of them but I didn't.

I set a leisure pace. There was no need to hurry. I had been averaging over twenty miles a day on actual travel days. I was already ahead of schedule. My feet felt better than they had for two weeks. That hot soak last night did them wonders. I stopped alongside the road and had my morning snack. Then at noon I had my midday meal. About ten miles down the road I met a man setting up a video camera. Bill had called the local television station in Missoula. I was interviewed as I walked along. A short time later, I met two men on bicycles headed the opposite direction. They turned around and wanted to know where I was going. They almost fell off their bicycles when I told them I was going to Florida. Again, I showed the *Lewiston Tribune* clipping. It saved me a lot of talk.

One of the men was Bob Harrington. He was a scoutmaster. He asked me if I would show my kayak and camping technique to his troop when I got to Missoula. We set it up for the next day. I reached Bill's store about 4:30 pm. He had his camper set up for me. His wife fixed us a nice dinner. They had invited some of their friends to come and meet me. We spent the evening exchanging adventure stories. One husky man in his mid-twenties was participating in the Missoula Little Brother program and he asked me if I would tell my story to his little brother's Boy Scout troop. I told him about Bob Harrington's troop and suggested that they get together; maybe we could do both at the same time. He knew Bob and said he would find out and let me know before I left in the morning. When the company left, I went to the camper. It was nice. Once again I slept well. It was quite comfortable.

Tuesday, May 5

After breakfast, I got under way at eight AM. I reached the small village of Lolo about noon. All along the way people waved and honked their horns. They had seen me on the evening news the night before. Shortly before I arrived in Missoula, a newspaper reporter stopped me. He asked me to spread my maps out on the ground beside the *Wind Dancer* and tell him about my journey.

While I was talking to the reporter, a woman stopped her car and pressed five dollars into my hand. That embarrassed me. I didn't intend my journey to be a money-making venture. At the same time, it made things a lot easier for me. I was surfing along the road on a wave of friendliness and generosity. When I planned this trip, I prepared myself emotionally for handling anger and misunderstandings, but I didn't foresee what was taking place.

The photographer asked me if I needed anything. I asked him where I could get some film for my camera. He told me he could get me some film at cost and he would bring it to me. After he left I was on my way again. I had not gone very far when I bumped into Bob Hoffman, the Boy Scout master whom I was to stay with. He was a telephone line worker out on a job but he had been watching for me. He explained how to find his house.

When I arrived I took a shower and went to a nearby mall to purchase a shirt and a pair of trousers. I wanted to look presentable for my talk. That was something else that I was not prepared for. When I got back from shopping, everyone was waiting for me. We loaded up the kayak and went to the church where the two troops were having their meeting. I gave my program and told them my personal history and described my trek to that date.

When I came to the part about going over the mountains, I explained my fears of the eighteen-wheel trucks and how I handled the problem. To demonstrate I picked up the radio and cried, "Trucker! Trucker!" Instantly, the radio came back with, "Red kayak, I hear you."

I was visibly shocked; I nearly dropped it. The boys laughed. When I picked the radio up, one of the scoutmasters anticipated what I was going to do and went out to his rig and turned his CB on. When I keyed the radio he replied. He had heard the story before. The boys had a good laugh from my surprise. When I told them about my blistered feet, one of the boys raised his hand. I called on him. He stood up. He could have been a model for a Norman Rockwell poster of the all-American boy. He told me he knew that I had never been a Boy Scout, otherwise I would have known how to take care of my feet. I asked him to explain.

He had been taught to inspect his feet after thirty minutes of hiking for red or hot spots, and if he found any he was to cover them with a layer of surgical tape. I admitted that I had never been a scout and that his suggestion was a good one. It was too late to save my feet, but I would get a roll of tape and apply it. Maybe it would help them heal. I had another 150 miles to go before I would reach the Missouri River. I had showed them my camping gear, told them my story, and delivered my message that being adventurous and physical fitness were better highs than alcohol and drugs. My program was well received. Everyone cheered.

When I finished they asked me to stay at the podium and close my eyes. They had a surprise for me. I did as they asked. While I had my eyes closed, I could hear the scraping of the chairs being moved. I wondered what kind of surprise they had in mind. I didn't have long to wait before they called for me to open my eyes. There before me was a huge, flat cake with a kayak and a man drawn in the icing, and "Happy Birthday" written on it. Forty boys sang the birthday song.

I stood there mute; my hair thin and gray, beard white, my face well weathered from tide and time, a veteran of three wars, and tears streaming down my face because a group of boys were singing to me. I must have been getting soft in the head in my old age. Everyone clapped and laughed at my surprise. Actually, my birthday was two days away.

The two scoutmasters told me that they had never seen their boys so interested. I thanked them all for their kindness and hospitality. We loaded up our equipment and returned to Bob's house, thankful for the quiet of the camper where I could regain my composure. The events of the last few days had been overwhelming. I wondered when it would stop. I wasn't used to this kind of fanfare. After about an hour of reflection, I wrote a few lines in my log chronicling the events of the day and trying to keep them straight in my head. It was difficult for me to believe these things were happening. They were not part of my fantasies.

Wednesday, May 6

That day I had breakfast with the Hoffmans. Bob went to work and I stripped everything out of the *Wind Dancer*, inventoried and inspected my gear, and gathered all my dirty clothes together. My plan was to wash them the next day. In general, I just loafed around and let myself unwind. Things had been pretty hectic lately and I felt sort of burned out. In the evening, family and friends gathered for a potluck dinner and listened to my story. Everyone had been treating me like a celebrity. I was not used to that.

Thursday, May 7

Today was my birthday but it had already been celebrated, so I didn't give it another thought. I washed, dried, and repacked my clothes. I replaced two washers on the carriage that I had lost and greased the axel with silicon. The photographer, Brian, brought me some film but he would not let me pay for it. These people were being too kind to me. That afternoon Bob showed me the easiest way to reach the freeway. He had called another scoutmaster in the next town. I was to stop there and give a talk to a group of school children. I had also been invited to join a Boy Scout troop in Helena for a float trip from Helena to Great Falls. It looked like my next two weeks were all planned out for me. I was ready to roll. I had another 150 miles to go.

Friday, May 8

I arose at six o'clock and had breakfast with the Hoffmans, gave them a hug, and told them what a great time I had with them. I promised them that when I reached Florida I would send them a postcard. I slipped into the harness, picked up the grab handle, and stepped off. The three days of rest had been good for my feet. I had taken the little Boy Scout trooper's advice and put a layer of surgical tape over my blisters. I was happy to be on the move again.

I had gone a couple of blocks when Bob Hoffman's son-in-law stopped me. He told me good-bye and wished me well. We chatted a few minutes then I was on my way again. I had gone maybe five miles when another Boy Scout master stopped me. He had his troop picking up trash in a park a couple of miles up ahead. He asked me if I would stop and have lunch with them and tell them about my trip. I laughed and said, "Sure." I had set off across the country to see what laid over the horizon and visit with the people, and I sure was doing that. I continued my march.

I went a couple of miles further and came upon an elderly man, about my age, sitting in a chair in front of his driveway. He too wanted me to visit with me. He was the grandfather to one of the Boy Scouts that celebrated my birthday with me. He told me that he admired my spirit of adventure and wanted to do something for me. He gave me a quart of grape juice. We talked for a few minutes and began my march again. In a short time I came upon two boys. They were my guides to the park, which was beside the Clarkston River. The Boy Scout troop gathered around me in a circle. We had lunch and I described my journey to them and once again headed out.

US Highway 12 joins US 90 at Missoula. Highway 90 is a four-lane freeway with a very broad shoulder. I was able to travel on the right side of the road with safety. The truck drivers hadn't forgotten about me. When they saw me back on the road, they wanted to know why I had disappeared. I explained my three-day stop at Missoula—including my birthday with the two Boy Scout troops.

Due to the newspaper article and the television coverage, a lot of people knew who I was and they would honk and wave to me as I walked along. One woman pulled over, stopped, and gave me a cold bottle of pop. She apologized because she didn't have more to give. I explained that I hadn't planned on anyone giving me anything on the journey, and a cold drink was really welcome.

My destination for the day was a rest stop near the town of Clinton. When I arrived, there was a notice that no overnight camping was allowed. This posed a problem for me. It was too late to go further. Even though I didn't like to break the rules, I decided to stay there for the night anyway. I would just modify my camping routine.

There was a restroom I used to wash up. The availability of water meant that I didn't have to go through my water filtration routine. Then I made notes in my log. When it was near dark, I pulled the *Wind Dancer* up next to the picnic table. Then I took out my ground tarps and draped them over the table, fashioning a shelter of sorts which I hoped would escape detection. If the powers that be did object to my being there, I could get under way immediately. Since there was no one around, I didn't think that was likely. I spread my sleeping pad and bag under the table and went to sleep.

Saturday, May 9

I slept pretty well under the table. I'm often told that I'm more animal than human. In fact, I'd been called a swine so often that it became a term of endearment. I fixed my breakfast of hot, freeze-dried coffee, orange tang, and mucilage. Then I slipped into my harness and headed to Highway 90 southeast for about sixty miles. My destination that day was Drummond; a ranch community of just over a thousand inhabitants. It was there that I promised Bob that I would stop and talk to the school children.

I was out of the Bitterroot Mountains heading toward the Rockies. The terrain was more open, but it was already on the rise. Going up a long, gradual slopping hill, I saw two cowboys about a mile ahead of me up the hillside carrying a cooler between them. I wondered where they were going. I was about to find out.

When they reached the highway, they sat the cooler down and waited for me. When I got up to them, they told me that they had passed me in their truck that morning and thought that I would like a cold drink. So, they put some pop and beer in their cooler and brought it to me. I thanked them for the pop but passed on the beer.

I'm not a teetotaler. On board the *Sea Venture* when the sun was over the yardarm, I liked an alcoholic beverage. But on a strenuous climb like I was on, I'd learned not to indulge. A little alcohol would turn my legs into chunks of lead. We stood there and talked for a while. They told me a little of the folklore of the area. Way off to the southwest of their ranch was a hill about 500 feet high. The hill had an almost vertical cliff that fell sharply to the ground below about a quarter of a mile to the Clark Fork River.

The ranchers told me that this used to be a buffalo jump. It seems that the Native Americans used to stampede a herd over the cliff and then go below and butcher the dead and dying buffalo. This seemed a cruel way to hunt, but a starving a person would use whatever means necessary.

After my chat with the ranchers, I continued on my way to Drummond. It was twenty-five miles from the rest stop. I arrived there at five pm, stopped at the edge of town, and called from a pay phone the number which Bob had given me; but I didn't get an answer. There was a middle-aged woman placing a duck figure on her lawn in front of a motel. I told her my story and that I wished to find Bill and Penny Wies. She said she knew them. She took me to the office and called around until she found them. They were at a Mother's Day dinner at some friend's home.

Bill came and got me. I didn't want to interrupt their party but they insisted. Later, Bill and Penny took me to their house. I was to stay with them. They had a very large home all made from natural logs. It looked like a setting from the old west. Penny fixed dinner for us and then prepared a bed for me. I was slated to give my talk to the children the following evening. Until then I was to stay with them. They were wonderful people.

What started out to be just a journey to see what lay over the horizon now had become the realization of the beauty of the American people. Each group of people seemed to out-do the ones I met previously—if that was possible.

Sunday, May 10

After breakfast Penny told me about a gulch out behind their place that was a very pretty place for a hike. Bill had gone to work early, but he had left word that I should meet him at the house at noon because he had something he wanted to show me. I took off with their dog for the hike. It was just as Penny had described it. The gulch extended up into the hills. It was cut by a babbling brook and lined with fir and ash trees. Once out of sight of the house there was no hint of civilization. It was a very quiet and peaceful place to walk. I was able to forget the cares of the world.

I had been gone about two hours when I realized I had to get back to the house to meet Bill. When I arrived, Bill was already there. We had lunch and then got into his four-wheel drive truck. He took me up into the wilderness a few miles away to the ghost town of Garnet.

Garnet had been established in 1860 as a mining town, after which, when the gold petered out, it became a timber community. When the trees were gone, the town was abandoned altogether. There were a few small log cabins—about the size of the one I stayed in at the foot of the Lolo Pass—still in existence but in near shambles. In the town itself there were a couple of old-time false fronted stores like in the Wild West movies. I took some pictures of the town for my slide program. The town got its name for the red sand stone formation found there. On the way back to the house we stopped at a cliff with a Native American hieroglyphic painted on it. I took a picture of it but I couldn't get close enough for it to show up.

We returned to the house and I hooked up to the *Wind Dancer* and pulled it down to Drummond Park where a reporter from the *Phillipsburg Mountain Newspaper* and a group of twenty children met me. Again, I told everyone about my trip, gave them the message about not using drugs and alcohol and staying physically fit. Then I threw in another little tidbit. I told them that a man with mediocre intelligence, but a lot of perseverance, could accomplish more in his lifetime than a genius would. My message was well received by both the children and the adults. I wondered if I would ever get used to giving speeches.

For a loner, I sure wasn't alone very much on this trip. I kept thinking about meeting Bill Bartlet on top of the Lolo Pass. If it wasn't for that chance encounter, this current adventure would have been missed. After my talk, we went home and Penny fixed us dinner.

Monday, May 11

I arose early and had breakfast with the Wies family. After breakfast I thanked them for their hospitality and said good-bye. My plan was to reach Garrison. At that point US-12 left US-90 and headed northeast toward Helena. Since I was pretty well rested, I didn't stop for my meals; I just kept marching along and ate my snacks as I marched.

I reached Garrison around two o'clock. It was a desolate looking little village with no place to camp, so I pressed on and made it to a rest stop on US-12 just before the town of Avon. I had covered twenty-eight miles; the longest distance that I had traveled in one day on my overland trek.

Shortly after I got my tent up and covered the cockpit, a thunderstorm broke out. While the rain was falling on my tent I was sitting inside warm and dry. I fixed my evening meal, sipped a hot cup of cinnamon stick tea, and made the notations in my journal. If I had been back on the *Sea Venture*, I would have laced my tea with a double shot of black Jamaican rum. That's what I called a *Sea Venture* tea.

Tuesday, May 12

Overnight the storm passed, leaving the sky clear with only a few cumulus clouds floating by. I pulled my tent down, shook the water off of it, packed it away, and soon I was on the march again. It was an easy day. I was only going to go fifteen miles. I passed through the village of Avon and continued on to Elliston. I stopped there because it lay at the foot of McDonald Pass with the summit just seven miles away. I didn't know what the elevation was where I stood, but I knew that it would rise to 6,335 feet where I had to pass. For that reason I elected to engage a room for the night.

The generosity of the people along the way had made it possible to rent a room now and then, without hurting my budget. After getting a room, I called Rick in Portland and told him that I would be arriving in Helena the next day. He said he would call the city chamber of commerce and see if he could get me a complimentary stay for two days. Helena was to be another of my major supply stops.

After the phone call, I went to a restaurant for a cup of coffee. It was too early for dinner. While I sipped my coffee, I met a young rancher named Jim Riefenberger. He had watched me pull the *Wind Dancer* up to the motel and wondered what I was doing. Again I presented the newspaper article which explained my trip. He reacted like everyone else, with amazement. He found it hard to believe that someone my age had pulled and paddled that craft nearly 800 miles. He invited me to a venison dinner at his house that night. He wanted his wife to meet me; at six that evening he came to the motel and picked me up.

While his wife cooked, Jim and I talked. They were a very interesting couple. He was a rancher and a blacksmith. His wife, Vicky, was an engineer working for the State Department of Energy Conservation. She was intrigued by my demonstration of crossing America by kayak using nothing but the energy of my own body. After dinner Jim took me back to the motel early so I could get some rest. I needed it to tackle the pass the next day.

Wednesday, May 13

When I awoke I packed my gear, checked out of the motel, and pulled my kayak over to the restaurant so I could have breakfast. I sat down at the counter and ordered pancakes, bacon, and eggs. An elderly gentleman came over and joined me. He had watched me pull the kayak over from the motel. The *Wind Dancer* was a magnate that attracted people's attention and fired their imagination.

As usual he wanted to know what I was doing. I let him read the newspaper story while I continued my breakfast. Then he told me his history. I was surprised to learn he was ninety-one years old and born right there in Montana. He was a spry old man and still quite active. He worked his ranch. He told me many tales of the things that had happened to him. He agreed with me that adventure was the spice of life. I could have spent the whole day talking to him, but the McDonald Pass was waiting for me and I wanted to get under way. So, I paid my bill and took my leave.

I started the climb at seven o'clock and I used the same technique as I did at Lolo Pass; setting a roadside post as a goal and sticking to it until I passed it. It didn't seem as difficult as the Lolo Pass. There was no self-doubt this time. I knew I could make it.

About three quarters of the way up the hill, I observed two horses grazing in a pasture next to the road some distance up. When they saw me, they came trotting down. They hung their heads over the fence and gazed intently at me with their ears perked forward. "What's the matter?" I asked out loud. "Haven't you two donkeys ever seen a man pulling a kayak before?" What happened then was astounding; the two horses backed away from the fence, dropped their heads between their forelegs, and for about half a minute they danced up and down, lifting all four feet of the ground and whinnying like crazy, like they were laughing their heads off. Then they stopped, looked at me again, and repeated the performance. Then they ran kicking up their feet for fifty yards, looking' at me again as if to reassure themselves that they weren't seeing things.

After their last inspection, they dismissed me from their minds and went back to grazing. Their actions struck me as so funny that I laughed out loud. I'm glad that no motorist had gone by. They would have thought I had gone crazy. That wasn't the first time an animal had acted strangely upon seeing me pulling the kayak. Back in Idaho, a dog came out of his yard to chase me. If I turned and growled at him, he stuck his tail between his legs and went yipping back to his yard like a monster was chasing him.

I continued my march. Soon I reached the summit. I stopped and took pictures first of the west side of the continent and then the east. There was a large sign there proclaiming it to be the MacDonald Pass, elevation 6,335 feet. I looked for someone take a picture of me and the kayak, but there was no one around. So, I maneuvered the *Wind Dancer* over in front of the sign and took the picture. At least I could show that it had reached the highest point of my journey.

From there all the way to Florida it would be down hill. It had taken me four hours to reach the top. I had my lunch sitting on top of the continent. I felt like I was on top of the world. Two more days and I would be back on a river.

Macdonald pass

On top of the cotinental devide 6325 ft.

I was taking a break when a guy in a panel truck pulled up beside me and asked if he could load my kayak on his truck and haul me the rest of the way to Helena. I thanked him and then explained my program. He didn't want to believe that I had paddled and pulled the kayak all the way from the Pacific. He took some convincing. Finally, he left and I continued on my way. Within an hour he was back with lunch, cold orange juice, and a free T-shirt from the Sports West Shop. He told me that he had called the newspaper and the television station. They would be along shortly.

After my second lunch, I picked up the grab handle and started down the pass. I didn't get very far when I was stopped this time by a couple in a van with a wind surfer board on top. Of all things—it was a couple from the Willamette Athletic Club.

They had recognized me and stopped to chat. As I talked to them, the Channel 12 news team showed up. They interviewed all three of us. I was so distracted by the events that I didn't get the names of the people from the club.

I got extremely nervous whenever I was being interviewed. I tried to avoid it when possible, though I hadn't had much luck in doing so.

The people from Portland continued on their way. The television crew headed back to their station and I was left to continue to Helena. When I got to the edge of town I called Rick in Portland. He had arranged a complimentary stay at the Aladdin Last Chance Gulch Motor Inn. He gave me the address.

I got to the inn at about six o'clock. I had come to the end of my twenty-two-mile hike over the pass. As I walked through the door I didn't have a chance to introduce myself because the news was on and they had just showed my interview. I received a celebrity's greeting. The manager put my kayak in a storage room. He told me that they would show the news again at ten that evening.

I lay down to rest a bit. I fell asleep and didn't wake up until eleven. I never got to see myself on the television.

Thursday, May 14

This day was a very busy one. First, I received a call from radio station KELL for an interview. Then, CACP called. Then, the *Independent Record* called and set up a two o'clock interview. Sports West called and wanted me to come to their store and pickup a pair of free shoes. Maybe they thought I had worn mine out. I also wanted to send the two wheels that I borrowed from the Ebb and Flow back along with some of my winter clothes. I needed to lighten my load as much as possible. I got that done just in time for my interview. Afterwards the photographer gave me a ride to the post office to mail my package home.

With that accomplished, I went to the Fish and Wildlife Department at the capital to find the shortest way to the Missouri River. I had twelve more miles to go, but the long over-land trek was finished. After my trip to the capital, I returned to my room to write some postcards and called Ruth to let her know I had made it.

I think she would have rather heard that I had fallen on my face.

Friday, May 15

I went through my usual morning routine and then located the manager to get the *Wind Dancer* out of the storeroom. By eight o'clock I was on my way. The day broke wet and cold. The temperature must have dropped by forty degrees. I didn't care though. It was well within my tolerance level. And besides, Montana needed the moisture. They had been experiencing a severe draught for months. The water level in all of the rivers was low. The farmers were worried about their crops and they had started to have forest fires. I made my twelve-mile hike out to the causeway at Lake Helena. There was a park where I could camp. When I arrived I pitched my tent and got ready to spend the night. Then it was time to put the *Wind Dancer* back into the water mode. I took the cycle flag off, stripped the pieces of tires and duct tape off, removed the wheels, and stored them once more in the aft storage compartment and reattached the rudder. Now I was ready to launch. I had traveled 815 miles in forty-eight days.

Chapter 5
Missouri River - Montana

Saturday, May 16

The head waters of the Missouri River were about fifty miles south of my campsite on the shore of Lake Helena at a place called Three Forks. That is where the Galeton, Jefferson, and the Madison rivers join. Lewis and Clark named the rivers on their journey in 1805. On their return trip they crossed near the Lolo Pass. At that point, the two explorers separated.

Meriwether Lewis took a more northern route and intersected the Missouri River near Great Falls. William Clark returned to the Three Forks area and explored the Yellowstone River. I chose to split the difference and join the river just above Helena, cutting about a hundred miles off my trip.

I had been informed that the Boy Scouts had postponed their float due to adverse weather conditions. Though it would have been fun to have them along, I got along quite well by myself. I didn't need people with me.

Ah! Blessed relief. I was back in my element—the river. At last my feet would have a chance to heal. I paddled out into Lake Helena, which joined the larger Lake Hauser. From there it was just a short distance to the Hauser Dam that backed up the water for both lakes. From here on I would be unable to lock through the dams as I had on the Columbia and the Snake rivers. There were no locks on the Missouri River. Portaging around dams would be a bitch. Not only were there no locks, there were no access roads around them.

Again I broke my own rule about not ignoring instructions. There was a log boom in front of the dam with a warning to stay out. It was meant to keep a person from being swept over the dam. I had no choice but to cross over it, get next to the bank, and pull the *Wind Dancer* up onto the rocks. Once that was accomplished, I emptied the kayak and carried all of the equipment down below the dam. Then I came back, put the wheels under the kayak, and maneuvered it down.

All that work took me a couple of hours. It was still early, but I decided to camp there for the night. I would be approaching the Gates of the Mountains—where the river cut through an extension of the Rocky Mountains—in a few miles. I could see them in the distance. Stopping there gave me time to clean the duct tape from my kayak, which I neglected to do when I left that morning.

Sunday, May 17

I purposely delayed leaving my campsite, hoping the weather would get better. I had wanted to get some good photos of the cliffs on either side of the river, but because of the weather conditions, it didn't look like I would be able to. Therefore, I started to paddle. As I got closer to the gates they seemed to open and close before me as my viewing angel changed. Lewis and Clark gave the formation their name when they passed through here in 1805.

With the weather being the way it was, the cliffs had an awesome surreal look. Like a scene from a movie, *Before Time Began.* I asked myself, if the sky had been clear and sunny would I have been more affected by its beauty? I think not. The dark brooding clouds hung down low. The tops of the cliffs disappeared in them. Patches of mist swirled around their faces. Birds circled in between them. There were Golden and Bald Eagles, hawks, osprey, and falcons among them. On the surface there were flocks of ducks and geese, and occasional

Wild Life

was not disturbed by my presence

stately Blue Heron could be seen standing on one leg watching me paddle by.

The biggest surprise of all was when a flock of great white pelicans flew by just above the river in a V formation on wings that appeared to stretch at a span of more than six feet. I had never seen pelicans on rivers that far inland.

My poor camera would never capture that scene. Taking a picture that was a thirty-five millimeter square from an area that stretched from horizon to horizon was asking too much from the film that I was using. It had an ASA of sixty-four, which would not catch enough light to make a good picture. But I took the pictures anyway.

No matter what the pictures captured they would mean something to me.

Mountain Goats

At a salt lick within The Gates of the Mountains

The gates opened up and I paddled through. On the right side of the river I came upon a herd of mountain goats at a salt lick. They appeared not to notice me. I started to paddle toward them taking pictures as I advanced, hoping to get as close as possible before they scampered away. I was able to get so close to them that the bow of the *Wind Dancer* showed in the picture. Further along, a deer stood on the bank under the cliffs and watched me paddle by. I felt that this was as close as I would ever get to see the country as Lewis and Clark had. I paddled on into the upper Holter Lake.

My destination was the Holter Dam recreation area. The map showed that there was a campsite, a lodge, and a boat ramp leading to a road that I could use to portage around the dam. It seemed like a good place to spend a day exploring the nearby area. Perhaps the weather would improve so that I could get better pictures for my slide program. At five o'clock that evening, I had reached the recreation area. As I had expected, they had a nice camping area and there were very few people. There was a spacious dinning lodge so it wouldn't be necessary for me to fix my own meals. I checked in at the lodge and was assigned a camping site. I pitched my tent and carried out my regular camping routine. Then I prepared for my activities on the following day. It was my plan to spend the day exploring the area.

When I finished my chores, I returned to the lodge for dinner. Several of the people there had seen my arrival and knew who I was. They came to my table, introduced themselves, and sat down for a chat. I really enjoyed those conversations because it gave me a chance to learn a great deal about the local history and the scenery nearby. It also gave me the opportunity to get the local news. This day was no exception.

Two weeks ago they had their version of the shoot-out at the OK Corral. I was told that two convicts had escaped from a mental institute in California and made their way to that campground and took over a trailer home. They had a woman with them. It was unclear if the woman was a hostage or if she was there willingly. The men were armed with automatic assault rifles. The locale sheriff called in a FBI swat team. At the end of the shoot-out, the two men killed the woman, set fire to the trailer, and committed suicide.

The manager of the lodge who told me the story made the point that it was unnecessary for the sheriff to have called in the swat team. The sheriff could have told the local game warden, Stan Peck, that the two men were poachers and Stan would have gone in to get them.

Stan had a reputation of being very strict. If he caught his own mother fishing without a license he would give her a ticket. While the lodge manager may have been exaggerating a bit about the warden's reputation, it was clear there was a great deal of respect for his dedication to duty. After dinner I lingered at the lodge and visited with the local people. Apparently, I was currently the only person there that you might call a tourist. It was too early in the season for most tourists. Mine was the only tent in the campground.

Monday, May 18

After breakfast at the lodge, I began my exploration of the nearby area. It was a pleasant day; cool, but the sun was shining. There was band of high clouds across the sky. I could see why they call Montana the land of the big sky country. Across the lake a mountain ascended above the surrounding hills. According to the manager of the lodge the locals called it "Titty Mountain," because it was shaped like a woman's breast. It was a near-perfect cone with a tip on it. I tried to find it on the map, but the only mountain that I could find in the general direction was named Green Horn Mountain, elevation 7,400 feet. It fit the description, but I couldn't say for sure it was that mountain. It wasn't the first time I found the local name for an object to be different than the official one.

Titty Mountain

Montana the land of the big_sky

After my exploration of the area, I took a walk over the route I would use for my portage around the dam. I wanted to see what I would be facing. I saw that it was going to be steep but, not as bad as it had been around the Hauser Dam. At least it was an easier entrance to the river below. After my hike I returned to the lodge for dinner and my evening's entertainment: listening to the stories of the old timers.

Tuesday, May 19

I broke camp, packed my gear, and pulled the *Wind Dancer* up to the lodge to have breakfast. After breakfast, I made my portage around the dam. There were a considerable amount of rapids just below the dam due to the low water level. I winced every time the kayak hit a rock. It was touch and go for quite a distance. But I made good time, covering about thirty-five miles. The river meanders back and forth with the mountains crowding right up to the channel.

The area's tortured past was in evidence. I could see where the lava flows came down the mountainsides. There were deer, an occasional bear, and several mountain goats. What really fascinated me were the flocks of great white river pelicans.

I made it to the Prewett Creek recreation area where I camped for the night. As I was setting up my tent, two fishermen caught four nice rainbow trout. They offered me one for my dinner, but I lacked the utensils to cook it, so I thanked them and declined. During my journey, people often asked me if I fished. My answer was no. Before my journey started, I realized that I would need to buy out-of-state fishing licenses for every state I would go through. That would have eaten up my budget. Besides, after swinging those paddles all day and setting up camp, I didn't have the energy to fish at night. So the fish I ate along the way were canned. I visited for a while then they packed up and went back to Great Falls. It had been a good day's paddle.

Wednesday, May 20

The following morning I was in for a surprise. When I opened my eyes, I saw that the rain fly was pressing in on the cabin portion of my tent. I couldn't account for it. I knew I hadn't been that sloppy when I pitched the tent the night before. When I unzipped my tent I saw what had caused the problem.

My tent was covered with an inch of snow. It was amazing, because I hadn't felt the drop in temperature. It had dropped by about forty degrees from the day before. I cooked my cereal and coffee while lying in my sleeping bag. After my morning meal, I pulled the tent down, shook the snow off, and packed it away. That was definitely not a fun day. It had stopped snowing, but there was a strong northeasterly wind blowing with freezing rain and sleet. The wind surfer goggles that Rick had given me protected my eyes from the ice pellets. I had sent back the gloves that I used in the first part of my journey with my other winter gear, so the sleet pounded my hands like steel shot.

My first goal for the day was to reach a town called Cascade. It was only about ten miles from where I was camped. The reason I wanted to stop there was to call Rick and let him know that I would be reaching Great Falls the next day. I hoped he could arrange for a place for me to stay. I wanted to stay in Cascade for two days before I continued on to Fort Benton.

When I reached the bridge at Cascade, there was a gravel boat ramp, but no town was in evidence. I pulled the *Wind Dancer* high up on the bank and saw a Forest Service four-wheel-drive minivan with a man in a uniform sitting behind the wheel. When I disembarked, he got out of his van and walked toward me. Was this the legendary Stan Peck? Even though I could think of nothing I had done wrong, I felt apprehensive.

He held out his hand and introduced himself. It was Stan. He said he had wondered if he would see me on the river. Stan watched as I peeled my hands from around the shaft of my paddles. While I was standing there talking to him, I was flexing my fingers and rubbing my hands trying to get the circulation back into them. My hands had practically frozen to the shaft of the paddles. Stan invited me to get into his van and get warm. While we sat there, I told him my reason for stopping and said that I was disappointed there was no town. He explained that the town was about five miles to the west. He told me not to worry, I could leave the kayak where it was and no one would bother it. He said he would drive me to Cascade and we could have breakfast and I could make my call.

While we were eating, I questioned Stan about the condition of the Missouri River north of Great Falls. I explained that I had been unable to get a float plan or map of that part of the river. He said no one traveled that part of the river because it was too dangerous. But he thought that I could make it alright in my kayak. He said he would go back to Great Falls after he dropped me off and get a set of maps for me from the BLM office, and that he would meet me under the bridge at Ulm where I planned to camp for the night.

I called Rick and told him that I would reach Great Falls at about four o'clock in the afternoon the following day, and that I would call him when I got there to find out if he had gotten me a room. Stan drove me back to the kayak then took off. I launched my kayak, buttoned myself in, and started paddling.

Several times I thought I saw Stan's car through the trees as I was paddling, but I couldn't be sure because it was just a fleeting glimpse. I thought he was keeping watch over me. When I reached the bridge at Ulm, Stan was there. He helped me pull the kayak up on the bank and showed me a flat spot where I could pitch my tent. He said it would be noisy but I would be protected from the snow and wind. He gave me a whole stack of maps of the Missouri River, all the way to the eastern border of Montana. He might have been a badass to the locals, but to me Stan is a saint.

I pitched my tent and walked up the road a hundred yards to a small restaurant for my evening meal. I was in no mood to cook that night. After dinner I returned to my tent. Since my sleeping bag was only comfortable to a temperature of forty degrees, I had to put on a couple of layers of clothing before I retired. There was no dishpan bath that night. I had a satisfactory day. I had covered thirty-two miles.

Thursday, May 21

When morning came I broke camp, loaded the *Wind Dancer,* and walked back up the road for my favorite breakfast of bacon, eggs, and pancakes. Afterwards, I returned to my kayak and cast off. My goal for that day was Great Falls. The weather had moderated some. At least there wasn't any freezing rain; it was just cold and windy. I paddled steady all day and reached the city limits at 3:30 PM.

I was met at the boat ramp by a television news team. They had been alerted that I was coming. They had actually been sent up river on another assignment, but when they saw me coming down the river they turned around to greet me. When they finished their interview, they helped me get to the Quality Inn where Rick had arranged for me to stay with the Great Falls Chamber of Commerce.

By five o'clock I was checked in at the inn, had a hot shower, and ate dinner. Then I called Dan Oakland. Bob Hoffman, who was the scoutmaster in Missoula, gave me Dan's name and phone number. Dan was the commissioner of parks and wildlife for Montana. Dan invited me to breakfast at eight the following day.

Again, I fell asleep before I got to see myself on the news.

Friday, May 22

Dan met me at the restaurant for breakfast and while we were eating he outlined his program for me for the day. He would take me shopping for the supplies I needed to carry me to Fort Benton, and then we would pick up a newspaper reporter from the *Tribune*. After that we would go out to the Morony Dam where I would be launching my kayak back into the river. That evening I was to go to his home for dinner. Dan had to go to his office before he could pick me up to go shopping. Before he left, he called a young fellow over who was eating at a nearby table. He introduced us and then left.

The young man was Neal Streeks, a river guide. That was a very fortunate introduction. As it turned out, Neal would save my bacon and solve one of the mysteries that had been on my mind: why was there no float map from Great Falls to Fort Benton?

While we were talking, Neal asked me, "Karl, where are you going to put it back into the river?" I explained that I was going to portage around all four dams at once instead of one dam at a time. I planned to put in just below the Monory Dam. He looked at me a minute and then said, "You know, there's a stretch of rapids and two four-foot waterfalls just below the dam.

A short while ago two canoes on a similar journey went over the falls and that was end of their trek." I gulped and almost swallowed my fork. In all my research on that river no one had told me about those falls. He said not to worry. If I knew what I was doing, I could get through them without a problem. Neal took a sheet of paper from his briefcase and drew a rough diagram for me.

If I left from the bank by the parking lot and cut diagonally across as quickly as I could, and kept about twenty-five feet from the bank, I would pick up a flume between the bank and the end of the falls as soon as I got to the bottom. I would have to swing back to the other side where there was another flume that would take me down. He told me he had done it in a canoe and he knew I could do it in my kayak. I was glad he thought I could make it because I didn't think I could. I had an unhappy feeling that I was going for another swim.

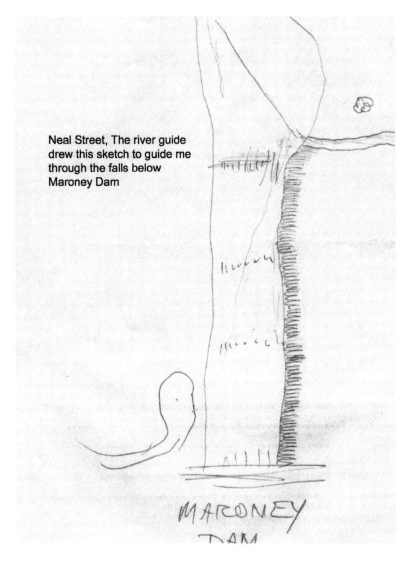

Neal Street, The river guide drew this sketch to guide me through the falls below Maroney Dam

MARONEY
DAM

We parted good friends; I thanked him for his chart of the falls.

Shortly after Neal departed, Dan came back with his seventeen-year-old son Brad. Brad had talked his father into letting him skip school so he could go shopping with us. Brad gave me tips on some of the food he took on his scouting trips.

He also cautioned me about snakes. He said a copperhead had bitten him once. And even though he was quickly taken to a hospital, he nearly died and was sick for a couple weeks. Those Boy Scouts taught me a lot.

We completed my shopping and picked up the reporter, Bert Lindler, a staff writer for the *Tribune*. We all drove out to the Monory Dam so I could see what I was going to face the next day. The rapids looked a little rough but they didn't worry me. Looking down river from where I was going to launch, I couldn't see any evidence of the waterfalls. If Neal hadn't told me they were there I would not have been prepared for them. Bert got his story. I told him about the conversation I had with Neal about the waterfalls. From there Dan returned me to the inn and told me he would be back at seven o'clock to pick me up for dinner.

Since I had a couple of hours to kill, I had enough time to satisfy another interest— the white pelicans. I wandered back to town and found a bookstore. The place was empty except for a woman behind the counter. I explained to her that I didn't want to by a book, I just wanted to find a little information about the pelicans I had seen on the river. She was a small woman, barely five feet tall, with graying hair. Her glasses were perched halfway down her nose and she looked at me over the top of them.

I told her I was just passing through and I saw the birds on the river and I had never seen them before. She smiled. "Oh!" she replied. "You're the fellow that is going to Florida by kayak that they showed on television last night." I admitted that I was. She told me that she also had seen the birds but didn't know much about them. She found a used book put out by the Audubon Society on birds of North America.

We found what I was looking for: the white pelican, Latin name, Pelecanus Erythororhynchos. It is one of North America's largest birds with a body length of over fifty inches and a wingspan of nearly ten feet. It listed its habitats as Oregon, Washington, Idaho, and parts of southwest Canada.

That surprised me. I had sailed and kayak those areas for years and had never seen one before. I wondered if they were a new arrival because I didn't remember reading about them in Lewis and Clark's journals. She didn't know. When I left her shop, she offered to give me the book. I declined and told her that the environment that I was living in would destroy the book in a couple of weeks. She laughed and wished me good luck on my trek.

I returned to the inn and waited just a short time for Dan to pick me up. Dinner was already prepared when we got there. Besides Dan, Brad, and his wife, two other families had come to listen to my story. That bothered me a bit.

My days in the wilderness with only the wildlife on the riverbanks to talk to affected my speech pattern. I forget how to talk to people. I tended to hesitate and grope for words to describe things. That embarrassed me. But people don't seem to notice; at least if they did, they don't show it.

One of the families had a boy in the fourth grade. He was a very intelligent child. He told me that he wanted to be a paleontologist when he grew up. He knew all the different dinosaur species.

That is another of my problems; I have an interest in all the sciences. So I know a little about a lot of things but not enough about anything that would really be worthwhile. I am able, however to understand and appreciate the things I observe on my journeys. We had a long conversation about the fossil beds that I would be passing after I left Fort Benton. The boy had far better knowledge about the subject than I did.

After dinner, we chatted for an hour and then I took my leave. Brad warned me about the snakes again. Just what I wanted to hear. As Dan was driving me back to the Quality Inn he told me he was going to purchase more supplies for me and ship them to James Kip, the recreation ranger. He was concerned, because my next stop, Fort Benton, was fifty miles away, and it was 240 miles from there to the next town at Fort Peck Dam. He was concerned that I would run out of supplies before I reached Fort Peck. He also told me to keep to the north side of the lake and to stay close to shore because hurricane force winds could build up quickly and I would need to get off the lake in a hurry.

I certainly couldn't complain about the great way I was treated in Montana.

Saturday, May 23

After I went to bed I didn't sleep too well. I kept thinking about those waterfalls. Neal's assurance that I would get through them okay left me apprehensive at best. He had more confidence in me than I did. Did he realize that my kayak was an ocean touring kayak loaded with two hundred pounds of gear?

I arose early, went to breakfast at the café, and headed down the road. There weren't many people out at that time, so I had the road to myself. I walked down the highway toward the dam with the *Wind Dancer*. Just outside the city limits, a pickup truck stopped near me. In it was a local rancher. He had read about my problem with the waterfalls in the morning paper. He wanted me to know that his ranch was just below the falls and if I wanted to avoid them I could cross his property. Also, I could stop and see Sacagawea Spring. According to his story, Sacagawea had become ill and when she drank from the pool she recovered. He believed that she had become dehydrated and drinking the mineral water replenished her electrolytes and made her well.

In his instructions of how to cross his property, he suggested that I be very cautious. In the pasture he had a very cranky bull that could be dangerous. I thanked him for his advice and told him that I would remember. I continued on my way. As I walked along, I tumbled in my head the information that I was given by the rancher. I was definitely not looking forward to going over the waterfalls, but being chased by a wild bull while pulling a kayak loaded with two hundred pounds of gear was not very high on my list of great adventures either.

By the time I arrived at the turn off to the dam I had convinced myself that my best chance of survival would be the waterfalls.

Sacagawea's Spring

North of Great Falls, Montana

I reached the parking lot above the falls at about two pm. As usual, I was way ahead of my timetable. I had planned to camp there for the night but I had more than four more hours of daylight left. With that much time I could be another sixteen miles further down the river. I knew that if I camped overnight I would lay awake half the night worrying about negotiating those waterfalls, just as I had the night before. So I said to hell with it. I would go now and get the falls behind me.

I pulled the wheels out from under the *Wind Dancer* and packed them away. I opened up the lockers and checked to make sure everything was loaded properly and then put the kayak into the river. I slipped into the cockpit and stretched the spray skirt tight. With my stomach turning flip flops, I pushed myself free of the rocks and started picking my way through the rapids heading for the far side of the river. When I got through the rapids the current picked up and it sucked me into the chute between the right end of the falls and the riverbank.

I was beyond the point of no return. I had the feeling that I was getting in over my head—literally. My stomach stopped flip-flopping and wedged itself firmly in my throat. I shifted the paddles to be ready for a quick brace. The kayak dropped into the cut and shot down the chute as if in a water slide. The bow punched through the standing wave at the bottom and threw the water into my face like a cold slap. The *Wind Dancer* handled it like a champ. But I didn't have time to gloat. Immediately I had to head back to the other side for a repeat performance.

Within fifteen minutes of arriving in the parking lot below the dam, the rapids and waterfalls were behind me. I had made it without taking a swim.

A quarter of a mile below the falls on the left-hand side, which was the west side of the river, there was a rocky point and a little further up the river bank was the old ranchers house. I should qualify that assessment of his age. His hair was gray and his face was well weathered, but he looked in good physical condition. So the odds were that he was probably younger than I was.

After pulling my kayak up onto the rocks, I picked up my camera and one of my water jugs. It was my thought that if a drink of the water from the spring made Sacagawea feel better, maybe it would quiet the butterflies left over from my trip through the waterfalls. I hiked up into the field where the gentleman told me I would find the spring. It was just a short distance, about a five-minute walk. I looked up into the field and there was a bull out there contentedly munching the grass. I kept my eye on him anyway. I had had enough excitement for one day.

I took a couple of pictures of the pond and the little creek that flowed from it to where it joined the Missouri River. There was no sign that stated Sacagawea drank there. In fact, there was no sign that anyone had drunk there. The water didn't taste very good either.

The map I had of the area said the pond was simply called Sulfur Springs. According to the Lewis and Clark's journals, they had spent nearly two weeks in that area portaging around those falls.

Would they have preferred that spring rather than the water in the river? I didn't know. I returned to the *Wind Dancer* and continued toward Fort Benton, the next major town. There were a couple of rapids after I left Great Falls, but after going through the falls, the rapids were a piece of cake. That night I camped on the riverbank near Carters Ferry.

Paddling

the wild and scenic Missouri River

Sunday, May 24

There was a touch of sadness in my trip that day that is hard to explain. It revolved around a conflict of emotions between compassion and the realities of nature.

It took me about two hours to prepare my breakfast, filter water, break camp, and get under way. I started paddling at seven am. The day was cold and gloomy. The river was flowing through a narrow cut in the mountains that were heavily wooded. But the surface was flat. I had paddled about two hours when I came around a bend and saw a mother mallard duck with a clutch of tiny babies. As I approached her I could see she became increasingly agitated. I started making low quaking noises trying to tell her that I meant her no harm and I directed my kayak to the far side of the river.

When I was abreast of her, she flew off, rising swiftly to an altitude of about fifty feet. When she did that I caught a glimpse of movement out of the corner of my eye. Coming at her like an interceptor rocket was a Peregrine Falcon. The mother duck made a diving turn to the left trying to evade the falcon. The two of them disappeared around the bend in the river so I didn't see a hit. I hoped the duck had escaped.

I nosed the *Wind Dancer* into the riverbank opposite of where the baby ducks took refuge. I waited there for fifteen to twenty minutes. I was hoping that she would return. But it was not to be. The chance of those little ducks surviving was remote. They would become food for other predators. It was quite probable that the falcon had a nest nearby with little ones of its own.

That was the law of the jungle: eat or be eaten; the survival of the fittest. The herbivores provide food for the carnivores.

On the river

I pitched my tent on the shore

Since I was in an area where there were bears and mountain lions, when I made my camp at night I took my machete with me and kept it at my side. If I were to be attacked it would be a contest of their fangs and claws against my paddles and machete; the survival of the fittest. How would I make out? I hoped I would never have to find out. Even though I had rationalized the law of nature, I still couldn't get the thought of those little ducks out of my mind.

I arrived at Fort Benton early in the afternoon. When I left Great Falls everyone told me it would take two days to get to Fort Benton. It took less than eight hours on the river. The current helped me a lot. I pulled the kayak up to the riverside park and pitched my tent. Then I browsed around town.

Back in the 1800s, Fort Benton was known as the bloodiest town in the west. They arrived by keelboats. The keelboats were later replaced by the steam-driven stern-wheelers. Fort Benton was as far west as a boat could go. The town probably played the most important role in the development of the Pacific Northwest more than any other city in the country. After Lewis and Clark came through in June 1805, the mountain men and fur traders made their headquarters there.

It was at this point that the westward traveler would go over the mountains of Montana, Idaho, and Washington on the Mullen Road. That road crossed the continental divide near Helena and ended at Walla Walla, Washington. That placed the traveler on the Columbia River. There was a statue of Lewis and Clark in the town square. I pulled the *Wind Dancer* up to the foot of it and had a passerby take a picture of me.

Near my campsite there was a portion of the old fort's mud wall, incased in chicken wire to hold it together and prevent further erosion. Along the banks of the river were several signs telling about other historical events, and there was a replica of a keelboat not too far from where I pitched my tent. During my walk around town, I met a man who invited me to his home the next day for breakfast. Later on, I met a preacher who was on vacation. He had parked his motor home near my tent. He invited me to dinner that night. His wife set an excellent table and the preacher and I had a very interesting conversation, even though we were poles apart in our basic philosophy.

I found one bit of information he gave me interesting. He said that there were no rattlesnakes on the north bank of the Missouri River. I was rather skeptical about that because earlier I had observed several snakes swimming across the river. In my research on snakes, I hadn't read anything that said the rattler couldn't swim like other snakes. I made up my mind to continue observing caution no matter what side of the river I camped on. I returned to my tent about ten that evening. I planned to continue my exploration of the town in the morning.

Monday, May 25

When I awoke the weather was rather dismal and a light rain was falling. I made my way to my newfound friend's house for breakfast. My favorite meal of bacon, eggs, and pancakes was served. The meals that had been provided on my journey had really been of great value to me. I sometimes wonder how I would have survived without them. They conserved my meager supplies and the information that the local people had given me was invaluable.

After breakfast I went into town in search of the BLM park ranger. When I left Fort Benton, I would be entering into the Missouri River wild and the scenic sanctuary area. Boaters were required to register. I found the ranger and he was very helpful. He told me that if I had been there two days earlier I could have joined four people in canoes. I explained to him that I liked people, but I got along quite well with just the company of the wildlife. He laughed and wished me a good trip.

I continued into town and visited the Union Hotel, built to accommodate the wealthy travelers of the steamboat era. From there I continued on to the museum where they had Native American and other artifacts of the early pioneer days. That was an era I would have liked to be born in. The world was still new then. There was still wilderness and places to go where no one had been before.

After my visit to the museum, I proceeded to a grocery store to top off my supplies. I had estimated that it was 450 miles from Fort Benton to Willston, North Dakota, which was the next town of any size where I could get supplies. If I averaged thirty miles a day, I would make it in fifteen days. I planned a one-day stop at James Kip Park. That was where Dan Oakland told me he would send some extra supplies. If for some reason he couldn't get the extra food to me, I would be in for some lean times; I could only carry fourteen days worth of supplies at a time. I was going to have to push for distance and conserve my food.

As soon as I completed my food purchases I returned to my tent. I divided my food into packets and repacked my kayak that night in order to cut to a minimum the things I would have to do in the morning. I visited the people that helped me and said my goodbyes, then returned to my tent and did my regular camp routine.

Tuesday, May 26

The sun was rising earlier with the coming of spring. That gave me the opportunity to leave my campsites earlier. From Helena to Fort Benton, I had been traveling northeast, roughly parallel to the Rocky Mountains, skirting their rugged terrain. The catastrophic events that shaped them were evident.

From the time I entered the mouth of the Columbia River, I often stopped and shifted my mind into a fantasy mode, allowing it to drift backward in time two hundred million years; then bring it forward in a sort of mental elapsed time photography and visualize the androgenic land forms as they emerged. I envisioned the internal forces that pushed up the coastal range of western Oregon and Washington; the plate movement over a series of hot spots as it formed the Cascade Mountain range; the erosion that brought about the deserts of eastern Oregon and Washington.

While going through the Bitterroot and Rocky Mountain range, I envisioned the tectonic plate forces that took on an even more spectacular display; the plates grinding together as they buckled up, pushing the mountains higher and higher; the earth's crust rupturing, allowing the lava to pour forth filling crevices and canyons; the lava held in place by the ash and earth around it taking shape as these crevices cooled, waiting for the exogamy forces to unlock their shape. Wind, rain, and the movement of the glaciers carved the soft material away, leaving the ancient lava flows in stark relief on the hillsides along the banks of the Missouri River.

While these events were taking place, the biological evolution was on going. The great dinosaurs arrived. It is said that they were wiped out by the climatic changes that took place or some other catastrophic events. The mastodons, giant sloth's, and the saber-toothed tigers replaced the dinosaurs. These were believed to be hunted to extinction by early man to be replaced by the animals I now saw walking on the banks of the river under the ancient lava flows; bear, deer, goats, and my favorite, the cougar. People have asked me why I traveled alone.

I wondered if I could adequately explain to someone my mental side trips back in time, or for that matter forward, as we traveled together. I don't think I could and that would make it an uncomfortable journey.

Lava flow

The lands tortured past is evident

Wednesday, May 27

I left Fort Benton at six in the morning. The portion of the river that I traveled on now is called the Missouri River Breaks. It has that name because the river channel had cut through the geological sediment that was laid down seventy to eighty million years ago by a vast inland sea that had covered what are now the plains states. The exposed layers showed the shifting of the shoreline. Due to the movement of the earth's crust, shale was set down in the marine area and sandstone along the shoreline.

I had acquired two heavy plastic folders which contained four maps at the ranger station. These were the most comprehensive float maps I had ever used. They included animal wildlife habitat information, geological and historical sites of the river, plus locations of campsite and river distance information. Anyone doing this journey should have a set of these maps.

When I reached mile marker forty-five at about four pm, I started looking for a campsite. Usually I tried to pick a shoreline where I could see the ground, but I saw a gently sloping bank covered with tall grass, and about twenty-five feet from the bank was a ten-foot square area with a flat shelf that looked like an ideal camping spot. I made my routine paranoid landing. I patted down the grass with the back of my paddle and then swept the paddles back and forth like a soldier looking for a land mine; at the same time, I carried my machete at the ready.

I had taken just a couple of steps when I heard a loud rattle. A rattlesnake has fiber-like muscles on either side of its tail that allows it to vibrate very rapidly. The end of its tail is equipped with a series of bone like buttons about the size of a large pea; one button for each year of its life.

I did not try to count his buttons to see how old he was. He was lying under a low shrub, not coiled but trying to get that way. I had interrupted his evening meal. His mouth was locked wide open with a ground squirrel about half the size of my fist in it. I admonished the snake for talking with its mouth full, backed up to my kayak, and continued down river a ways and repeated the landing operation.

I did it successfully that time. I suffer from a malady called ophidiophobia—an uncontrollable fear of snakes—which is ironic because I grew up in the wilderness of Nevada and Idaho without any fear of them. However, in 1945 in the Philippines, a seven-foot boa crawled in bed with me. How did I know he was seven feet? Because he was a foot longer than I was.

It took me a couple of hours to get up the courage to throw him out but it left me with a fear I haven't been able to conquer. To appreciate why I didn't kill the snake you would have to understand the code that I live by.

In my world travels, as I moved from the primitive societies of the aborigines to the sophisticated societies of Europe, I lived by my own rules with little or no friction. I fantasized that if I could get the attention of the world population and get them to live by the same laws, I could stop the chaos.

Since I had little influence in this world, I would have to create one that I could. My boat the *Sea Venture* was my world.

> I am monarch of all I survey,
> My right there is none to dispute;
> From the centre all around to the sea
> I am lord of foul and the brute.

Except for the physical laws of nature, Ruth, and the US Coast Guard, this stanza from a poem by William Cowper is true. Therefore, on the first page of the log book I wrote the *Articles of the Sea Venture.*

> Be it known to all Landlubbers, Pollywogs, and Shellbacks having placed your feet on the deck of this vessel, you have departed that part of the world known as land; where humans labor with backs bent and heads bowed following

weed eaters lawn mowers and other instruments of torture; and have entered into the domain of the ancient mariner; where all eyes seek the sun stars and the far horizon.

THEREFORE, it is understandable that the laws pertaining to land are not applicable here. In their stead, you are governed by of this ship as administered by her skipper. These articles are as follows:

ARTICLE I.
Each individual will live their life according to their own philosophy and morals, and will not be interfered with either force or intimidation, so long as said individual grants others these same privileges. Gentle persuasion is allowed when no real objection is met.

ARTICLE II.
Harm no creature great or small except in the defense of the ship, or to protect the life and health of the ship's company. A life may be taken for food, but never for vanity.

ARTICLE III.
Protect all creatures large and small except when they are a hazard to the ship's company.

ARTICLE IV.
Each individual shall make a significant contribution to the systems that support them. If they don't at least pull their own weight, they should not have born.

ARTICLE V.
Each individual shall enjoy living. If Articles I through IV are observed, there is no other purpose to life.

BE IT FURTHER KNOWN, those persons finding these articles a desirable way of life, and so indicating in the log the day on which they read them; then give their name and address; they will be considered permanent members of the ship's company. They will be kept informed of the *Sea Ventures* whereabouts, and will be given the hospitality of the ship in port or on the high seas, wherever she may be found.

According to Article II, the snake was not harmed. It is my law and I live by it.

Overall, I was quite pleased with myself. I had been under way now two months and covered nearly 1,500 miles. I had met some of the most wonderful people and seen some of the most beautiful scenery in the world. I was well ahead of schedule and within my budget.

It couldn't get any better than that.

Thursday, May 28

The blade of my paddle first hit the water that morning at six am. With the current pushing me along, I was able to travel quite rapidly. My only delay was when I quit paddling to indulge in my elapse time fantasies, which I did a lot on that stretch of river. White sandstone cliffs, towers, spires, cathedrals, and castles looked as if a master abstract sculptor had created them. Massive lava flow walls came down to the river's edge, clinging to the hillsides at impossible angels. One mountaintop had a hole worn through it by the forces of nature. It carried the name "Hole in the Wall." It all seemed to be so permanent it was hard to imagine that the same forces that created them were still working on them, and a thousand years from now they would be far different than they were today.

I couldn't help but think back to my days of kayaking on the Rhine River in Germany and contrasting these mountains with the neat castles sitting on the hilltops there. Along with the geological wonders, the float maps stated that there were some sixty species of mammals; 233 species of birds; twenty species of amphibians; and forty-nine species of fish in that area.

The nature of the river had changed from what it was in the Rockies. It was now wider and had several islands. There had been a few rapids, but nothing very exciting. The kayak handled them well. After I had been paddling a couple of hours, I saw two canoes. I had caught up with the two couples that had left Fort Benton two days ahead of me. That wasn't surprising.

Generally, a kayak is faster than a canoe and two couples would have been talking along the way, departing later in the mornings, and setting up camp sooner in the evenings. The canoeists were four young people from Grangeville, Idaho: Jeff DeBowes, Valerie Guanders, and Tim and Laura Button. It was getting late in the afternoon and they invited me to camp with them. Their destination was Cow Island. It was near here that the army trapped Chief Joseph and the Nez Perce tribe and forced them back on the reservation. Cow Island was a good campsite and the two couples got a big kick out of my camp routine. We got along well. They were the first people that I had seen in three days.

Friday, May 29

I was first to get under way that morning. They were still having their breakfast but they came down to the river to see me off. I took a picture of them waving to me, and then I paddled back to the bank, passed them my camera, and asked them to take a picture of me on the mighty Missouri River with the sand stone cliffs in the background. Then I was on my way. The two couples were going to camp one more night on the river. They had rented canoes at Fort Benton and were not due to be picked up for two more days. I had only twenty-six miles to go so I was in no particular hurry. I would be at the James Kipp State Park at about two o'clock in the afternoon if I continued at the rate I was going.

Art

Mother Nature's private showing

I came around a bend in the river and observed a fisherman in a seventeen-foot motorboat. I could see that he had hooked a fish and from the struggle he was having, it had to be a big one. I stayed away a short distance and back paddled to keep my kayak in position so I could see what he caught. He was fishing with a three-pronged hook and he had snagged the fish in its back. He was really fighting it to get on board.

When he finally got it up where I could see it, it was the strangest looking fish I had ever seen. It was a fish straight out of the Jurassic era. I asked the fisherman to hold it up so I could take a picture. It was about five feet long with a heavy body. Its nose was over a foot long and shaped like a canoe paddle. Hence it's name, paddlefish; I have been unable to learn its scientific name. It belongs to the sturgeon family.

It doesn't feed on flesh but on algae and plankton. Therefore, the only way they can be caught is to cast out across the water and jerk the line back toward the boat and hope you can snag one. The man told me they can only be found on the Missouri and Mississippi rivers and in China. They grow to about 150 pounds. The fisherman told me he thought it weighed about seventy-five pounds. He wasn't exaggerating. I thanked him for lifting the fish up for me and for the information. I continued on my way. I reached the Fred Harvey Bridge at two-thirty that afternoon.

I placed the wheels under my kayak and pulled it up to the James Kipp Sate Park campground. I left the kayak and hitchhiked out about four miles to the park headquarters. The park ranger was a very pleasant middle-aged woman. I introduced myself and asked if anyone had left supplies for me. She broke out in a big smile and said she had wondered if I was going to show up. She gave me my package and arranged transportation back to the park. My luck was holding. I was making out like a bandit.

I got back to my campsite early enough to wash my clothes. The park had a fresh water pump so I broke out my camp stove and heated some water. While the water was heating, I pitched my tent. After that I filled my plastic dish pan with the hot water, poured in some liquid dawn, washed my clothes, rinsed them, and hung them over limbs and the picnic table to dry. With that done, I sat about my other evening routine. Having access to fresh water, I didn't have to filter water. I could go directly to mixing my milk for the next day's breakfast. With that out of the way it was time for my evening meal. With all my chores done, I sat at the picnic table and made a few notes in my spiral book, walked around, and visited with some of the other campers. When the sun went down I returned to my tent and retired.

Saturday, May 30

When morning came the first thing I did was check my clothes. They weren't dry. Not to worry. I proclaimed another lay day. I completely emptied all the equipment out of my kayak and washed it inside and out. I opened the storage lockers to dry. I took all my equipment apart and checked it out for serviceability and set it aside to dry. I touched up the edge of the machete. My equipment was lying all over the place around my tent and on the tables. A camper came by that I had talked to the night before and asked me where I had gotten everything. I told him it had all come out of the kayak. He couldn't believe it. He said there was no way in hell that I had all that stuff inside that little kayak. I told him to come by the next morning at six am to see for himself.

Sunday, May 31

My first act after my morning chores was to reload my kayak. I was surprised to see the fisherman that I talked with the night before get up at six in the morning to watch me load my kayak. He sat at the picnic table and smoked his pipe. When I had finished he told me that he wouldn't have believed it if he hadn't seen it. He helped me down to the ramp and held the kayak while I folded the carriage and stored it in the aft storage compartment. I tied the painter off to the cleat in front of the cockpit and tucked the life jacket under it. It was too hot to wear it or the spray skirt, but I keep it handy in case I needed it. I waved to my friend and cast off. I picked up the stroke and I was on my way.

The nature of the landscape was changing. I was moving away from the sculptured cliffs and moving into the broad expanse of the ancient sea bottom. The character of the river was also changing. It got wider and murky. I couldn't judge its depth. It had become so shallow that with only a draft of a couple of inches, I was running aground even in midstream. I was coming into the delta area of the lake. There were many islands and water reeds. Sometimes I would have to use the paddles and push the kayak through the mud to get it into deeper water. As the river entered into the lake, its current slowed and dropped silt. There was no way that a motorboat could get through there.

I continued paddling. The sky was blue, the sun was warm, and after a few miles I moved out into the lake where the water was deeper. The wooded area was replaced with low barren hills of granulated sandstone and shale. I let my mind wander back in time seventy million years. I was no longer kayaking on a manmade impoundment. I was paddling on an ancient inland sea. I could see a Tyrannosaurus Rex feeding on the shore while a brontosaurus wallowed in the shallows and a pterodactyl flew overhead. Never mind that the pterodactyl happened to be a buzzard.

One of the things that Dan Oakland, the park rangers, and the local fisherman all had in common, besides being friendly, was that they all warned me about high winds in this area. Not to worry; I had dealt with that phenomenon before. Right now the wind was calm. I would worry about that when it happened.

At high noon I paused in mid-river for lunch. I pulled out a can of sardines, cheese and crackers, a chocolate milk shake, and dried fruit, and put together a slice of bread with peanut butter and strawberry jam. With my hunger satisfied, I continued to paddle. About two o'clock a gentle breeze popped up. That was fine though; it did get warmer. I continued to paddle. In about an hour it was no longer a gentle breeze. It was getting nasty.

I pulled on my spray skirt and put on my life jacket and continued paddling for about another hour. I realized that I was going to have to get off the lake. I found a cove about two hundred feet ahead that looked promising. It was just below a recreation area called Crooked Creek. I pulled the kayak up on the beach as high as I could get it and set out to find a campsite. There was a hill about one hundred feet high with a gentle slope. There were no rocks or cliffs that I could use for protection, but there was a gully which cut through the hill about twenty-five feet deep.

Camping in a gully was the last thing I wanted to do. Even in a semi-arid area, a sudden rainstorm could quickly send me swimming. I found a flat spot nearby and proceeded to pitch my tent. I laid out my ground cover weighing down the corners with rocks to keep the wind from blowing it away. After that I placed the inner portion of the tent on the cover and, working from the up-wind side, I staked it down, driving the pins clear to the heads to give them the maximum holding power. Next came the bows; these were three fiberglass rods, one-quarter inch in diameter, in five sections held together with a one-eighth-inch shock cord. When assembled they were twelve feet long.

I placed the rods in their sleeve and pushed them through. With that done I raised the rods, placing each one in an eyelet, and raised the tent to the standing position. That made a round structure four feet tall and seven feet in diameter. Now all that was left to do was put the rain fly over it and it would be waterproof. I turned and bent down to pick it up when a sudden gust of wind hit the tent, pulled the pins out, and sent the tent flying down the hillside like a seven-foot diameter balloon heading right for the lake.

I dropped the rain fly and took off after it as fast as I could run; my legs flaying like pistons. I wanted to catch it before it got to the lake. I didn't make it.

When the tent hit the lake, it rolled right across the surface like a huge beach ball. I went right in after it. Wallowing in the mud and water, I threw myself in a flat dive, plowed through the mud, and swam as fast as I could after it. Fortunately, about fifty yards off shore it got enough water in it so that it stopped rolling, but the wind was still pushing it. I swam out to it and popped the bows out off the eyes and collapsed the tent. Now I had a mass of fabric seven feet wide and twelve feet long to get back to shore. I grasped the center of the bows in my left hand and doing a scissor kick and a one-arm paddle, I made it back to shore. I crawled back through the mud and shook the water out of the tent and carried it back up to my campsite.

This time I carried it down into the gully. I found a flat spot a little bit above the very bottom and I scouted the bank for an easy exit. Before I could put my tent up, I had to go back to my original site and find my tent pins. I found them scattered clear back to the water's edge. I washed all the mud off the tent, my clothes, and myself, and did my camp routine.

That whole operation started at four o'clock. It was nine o'clock when I finally rolled up my life jacket, put it under my head, and stretched out on my sleeping pad. I had paddled the *Wind Dancer* over forty miles and once again beat the Grim Reaper. However, this time there was no adrenaline rush or feeling of elation. That sorry sucker caught me off guard on land. I was angry.

Monday, June 1

I left my little cove at six o'clock in the morning. I was getting deeper and deeper in the lake and it was getting wider. Dan Oakland had suggested that I keep close to the north side of the lake and follow the shoreline. But I didn't like that idea. It would make the passage too long. I chose to stay near the center to make a straight line. I paddled steady and was making pretty good time. By one o'clock, the wind started picking up again. At two o'clock, it was impossible. The waves were breaking over the top of me. I headed for the south shore to the Devil's Creek recreation area. The boat ramp was constructed of steal-pierced planking. The planking was developed back in World War II for airstrips and amphibious landings. I had made landings on them myself with an amphibious truck at Inchon during the Korean War.

I pulled my kayak up on the planking, well away from the shoreline, and went to see if I could find a place out of the wind.

At the main entrance to the park there appeared to be a building. I fought my way up, or I should say, I was blown up there. It was a partially destroyed concrete structure. There wasn't much of it left to provide enough shelter to pitch my tent, so I made my way back to the kayak.

Near the ramp was a parked semi-tractor and trailer rig. It looked like it had been abandoned there for months. The door was unlocked and the windows were intact. I crawled up into the cab and closed the door. It wasn't comfortable but I was out of the wind. That was a blessing. I thought I could stay there until the wind would die down and I could continue paddling. That was not to be.

By seven pm, the wind had reached hurricane strength. I realized I was stuck there for the duration. I left the cab of the truck and fought my way to my kayak. The flying sand and gravel stung my face. I got a bottle of water, a packet of food, and my sleeping bag, and returned to the truck and tried to make myself as comfortable as possible. The bench seat in the cab was about two feet wide and five feet long; a little uncomfortable, but far better than being out there in that wind.

Tuesday, June 2

The Devil's Recreation area was very aptly named. The wind blew like the devil. I thought by morning it would die down, but that didn't happen. If anything, it got stronger. It looked like I would be stuck here another day. I had to make another trip to the kayak for food. I had to get the water from the lake and use my water purifier. I had to do the filtering process inside the cab. That was easier said than done. But I took my time. I only left the truck during the day to relieve myself. Nighttime came and the wind shrieked around the truck and tried to turn it over. It was impossible to get any rest.

Wednesday, June 3

Sometime in the early morning I must have dozed off. I woke up with a start. What woke me up? Silence! After two days of listening to the shriek of that wind, the absolute absence of sound was deafening. I got down out of the cab. It must have been four in the morning. There was not a breath of air stirring. It was just as if someone had shut off a fan. There was just a hint of a glow in the eastern sky. The stars were still out. I wanted to get out of there as soon as possible. I fixed myself a hot cereal breakfast with coffee. I had already filtered my water and made my milk, so within an hour I was ready to go. With the sun rising above the eastern horizon, I was happy to be under way. In the last two days, I had barely made twenty miles. There were no spectacular vistas to distract me so I made steady progress.

I had paddled about five hours when I heard the engine of a small plane. It was coming up behind me and it sounded quite low. It passed me on my left and swung north to fly over the north shore. It was a single engine; a high wing monoplane that looked like it was carrying two passengers. It circled over the area like it was looking for something. Then it turned to the right, crossed the lake, and made a couple of passes over the south shore. After that it came out again, over the lake and once again up behind me to my left. When it got past me, it swung to the right about a hundred yards in front of me and dropped to an altitude of fifty feet. When it was directly in front of my bow, an arm came out of the starboard window and made stabbing motions toward the south shore. I sat there for a moment dumbfounded. For some reason they wanted me to go over there. I looked in that direction; there was nothing there but barren hills. I hesitated. The plane turned, leveled off, cut its engine, and landed. I wondered what the hell was going on.

It was over a mile away so it took me fifteen to twenty minutes to get there.

I landed on the lakeshore and pulled myself out of the cockpit and walked toward the plane. I needed to stretch my legs anyway. There were two men standing by the plane. I was absolutely astounded. It was Dan Oakland, the parks and wildlife commissioner from Great Falls, and his pilot.

I asked him what was up. He told me he had heard about the hurricane force winds on Lake Fort Peck. He had called the ranger station where he had sent the food and learned that I had picked up the food five days ago and realized that I was right in the middle of the lake when it hit, and he wanted to know if I was alright.

I described to them my two-day stay in the cab of the truck at the Devil's Creek campground and that I had just left there five hours ago. He had seen the truck when he passed over it and knew who it belonged to. It belonged to a fishing company that supplied buffalo fish to a fast food chain for fish and chips. I told him that I wished they had parked a truck with a bigger cab, but I didn't know how I would have survived without it. I thanked him for sending the food and for coming out to check on me.

They both laughed at my story and they were happy that I was okay. They told me they were amazed at how fast I was traveling. I told them I was too. I had already traveled over twenty miles that morning and if I didn't get hit with any more high winds, I would reach the Fort Peck Dam the next day. We shook hands. They wished me well, climbed into their plane, and took off. As I walked back to the kayak, I marveled at the response I was getting from the people along the way. If they weren't standing by the roadside or the river, they dropped out of the sky.

Since it was ten o'clock and I was already on land, I decided to have my lunch. I did a few stretching exercises. Two days cooped up in that damned truck had left me a little stiff. Then

I slid the kayak into the water, slipped into the cockpit, and started paddling. I set the lubbers line on ninety degrees due east and engaged my body to swing the paddles fifty to sixty strokes per minute, and continued my journey.

I had been paddling about two hours and I began feeling depressed. Why? I didn't know. There wasn't a breath of wind or a cloud in the sky. The sun was directly overhead, not casting a shadow. Then I realized there were no birds or insects. The air was empty. Except for the metronome dip of my paddles, there was no sound. The lake was like a mirror; no fish jumped; there wasn't even a bubble. The stroke of the paddles made little swirls in the water beside the kayak. The bow cut the water and the wake of the *Wind Dancer* spread out behind me in a wide V only to disappear shortly as the surface of the lake pulled itself together. The lake was a mirror image of the sky above. In front of me, where the horizon should be, was nothing but a blue gray haze. It was like looking into infinity.

Now the feeling of depression became anxiety. I was no longer paddling on a lake or even an inland sea. I was trapped in a huge globe and I wasn't moving. The globe was turning like a squirrel cage and I was at the bottom of it. My arms became tired and didn't want to swing the paddles anymore. I let the paddles rest across the cockpit. All motion ceased. I became panicky. I wanted to resume paddling but I couldn't get my arms to function. I wanted to turn my head to look at the shore, but my head was locked in the straightforward position.

Now absolute terror set in; I was paralyzed in the middle of a lake a hundred miles from nowhere. I had no memory of ever having that feeling before. I was not in control of even my own body and, yet, my mind was completely lucid. I could think but I couldn't act.

Somehow I had to regain control...but how? I felt if I could somehow inflict some pain I could make it happen; but if I couldn't move, how could I do that? I began to rationalize. First, I would have to squash my fear. Then, I needed to concentrate on winding up my strength and releasing it in one jerk. If I could bang my knees on the inside of the kayak, the resulting pain would unlock my body. Kapow! It worked. I snatched my hat off my head, filled it with water out of the lake, and dumped it over my head unmindful that it ran down into the cockpit.

I turned the kayak toward the north shore and paddled like crazy. The old man needed a nap.

When I reached the shore, I pulled the kayak up and dug out my sleeping pad, laid it out in the shade of a cliff, and relaxed and went to sleep. After an hour I woke up. I stripped off my clothes and dove into the lake. That cleared the cobwebs out of my mind and I felt pretty good. My kneecaps were bruised but, what the hell, not to worry. They would feel better when they quit hurting. I ate a snack, drank some water, and resumed my journey at two o'clock. I had at least seven more hours of daylight and I had already covered over thirty miles.

I continued on my way for four more hours. I picked a good campsite near the lake and did my normal camp routine. When I finished driving the last pin holding the rain fly down, I became aware that I was under surveillance.

A hundred yards down the shore, a prong horn antelope stood watching me. I picked up my camera and found it in my viewfinder. But with the twenty-eight millimeter lens, it looked like it was a mile away. So I started to walk toward it to see how close I could get before it would take flight. It started to walk toward me. There was less than fifty feet between us before she bound over the hill. I took her picture. I returned to my tent and completed my chores. It was still daylight when I retired. I had covered over forty miles and if I had calculated right, I would have only twenty-six miles before I reached Fort Peck Dam.

After I laid down, I thought about the events of the day. I wondered how long I spent in that out-of-control condition. It seemed like hours, but it could have been minutes, maybe only seconds. I don't know. I never had that happen before and I hope it never happens again. I was just plain pissed. That son of a bitch the Grim Reaper had used my own body against me. I was not going to let that happen again.

Thursday, June 4

The grand plan for that day was to reach the Fort Peck Dam. That wouldn't be too difficult, I believed, if my calculations were correct. I had less than thirty miles to go and no distractions. The weather was near perfect and there wasn't much to see except a lot of space. That made me think back over the last month of all the thing I was able to observe, both landscape and wildlife. Fresh in my memory was the antelope that wasn't afraid to approach me.

I reached the Fort Peck marina at four pm. I put the wheels back under the kayak and pulled it up to the camping area and pitched my tent. They had a restaurant and water there that cut my camping routine in half. Then I made a scouting trip to find the best way to get my kayak down below the dam. That would be my last portage in Montana. I estimated that the distance from there to the North Dakota border was one hundred miles.

When I came off the lake, boaters wanted to know where I had started from. They didn't want to believe that I had come all the way from the west coast. They asked me if I had weathered through the storm on the lake. I told them about my stay in the truck at the Devil's Creek campground. They shook their head and told me I was lucky. After dinner I stayed around and visited with them before returning to my tent and retiring.

Friday, June 5

I didn't push that day. I didn't intend to go very far. I went to breakfast, came back to the tent, and packed up to make my portage. One of the boaters showed me a shortcut. So, I paddled over to the control house where there was a ramp; it wasn't improved but it was passable. Then it was a two-mile portage to what they called the down-river recreation area; a very nice campsite with trees and grass. It had restrooms and showers, and also a place to wash my clothes. I was going to rent a motel but the place was so nice I didn't need to. I was more comfortable in the tent. I even washed my kayak. It needed it. That Missouri River mud was like glue.

I just killed the day there. I deserved it. After washing my clothes and kayak, I pulled my sleeping pad out and placed it under a tree for an afternoon nap.

For a while I laid there thinking back over the events that took place the day before. Just how dangerous was my situation out there? Was my loss of control a physical or a mental problem? I had never experienced anything like that before, or read anything about that happening to someone else.

Maybe I should see a psychiatrist. On occasions Ruth had told me that I should be committed. She had threatened me with divorce if I continued the journey. That confused me. We were planning to meet the thirtieth of August in New Orleans to celebrate our twenty-fifth wedding anniversary. Was it logical that she would divorce me when I reached Miami?

I am not going to say that women are more intelligent than men, but they sure as hell are more cunning. Miami was 4,000 miles away.

I was not going to worry about it until I got there.

Saturday, June 6

When morning came, I began by taking a hot shower. The campground had a coin-operated shower unit. A quarter provided five minutes of hot water. It would probably be a long time before I would get that privilege again. After that it would be back to bathing in the river. After the shower, I set up my camp stove on a picnic table and cooked a bowl of cream of wheat. I drug my feet that morning, reluctant to leave such a nice camping area. I didn't make it to the river until nine o'clock. About two miles down the river I hit a stretch of rapids, but I had found that the *Wind Dancer* handled rapids better than I thought she would. After the waterfalls at the Monory Dam, rapids were a piece of cake.

I camped that night at a place above Wolf Point. I was using a Montana road map to navigate with; I didn't know how far I had traveled. The day passed without incident. The weather was good. I was well rested. My kneecaps ached a little but already the pain was starting to go away. There was no campsite there, so I just camped on the riverbank.

Sunday, June 7

I resumed my early morning start. I liked the early mornings. Everything was fresh and the temperature was cool. By midday it got quite hot. The summer solstice was in a few days. I am always a bit sad on that day because the sun starts its journey south and from that time on the day gets a little shorter. I passed by Wolf Point about two o'clock and continued on to the town of Popular. Bill Harp, one of the people who I visited in Great Falls, asked me to call his brother when I passed through there. But when I called there was no answer. Popular sits about four miles back from the river. So I didn't stop, but paddled on for a while until I found a campsite.

Monday, June 8

When daylight came, I was on the move again. The landscape had changed. I had moved now deeper into the ancient seabed of seventy million years ago that made up the Great Plains states. Now on either side of the river were rolling hills which were quite barren, except where farmers had planted trees. The wildlife had been replaced with cattle and horses. Along the riverbanks, the wild roses were blooming and I could smell the blossoms clear across the river.

It was a pleasant contrast to traveling down a ribbon of asphalt and breathing exhaust fumes. I stopped at the town of Brockton for supplies and water. Brockton is on the Fort Peck Native American reservation and is the last town on the Missouri River before the North Dakota border. I camped for the night on the riverbank below the confluence of the Big Muddy Creek. It was only a few miles from here to where the Yellowstone River joined the Missouri, just inside of North Dakota. I would be there the next day.

I had completed 1,500 miles, one quarter of the distance of my trek.

CHAPTER 6
MISSOURI RIVER - NORTH DAKOTA

Tuesday, June 9

I reached the point on the Missouri River where it joined the Yellowstone River in a blinding rain. It wasn't hard to tell where I was. The water had turned yellow from the amount of yellow silt that it was carrying. Just like at Lake Fort Peck, the river's silt created a vast marshland with many ponds filled with reeds and tulle plants. It was a regular maze. I had a hell of a time finding my way through it. I knew from my map that the city of Williston was to my right, but because I was sitting so low in the kayak, I couldn't see where it was. I had taken so many blind alleys that I had lost count of them. It took me two hours to work over to the bank, when I saw a farmhouse sitting on a hillside overlooking the lake.

I was now in Lake Sacagawea. It was named after Lewis and Clark's interpreter, Sacagawea. I needed to go ashore to find out where I was. I was afraid that I had bypassed the town and I needed to resupply here and get a map of the lake before I could go on. I made my way over to the shore and forced the kayak up onto the mud. I reached down with my fist and pushed to see if it was solid enough for me to stand on it. It seemed so.

I stood up, swung my left foot over, and tried again. It seemed solid enough to support my weight. Then I put all my weight on that leg and started to pull my right leg out of the cockpit. It was a big mistake. My entire left leg disappeared in the ooze. I laid myself belly down to get as much surface area as possible to keep from being sucked down. I couldn't get back in the kayak, so I reached up and loosened the painter from its cleat and slithered through the mud like a snake, pulling the kayak behind me until I could get it up on dry land.

I walked up to the house and saw two men, one elderly and the other my age, working on a piece of farm equipment. They both looked at me as if I was some prehistoric creature that had just crawled out of the ooze of the lake. I introduced myself, and explained what I was doing and what happened. They laughed hilariously at my condition.

The owner of the farm was named Charley Nelson. The other man was his neighbor. They confirmed my fears. I had bypassed Williston by three miles. Charley told me to camp where I was and he would take me to town the next day. He invited me to have dinner with him and his mother that night, and he brought me a bucket of water to wash the mud off of me. I carried the water back to my kayak, stripped down, washed, and put some clean clothes on. It had quit raining by that time. I did my camping detail and went up to dinner.

I do believe I could had fallen in an outhouse and came out smelling more like roses than what I smelt like at that moment.

Wednesday, June 10

I had breakfast at my tent and walked up to the house about nine o'clock. Charley took me into Williston which was about one hundred miles south of Canada. That was as far north as I would get on my trek. From now on, I would be traveling southeast until I reach Miami, Florida.

I washed my clothes at a laundry mat, bought food for my journey, and got a badly needed haircut. Charlie then took me to a radio and a television station for an interview. Our next stop was the BLM headquarters for the lake area. They gave me a map of the lake showing all the campsites. The lake is long and narrow, about 180 miles, and subject to the same high winds that I found on Lake Fort Peck. It would take me two more days before I reached the Mississippi. I had a very busy and productive day. Charlie's mother fixed us dinner. I had already packed my kayak as much as possible. They had invited me to breakfast at seven o'clock so that I could get an early start.

Thursday, June 11

After I had breakfast with the Nelsons, I returned to the *Wind Dancer*. I had completed the loading so I walked along the shore and gathered driftwood, which I used to build a walkway to pull the kayak through the ooze to get it to a place where it would float. Even then I had trouble with my weight in it; the kayak sank into the mud and I had to use the paddles to push it further out until it would float.

The next two hours were very frustrating because it took that long to maneuver my way through the bull rushes, tulles, and reeds. I was really happy when I finally got out of that marshland area and started making good time paddling. The land was sparsely populated; there were no towns and only a few farms. Sometimes the farms would be close enough to the edge of the lake that I could smell the aroma of the newly mowed hay. My maternal grandfather brought me up on a ranch in central Idaho, so the smell of the barnyard brought back pleasant memories of my youth.

I made thirty miles that day and ended up at the Lewis and Clark State Park. It was a nice campsite with hot showers and full camping facilities, but expensive at six dollars a night. I guess it was worth it, but it sure ate into my budget. Enjoying a hot shower after a day's paddle was nice, though. After I had returned to my tent, a gentleman brought a full fried chicken dinner with all the trimmings over to my picnic table. He had heard about me from the television programs. He sat there and chatted with me while I wolfed down his offering.

Friday, June 12

This was an atypical day. Nothing happened. I made forty miles without half trying. I took off about daybreak and swung my paddles at a steady rate. Every two hours I would pause and eat a snack. At noon, I stopped and fixed lunch and did some stretching exercises to keep my back from kinking up. Then I continued. No wind, no rain, and the terrain on either side of the lake was just rolling hills dotted with an occasional ranch. Nothing inspired my mind to make elapsed time sojourns. I sometimes passed through a patch of dead trees with cormorants perched on the branches. That evening I camped on the shore beside the lake.

Saturday, June 13

I made it to the Red Butte Campground. There was no hot shower, but it was quite nice with a fresh water source and toilets. I had covered over forty miles. At that rate, I would be able to make it to the Buela Campground the next day, leaving only two more days on this lake. That would be of little consolation though because the next lake was Oahe, and Oahe was even longer than this one at two hundred and forty miles. That would make for a long and rather boring paddle because there seemed to be little there to inspire my imagination into my flights of fantasies.

Paddling in the middle of the lake with little change in scenery was like paddling in slow motion. It got monotonous as hell.

Sunday, June 14

I arrived at Buela Campground late in the afternoon. It was a great campground with first-rate facilities. I tried to use the better campgrounds whenever possible. Not only for the creature comforts they offered, but because of the presence of lots of tourist. It seemed that the more people, the less likely I would run across the local residents who liked to shake their tail at me. That was a constant worry of mine. To be bitten by a poisonous snake was not high on my list of things to experience; since the instance out of Fort Benton I hadn't seen any snakes.

Monday, June 15

I left the campground at seven o'clock. Again it was nice weather. The sky was blue and the winds were calm, but sitting a half mile out on the lake didn't offer much to see as far as interesting landscape or wildlife. Just an occasional crow or a buzzard flew overhead. There was nothing to occupy my mind except to maintain the rhythm of my stroke. The hills in the distance flowed by in slow motion. Every two hours I ate a snack and drank copious amounts of water. Sweat trickled down my rib cage. My white T-shirt soaked it up. The slight breeze caused by the movement of the kayak allowed the moisture to evaporate. That acted like an air conditioner to keep me relatively cool. At noon I went ashore, then took a swim and fixed my midday snack. Afterwards I did a few stretching exercises, then continued on my way. By five o'clock, I had reached the Garrison Dam.

I had a two-mile portage around the dam. Unlike the Columbia and the Snake rivers, the Missouri River had no locks at its dams, which made it necessary to portage around them. The Garrison campground is operated by the Army Corps of Engineers. It was the nicest campsite yet, but expensive. They charged me nine dollars a night. I tried to talk the camp ranger into letting me stay for less money, but he told me he didn't make the rules, he just followed them. I appreciated that.

Tuesday, June 16

I got off to a late start that morning. I didn't have a problem; it was just that it was a really pleasant campsite and I was loath to leave it. Also, I was heading to the city of Bismarck, the state capital. Bismarck was one of my designated resupply points and I needed to get my tent repaired. The distance between Garrison and Bismarck was only about fifty miles and the river flowed freely, but I wanted to split the trip up and get there early on Thursday. I would reach the Oahe Reservoir after Bismarck. It was a pleasant paddle on the Missouri River after the monotony of the endless lake. That night I camped by the side of the river near the small town of Price, population of about 2,000 people.

Wednesday, June 17

I left my campsite as quickly as I could that morning. I only had about twenty miles to go. As soon as I got under way, I started looking for a store or office where I could use a phone. I wanted to call Rick in Portland to see if he could get me a complementary room for the night. A short distance above Bismarck, I saw a stern-wheeler pulling up to the dock. There was a rock breakwater forming the harbor. I pulled my kayak up on the rocks and dug my battery-powered shaver out and shaved before I went into the office that operated the stern-wheeler. I don't mind being a primitive old barbarian, but I don't like looking like one. It was my belief that if I made myself halfway presentable people would be more willing to help me. So far that seemed to work.

I approached the woman behind the desk and introduced myself. I told her I wanted to make a long distance call using a toll-free number. Kitty Schuler was the marketing director for the stern-wheeler Farwest. I told her my story and she let me use the phone. She had been looking out the window watching the arrival of the stern-wheeler and had seen me enter the harbor and shaving on the rocks before I came in, and was amused that I did that. I told her that I had been under way for two and a half months and had traveled over 2,000 miles. I was getting a little raggedy and I didn't want to frighten anybody. She laughed. After about an hour, Rick called back and gave me a list of people to call. Kitty took charge and made the calls for me. She got a hold of two television stations, one radio station, and the local newspaper; all of which wanted to interview me over the phone.

After the interviews were finished, she called the Ridder Marina in the town of Mandan and arranged for me to store the *Wind Dancer* there. Mandan is smaller than Bismarck and just across the bridge. Lewis and Clark spent the winter there where they made their most important acquisition: Sacagawea, a sixteen-year-old Native American girl and the wife of a French fur trader. Her husband, Charbonneau, was hired as an interpreter, but it was Sacagawea who actually did the interrupting. And because of her, her brother gave them the horses that the expedition needed to cross the Bitterroot Mountains. Her presence convinced the Nez Perce tribe to let them pass unharmed. I am firmly convinced that without her they wouldn't have made it.

When I arrived at the Ridder Marina they helped me secure the kayak. Then they took me to Bismarck where I got the zipper in my tent repaired. Later they took me to the Colonial Inn where I was to stay for the next two days.

So far on the trip, people would stop whatever they were doing to help me. The world is still full of nice people.

Thursday, June 18

That morning I had breakfast with Dick Bratten from Billings, Montana. He was a young drummer playing at one of the local bars. He saw me on TV and wanted to talk to me. Later, the band gave me a ride into town in their bus so that I could by my supplies. After I made my purchase, I returned to the inn and washed my clothes in the coin-operated machines. Lewis and Clark never had it so good. In fact, they spent a long and very cold winter here.

Friday, June 19

On this day I made it to Fort Rice. As I was paddling along, I looked back over my shoulder late in the afternoon and saw a huge cloud forming. I knew what that meant. In a short while I would be engulfed in a severe electrical storm. I headed for the shore. I no sooner got my tent up when the storm broke. I dove into my tent and zipped it up. The storm was horrendous the lightning bolts lit up the inside of the tent. The thunderclaps were deafening, but I didn't worry. I laid back and waited until the storm slacked off, then continued with my camping routine.

Fort Rice is located a couple miles inland from where I was camped, and near the headwaters of Lake Oahe. Lake Oahe is the longest of the six lakes on the Missouri River and the lake is relatively narrow, but it has many bays backed up into the Dakota badlands filling canyons and valleys. Some of them were over six miles wide, taking me over an hour to cross. That made me vulnerable to those high winds that could pop up in a matter of minutes and last for days. The Native American word *Oahe* means a foundation or a place to stand. Along the banks of the Oahe there are several historical sites. Sacagawea is said to be buried at the Fort Manuel Trading Post and Chief Sitting Bull's gravesite is near the banks of the lake.

Saturday, June 20

Each night I picked the following day's goal based on a forty-mile run. The goal was not difficult... if the winds were kind to me. On this day, the winds were calm and I had a comfortable run. In the days before the dam was built, there were considerable woodlands that were the home of deer, elk, and pronghorn antelope. Now much of the animal habitat was under water and biologist are trying to reestablish both the woodlands and the animals. There are a few ranches located on the east side of the lake, while the west side belongs to the Standing Rock Reservation.

I completed my forty-mile run and camped at the Fort Yates recreation area. At that point, I was only ten miles north of the South Dakota border.

CHAPTER 7
MISSOURI RIVER - SOUTH DAKOTA

Sunday, June 21

I really didn't look forward to this day. While it was the longest day of the year, being the summer solstice, from now on I would lose approximately two minutes of daylight every day. That may not sound like much, but in a month I would lose a whole hour. I like daylight. Up to this point, I could paddle ten to fourteen hours a day, which contributed to the distance that I could achieve in a day. It started getting light at four am, and by six I was on my way.

I crossed the South Dakota border at ten in the morning. The sky was blue, the winds were calm, and the long paddle boring.

I was too far away from the shore to clearly see the presence of the animals. But I could see the cattle grazing on the hillsides. Other than that, I had to content myself with watching the prow of my little craft cut through the surface of the lake. There were more fishermen now on the lake. Sometimes I visited with them a few minutes just to see what they were fishing for. The fish were northern pike, walleye, and once in awhile trout. When I figured I had traveled forty miles, I started looking for a campsite. I found one at a place called Cattail Bay, near the town of Pollock, which was deeper in the bay.

Monday, June 22

When daylight arrived, the wind was calm and I resumed my paddling. However, about ten o'clock, I began feeling little puffs of wind which indicated that the calm was going to change, so I moved closer to shore. By midday, the winds had become downright uncomfortable and paddling against them was unproductive. I fought my way to a boat ramp with a connecting access road. I pulled the kayak up on the ramp and sought shelter behind a rock cliff.

I removed my map from the cockpit, and with a pair of dividers measured the distance to the city of Mobridge. The distance was approximately seventy miles, but I noted that if I cut across by road, I could bypass Mobridge and arrive on the other side of the city in twenty-five miles. Since I didn't like sitting around waiting for the wind to drop, I decided to put the wheels under the kayak and walk. I didn't mind going slow, but I wanted to keep moving toward my goal.

I sat down on a rock and took off my shoes and socks. I could see the pink scars left by the blisters from my last long-distance march, so I covered those areas with a layer of surgical tape like the Boy Scout told me to do back in Missoula, Montana. Don't tell me an old sea dog can't learn new tricks. I slipped into my harness, ran the painter back to the cleat in front of the cockpit, picked up the grab handle, and started walking.

After walking for two hours, I noted a change in the weather. The afternoon sun had disappeared. When I looked back to see what was the cause, I saw that a huge wall of black clouds had formed clear across the western horizon. I knew what was coming: an electrical storm. I consulted my map. I was six miles east of Mobridge. It would take me two hours to reach shelter. I continued to march. In about an hour, all hell broke loose.

I'd been in electrical storms before, but this one was the granddaddy of them all. Great bolts of lightning were arcing from cloud to cloud, creating a fireworks display like I had never seen before. Bolts of lightning were hitting so close to me that I could smell the acrid odor of ozone. The air was so full of electricity that the hair on my forearms was standing up.

It was now completely dark and the rain was coming down in sheets. I looked down the road and saw a neon sign proclaiming the presence of shelter: The Twilight Bar and Motel. I had found a sanctuary.

When I approached the entrance, I saw the no vacancy sign and my hopes dropped, but I went in anyway and sought the manager. I asked him if he had a tool room or store room that I could take shelter in. He told me no, but if I drove another five miles down the road there was another motel. I told him I was not driving I was walking and pulling a kayak behind me.

His mouth fell open and he looked at me in disbelief. He could see me standing before him soaking wet; he went to the door and looked out and saw my kayak there and the lightening striking all around. I told him that I had come two thousand miles and I had another three thousand to go. He said I must be crazy. I replied that he wasn't the first to say that.

He laughed, and sympathy for my situation overtook him. He said that his name was Steven Blummer and that he had a room that he had set aside for renovation. It had a bed and mattress but no bedding. I said that I had a sleeping bag and the room would be fine. He took me to the bar and gave me a bowl of chili topped with chopped onions and cheese and a saucer with a slice of cornbread on it. When he came back with the key, he told me he had called the newspaper office at Mobridge and they would send a reporter out to interview me in the morning. He asked if I would wait until the reporter got there before I took off in the morning. I said that I was so happy about getting a room that I would agree to anything. Along with the key he brought me a towel so that I could take a hot shower.

Once again I was the recipient of someone's hospitality and lucked out far better than I had any reason to expect.

Tuesday, June 23

The reporter from the *Mobridge Tribune* arrived at eight o'clock in the morning and interviewed me. It didn't take too long. But because of my rather lengthy breakfast, I didn't get a very early start. Steve described a shortcut to the lake that cut out about five miles of paddling, so I still made my goal of forty miles to West Whitlock Bay, where I camped for the night.

Wednesday, June 24

I was still at West Whitlock Bay. Early in the morning there had been another of those severe electrical storms with high winds. It broke one of the fiberglass rods in my tent and ripped the rain fly. The high waves beating on the shore filled my kayak with water. I spent the day drying out my kayak and repairing my tent. I used a trashed section of fishing rod, the same diameter as the broken tent rod, to fix the tent. It fit together rather well. To repair the rain fly, I brought out my sewing kit and sewed it back together using a cross-stitch. Afterwards, I covered the stitching with a layer of duct tape to make it waterproof.

While I was repairing my equipment, a reporter came from the town of Gettysburg to interview me. She had been notified I was in the area by the park ranger. By evening, I had everything back in serviceable condition. The next day I would be on my way again; weather permitting.

Thursday, June 25

On this day, I only made fifteen miles. At ten in the morning, the winds picked up and in a couple of hours it became impossible to make any progress. There was no sense taking chances so I decided to pack it in. I backed into Sutton Bay. Turning the bow to the wind, I paddled just strong enough for the kayak to split the waves and let the wind push me back into the bay. This time I didn't pitch my tent. I selected a picnic table next to the restroom and out of the wind. I covered the table with one of my ground tarps, placed my sleeping pad and bag under the table, and that was where I spent the night.

I didn't set up the tent because I wanted to get out of there as soon as possible in the morning. I was nearing the end of the lake and I wanted to get off of it before it killed me.

Friday, June 26

I got under way at daylight, but I only got fifteen miles to a place called Bushes Landing before I had to land due to the weather. I took some measurements from my map and found that there was a narrow neck of land sticking out into the lake that measured twenty-five miles. If I paddled around it, it would be nearly eighty miles to Pierre. But if I went across it, I would save sixty miles.

It was a steep gravel road getting out of there. Once I got out on the flats, I made good time. By late afternoon, I reached a park on the outskirts of the city of Pierre. According to my map, this was supposed to be a campground, but a sign was posted said no camping allowed. I stood in front of the park with my map in hand, pondering my next move.

As I stood there, a gentleman walked out of a house across the street and called to me. He wanted to know if I was having a problem. I explained to him that I had expected to camp there for the night, but since there was no camping allowed, I would have to move on. He offered to get his truck and help me move to the next campsite which was just passed the dam. I told him that would not be necessary, but that I could use some water.

He introduced himself as Jim Hoag. I judged that he was in his fifties. His home was also his place of business. He ran a charter fishing and adventure guide service. He took clients fishing for lake salmon. Jim told me he had seen a lot of boats towed past his home, but he had never seen a kayak pulled by a man before. He invited me in; he wanted to hear my story.

After I was finished relating my journey and plans, I told him I planned to spend a couple of days in the area and that I needed to go to a bank for some money and buy more supplies on Monday. My method of financing my operation was to go to a bank every two weeks and get a hundred dollars on my credit card. I carried very little cash on me. When the bill would come in, Ruth paid it in full; that way I wouldn't incur any interest and Ruth could see that I wasn't exceeding my budget.

Jim lived with his son who was out of town for a while so he invited me to stay with him. He also offered to give me a ride into town on Monday to go to the bank and do my shopping. I accepted his invitation with gratitude.

My luck was phenomenal.

Saturday, June 27

Jim had clients to take out on the lake fishing. He invited me to come along, but I declined. I wanted to use time to inventory my supplies, clean my equipment, and repair the hull of the *Wind Dancer*. A couple of days before, I had hit a rock and cracked the hull. I put a duct tape patch over the crack, but in a day or two the tape would deteriorate. Here at Jim's place I could give it a permanent fix.

After he was gone, I emptied the kayak and cleaned it out, turned it over and pulled the soggy tape off, then cleaned the fracture with acetone. The next step was to mix up a little epoxy and spread it over the crack. It takes twenty-four hours to reach full strength, but then it wouldn't break if hit with a hammer. I would never put to sea without two things: duct tape and epoxy. After my kayak repairs were completed, I set about inventorying and inspecting my equipment, cleaning and repairing as I went. After I left Pierre, there would be another hundred miles of rolling hills of Native American reservations, without a chance of getting any help. Then, after reaching Chamberlain, I would be entering into another long lake, but not as long as Oahe.

After cleaning and repairing my equipment, I hitchhiked to Fort Pierre. It was established in 1832 as a fur trading post. It had many historical items from that era which I found very interesting.

Across the river from Pierre is the Teton Council Site. It was here on September 24, 1804 that Lewis and Clark faced down the Teton Sioux Warriors when they turned hostile.

When I returned, Jim took me into town to get my supplies.

Sunday, June 28

After breakfast, I sanded the epoxy patch on my kayak smooth and inspected it for strength. It wasn't very pretty but it was serviceable. I turned it right-side up, put the wheels back under it, and then repacked so that I could continue my journey in the morning. I fixed lunch for myself from Jim's refrigerator. He told me to make myself at home and I did. From his kitchen, I moved to his living room.

I called Rick Runckel, my contact in Portland, so he would know where I was. I told him that he would not have to make arrangement for any overnight stays. That taken care of, I sat down at his table and wrote postcards to all of the people whom I had promised to write, including Ruth.

I had called Ruth collect a couple of times in the past, but she got mad that I was increasing the phone bill, so now I just sent a card.

As of this day, I had traveled three months and covered nearly 2,500 miles. That put me at about the halfway point.

If I continued at my current rate, I would be down in the Gulf of Mexico in September; just in time to catch a hurricane. That was just what I need to make the journey complete!

According to Jim's bathroom scale, I weighed 165 pounds. I had dropped twenty pounds since I started this trek. I felt in excellent health—no aches, pains, or afflictions—and I was rested and ready to swing my paddles some more.

Monday, June 29

I got up early that morning. After breakfast, Jim took me to Pierre to go to the bank and post office and get a chart of Lake Sharp. I had two interviews with the news media. Jim and I got back to the house at ten o'clock in the morning. I harnessed up and headed for the river. Jim drove in front of me to show me the way.

I got to the river at noon. I shook hands with Jim and thanked him for all of his help and then launched the *Wind Dancer* and started paddling. I had good weather with a light wind and the river current was with me. By 6:30 that evening, I had made twenty-five miles to a campsite named DeGrey. That is where Chapelle Creek entered Lake Sharpe. The lake started sooner than I thought. I camped for the night.

Tuesday, June 30

The next day the weather started out rather nice and I thought it was going to be another day like the day before, but by midmorning the wind picked up and I was having trouble making headway. I made it to a recreation area called Iron Nation. I looked at my map. The lake made a big loop around a high hill. It almost came together forming a complete circle. It was only a mile across the neck.

Back in the eighteen hundreds, the steamboats would let the passengers off here, and let them walk across and then pick them up again on the far side. It was thirty miles around the loop However, the distance following the trail across land was only six miles from Iron Nation to the Native American village of Lower Bruel, which was my destination for the day. Walking, I could make that in two hours.

All along the way people told me to stay away from the Native American reservations. When I asked why, I was told that the Native Americans didn't like whites. I wondered why. But living dangerously was my way of life, so I decided to just go for it. I have always gotten along with all types of people.

As I was putting the wheels under the kayak, a police car arrived. A Native American policeman got out of the car and started walking toward me. He came up to my rig and asked me what I was doing. I told him my story and explained that it was thirty miles around the loop, and I asked him if it was alright if I walked across his reservation. It would be shorter for me.

He said, "Sure, be our guest." He got back into his car and took off in a cloud of dust. I pulled on my harness and started walking.

I had walked about fifteen minutes when up behind me came a pickup truck with a young fellow in it. He was a husky lad about thirty years old. He told me he recognized me from the radio broadcast from the night before and wanted to know if I needed help. I said that I had to do this on my own, but if he had a cold drink in his pocket, I could go for that.

He laughed and told me that if I stopped by his office, at the Bureau of Indian Affairs, he would get me something cold to drink. That was Ken Parr, the Bureau of Indian affairs biologist. He took off and I continued on my way.

After an hour passed, Ken was back. This time he had his boss with him. Mr. Edwin Miller was the director of Indian Affairs. They brought a half gallon of cold lemonade and a half dozen chocolate chip cookie, still warm from the oven.

They explained that they were having a meeting on alcoholism that afternoon and they wanted to know if I would be the guest speaker, and tell the people of my journey and why I was doing it (advocating adventure and physical fitness rather than drugs and alcohol). I told them sure. I wasn't much of a public speaker, but if I would serve a useful purpose I would do it.

"Good," they said. They directed me to their office building and took off. I continued on my way. In about an hour and a half, I entered the town and proceeded to the administration building. Ken met me, took me to his office and gave me a can of cold root beer, my favorite soft drink. Then Mr. Miller came and they showed me where I could wash up and make myself look presentable. After I completed that task, they told me what they wanted me to do. I was to wait for the police chief to come, and then we would go to the meeting building where I would give my presentation. I agreed; I wanted to serve a useful purpose.

About fifteen minutes went by when Captain Randel, the police chief, arrived. He was the same police officer that I had met at the Iron Nation recreation area where I emerged from the river. Then the parade was assembled. Captain Randel took off slowly with his police cruiser, lights flashing and siren blowing. I harnessed up and followed him, and Mr. Miller followed me in his vehicle, a three-element parade.

I don't know how they got the word out of what was happening; I had only been there an hour. There were hundreds of people lined up along the street cheering and waving. I smiled and waved back, but inside I was laughing my head off… not at the Native Americans, but at myself. This had to be the most hilarious happening in the history of the west: a white man pulling a bright red kayak behind a police car with lights flashing and siren sounding through a Native American village with the Native Americans cheering. My mind flashed to Chief Joseph and Sitting Bull.

Were they lying in their graves crying or laughing?

It was about a quarter of a mile from the Indian affairs office to the meeting place, and all along the way I asked myself how I was going to approach this anti-alcohol message without sounding judgmental. My maternal grandfather had said,

"Sonny, never judge a person until you have walked a mile in their moccasins." I asked myself, "If I walked a mile in their moccasins, would that qualify me to judge them?"

Logic told me no, because I would still be judging with a white man's mind. This land has been their homeland for ten thousand years. When Lewis and Clark came through here, they gave the Native Americans peace medals and promised them the white man would not take their land, but we did. We took their land and killed nearly all the animals they used for food. Then we crowded them into reservations and sold them whiskey to drown their sorrows. Now I was going to tell them they shouldn't drink it? How could I do that, I asked myself? I didn't know.

When we got to the meetinghouse, they had their business meeting and I was introduced as the guest speaker. I told them about my many adventures and misadventures and described my camping procedure. I still hadn't given the anti-alcohol message when I entered into the question-and-answer portion of my talk.

A woman about my age gave me the opportunity I needed. She was only about five feet tall, a little on the roly-poly side, with a long braid of graying hair hanging down her back. She looked at me with solemn eyes, and asked me if I carried whiskey in my supplies.

I addressed the whole group explaining that I had three reasons for not carrying alcoholic beverages with me. First, every item I carried had to be of the highest nutrition possible; while alcohol was high in calories, it had zero nutritional value. My second reason was that when I was camping in the wilderness, I had to have my wits about me; I needed a total awareness of what was happening at all times. My third reason was that when I was swinging my paddles on the river, if I had any alcohol in my system, it would go right to my head and all I would want to do is go ashore, lay down under a tree, and take a nap.

"But," I said, "at this moment, I'm so nervous because I'm not used to talking to groups that I would love a stiff drink." That brought a hardy laugh to my audience and a smile to the old woman's face. I was happy that I could end my presentation on a humorous note. Each person came by and shook my hand and thanked me.

After my talk, I took the kayak to Mr. Miller's house. He had invited me to camp there for the night. He said he would give me a tour of the reservation and then dinner that night. I was taken down to a marina that was under construction. The Army Corp of Engineers was opposing the marina, which had started a conflict between the Bureau of Indian Affairs and the Corps. Mr. Miller said that he had asked the South Dakota state senator to intervene and get the marina approved.

From the marina, we went out into the prairie to see the bison. In the early 1800s, the reservation had millions of heads, now they only had a few hundred. Even so, it was a thrilling sight. As we continued our tour, he took me to a high point overlooking the reservation to see their farm. It was lush and green. It was part of the University of South Dakota's agriculture project and reportedly one of the most productive farms in the state.

From there he took me on a rough foot path up the mountain that formed the big bend in the river. It was so steep that I thought the four-wheel drive vehicle was going to tip over backward. At the very top was a large rock, over three feet tall, with a flat, oval-shaped top about four feet in diameter. I was told Lewis and Clark stood on that rock for a view of the river. It was exciting for me to stand at the same place and see the same scene nearly two hundred years later.

I took a picture of the river from there, then posed Mr. Miller's son on top of the rock in a Lewis and Clark pose. That was the end of our tour of the reservation. We returned to Mr. Miller's home for dinner. After dinner, I thanked them for their hospitality and explained that I was an early riser and would be on my way at dawn. I pitched my tent on their front lawn so I wouldn't disturb them when I left in the morning.

To recap the day: I paddled twenty-five miles, walked ten miles, participated in a three-man parade, given a speech, and taken a tour of the reservation.

For an old explorer who only wanted to see what lay over the horizon, I had quite a day.

Wednesday, July 1

As I predicted, I was awake and on my way at first light. The streets were deserted. Before I entered into the marina, I turned and took a picture of the sign marking the village of Brule. The sun was just rising above the horizon, casting a long shadow. I will remember that village for the rest of my life.

I stayed close to the shoreline to lessen the impact of the wind. That was the windiest country I had ever seen. It would be an excellent place for a sailboat, but I had seen only one sailboat since I left Portland.

I reached the Big Bend Dam at ten o'clock. I put the wheels back under the *Wind Dancer* and portaged around the dam to the lower level, and was on my way by eleven o'clock. At two, the wind switched directions and was now at my back. That was a help. I arrived at the city of Chamberlain at 4:30 PM.

As I approached the marina where I had planned to camp, I overtook a young canoeist paddling alone. He was also planning to camp at the marina for the night. We exchanged greetings and pitched our tents close to one another. He was a pleasant young man in his early twenties; tall, slender, and well mannered. In a matter of a couple of hours, we became good friends. On our way to the marina, I had observed that he was an accomplished canoeist. I was impressed. His name was Bill Baumgart.

After we pitched our tents, we walked to the bait shop to get maps of the Frances Case Lake. Their maps were all sold out. We returned to our tents and spent the evening telling each other our adventures. It was a most enjoyable evening.

Thursday, July 2

That morning Bill and I had breakfast together and then I broke camp. Bill was going to spend another day there and then return home. He walked with me to the Corps of Engineers to get my map. The ranger told me the television station KELO was monitoring my journey. The rangers along my route were asked to report my progress. He also called the local newspaper and arranged for a reporter to come out for an interview.

Bill and I said our good-byes. He told me he was happy to have spent the evening with me and that he could see he had a long time to pursue his adventure, since I was sixty-one and still going strong. I was saddened to learn that Bill did not live to fulfill his dream. When I returned to Portland, I wrote to him. His brother answered my letter. They found Bill's boat capsized and he had drowned. All I can say is that it was not carelessness on his part. Something must have caught him off guard. The specter of death hovers over the river and if he can catch you off guard, he'll nail you.

I finally got under way at 9 am. The weather was good and I had a mild, following breeze, so I made good time. I reached the Platte Creek Recreation Area at seven o'clock, having made fifty miles. A boater, Mr. Ken Kredit of Platte, met me. He had heard of my journey over the radio. Mr. Kredit reported my presence to the ranger and paid my camping fee. That was another plush place to camp.

Friday, July 3

If I made good time the day before, I sure paid for it this day. I got under way at seven am. My goal for the day was Fort Randall Dam, a distance of about forty miles. Under normal conditions, I would have been there by six pm, but I ran into heavy headwinds all day. If I stopped paddling even for a second to take a drink or to eat something, I was blown backward.

At noon I pulled into a protected cove and prepared my meal. After I had eaten, I did some stretching exercises, climbed back into the *Wind Dancer,* and resumed paddling. All afternoon I swung those paddles fifty to sixty strokes a minute, only pausing long enough to take a bite of a granola bar or a handful of dried fruit and a drink of water. By 8:30 PM, I reached a bay on the south side of the lake, just above the dam. I could see the boat ramp, but I didn't have the energy to make it. I pulled my kayak up on shore and pitched my tent without my usual ritual. If there was a snake there that wanted to bite me, well, to hell with him; he could suffer his own fate.

By the time I got my tent up, darkness had fallen. I threw my sleeping pad and bag into the tent along with a packet of food and a quart of water. As soon as I entered my tent, I flopped down on my bed and took out a can of Van Camps pork and beans for my evening meal. I chose that because it was the one item that I could eat cold. I opened the can with my P38.

For those of you that don't know what a P38 is, it is small inch-and-a-half folding can opener that enabled the GI's of World War II, and subsequent wars, to open their canned rations. When I was preparing for my journey, I went to an army surplus store and bought one. I wore it on a thong around my neck. I ate the beans out of the can with a spoon. Afterwards, I threw the empty can in front of the tent, rinsed my spoon, dried it, and put it away.

Since I am a no-visible-signs camper, I carried all items I used with me when I left. This was the first time on my journey that I pushed myself to the point of exhaustion. I covered the forty miles that I set for myself, but I had to paddle fourteen hours to do it.

On the next day my goal was rather modest. All I would do is hike around the dam.

Saturday, July 4

I was still a little burned out from my ordeal the day before, so I was sort of dragging my feet. I slept longer than normal. I prepared a leisurely breakfast and took my time breaking camp. I could look across the bay and see the boat ramp where I would take the kayak out of the water. It was just a short hike up over a slight hill and down through the historic site of Fort Randall, established in 1856 as cavalry fort during the Native American wars.

I finally got my act together and paddled across the bay. When I reached the ramp, I placed the wheels under the kayak and proceeded over the hill past the fort. Some of the old mud walls of the fort were still intact so I paused and took a picture for my slide program, and then continued on my way.

I made the portage that morning and reported into the park ranger. Again I was told about the television station KELO. I told the ranger to let them know that if all went well, I planned to be in Yankton in two days. I expressed my gratitude to the ranger for having campsites just a day's paddle apart, then I told him that if he would turn the damn wind off, I would be really happy.

He laughed. He asked me if I would tell my story to the other campers. I said sure. He went off to arrange a storytelling time and I set about my camping routine. After setting up camp, I stripped down my kayak, washed it, inspected my equipment, laundered my clothes, and took a hot shower. This site was another of those super luxury camping sites. I don't know why Lewis and Clark had so much trouble. I was having a ball.

Evening came. I packed up my gear and pulled the kayak down to a camp theater where the ranger had gathered a group of about fifty people to hear my story. I explained my lifestyle and recounted my adventures. It went over pretty well.

After the presentation, a boy about five years old came and pressed a twenty dollar bill into my hand. This was always an embarrassing moment for me because I didn't quite know how to handle the situation. I protested that I wasn't looking for money. The boy's father told me that they wanted to feel that they were a part of the journey and asked me to accept it. I did and thanked them.

I also met couple by the names Chuck and Carolyn Nepodal. They asked me to call them when I reached Omaha, Nebraska. They wanted to see if they could arrange for me to give a talk about my journey at the Boys Town, a haven for orphan boys. That brought back the memory of the movie starring Spencer Tracy about the development of the first Boys Town. I said that it would be an honor to give a talk there.

Sunday, July 5

I was up and on my way before the other campers began stirring. I pulled my kayak down to the river and the first stroke of the paddle hit the water at seven o'clock. The day was beautiful. There was a soft following wind and the river current was carrying me along quite nicely. I was just entering into the Lewis and Clark Lake that was formed by the Gavin Point Dam. Lewis and Clark Lake is the last lake on the Missouri River.

Lakes seemed to be a nemesis for me; my first misadventure happened on a reservoir in central Idaho when I was ten years old. At this point, I started reminiscing about my first experience on a lake, or rather my first catastrophe.

To fully tell the story, I need to go back to when I was four years old and abandoned by my father, and rejected by my stepfather. My sister was three years younger than I was. She was acceptable to my stepfather. My mother had little choice; it was either all three of us going to my grandparents, or just me.

I was the odd man out, which was the luckiest thing that could have happened to me. I was put into the hands of the world's greatest man.

My grandfather was born in southern Arizona to Mormon settlers in the late 1800s, and became a pistol-packing cowboy of the Old West. He married an English woman and they began migrating north; first into Utah and then they settled for a short time at a gold mining town called Jarbidge, Nevada. That was where he was when he acquired me.

When the gold ran out, he moved farther north to the farming community of Emmett, Idaho. I went with him. Grandfather's ranch was located at the foot of an extinct volcano named Black Butte. A mile away was the Payette River. Five miles northwest of the ranch was the Black Canyon Reservoir.

I had constructed a raft from driftwood with a six-foot section of a lodge pole for a mast, a broken broom handle for a yardarm, and a broken board for a rudder. It was a work of art; it was my clipper ship, the *Star of India.*

One Friday after school let out early, I hurried home to ask Grandpa if I could go to the lake to try my raft. No one was home, so I took matters into my own hands and went. I parked my bicycle on the shore. I pushed and pulled and finally got the raft launched, and with a discarded saddle blanket for a sail the wind propelled it across the lake. That was when I realized I was in deep trouble. I was beached on the lee shore. I couldn't get back against the wind.

When grandpa came home and I wasn't there, he stated looking for me. He found out from the neighbor girl what I had bragged that I was going to do. My grandfather and a neighbor found me long after dark. Upon arriving home, my grandfather invited me to a critique of my adventure. The critique was conducted in the barn and he emphasized his points with a well-laid-on harness strap. My problem that day is best described in military terms as the four Ps: piss poor prior planning.

I learned two things that day: square-rigged rafts don't sail worth a damn, and never put to sea on a Friday. That was my last trip to sea before I joined the navy, which was three days after my seventeenth birthday, May 10, 1943.

In spite of spending the day daydreaming of my youth, I made forty miles to a park at the city of Springfield. I was only twenty-five miles from my next destination, The Gavin Point Dam.

Monday, July 6

This day was a real winner. The weather was bright and sunny and blessed with a gentle following wind. I made the marina above the Gavin Point Dam shortly after noon. I was nearly hit with a ski boat as I entered the approach to the marina. When I docked, I made my way toward the boat to give them a piece of my mind. However, when I got there, they were loading a young water skier into an ambulance. He had gotten caught in the propeller of the boat and was badly cut up. I could see why they were in such a hurry to get him in, so I stayed out of their way. I never did learn how he was. He looked like he was in critical condition.

The park ranger and the owner of the KELO television station met me. He was also a partner in the marina. He was on vacation on his sailboat, a thirty-foot cutter rigged sailboat named *Assignment*. He said that if anyone called the station and asked for him they could just say that he was on assignment. Right away I knew he was a true sailor. He had a television crew there to interview me.

During the interview, one of the crew asked me if there was anything that could stop me. "Yes," I blithely replied, "a pretty girl's smile." Little did I know that I would end up regretting that flippant remark. KELO's sister station in Portland broadcasted that interview while Ruth was at work and one of her co-workers was watching it. She called, "Ruth, they're interviewing Karl somewhere in South Dakota." Ruth heard that remark. When I got home Ruth said to me, "So! I couldn't stop you but a pretty girl's smile could."

Sometimes I think I'm my own worst enemy.

After the interview, the owner took me to dinner and then for a sail on his boat. I sailed and he was the crew. I was happy to see I hadn't lost my touch. It had been nearly a year since I had been sailing. Sailing is my first love. We had to cut short our sail because we could see there was another storm building in the west and I hadn't pitched my tent yet.

Before I went to pitch my tent, I called Rick and told him where I was so he could see what kind of arrangements he could make for me for the next stop at Yankton. That task completed, I hurried to the camping area to pitch the tent. I got the tent up just before the storm broke. It was another electrical storm; it was a real hummer. I had put the tent up back in the trees, even though I knew it was dangerous, to protect it from the wind. I took a chance and got away with it.

Tuesday, July 7

I packed up my gear and pulled it up to the marina for breakfast. Afterwards I continued around the dam and down to the lower level, only to find that I was going to have two portages. Below the dam was a small lake, or you could call it a large pond, about one hundred yards wide, that seeped up out of the ground. It had no inlet or outlet so I had to paddle across it and then put the wheels under the kayak to cross a narrow neck of land to get to the river. Then it was only five miles downriver to Yankton.

I arrived there at noon. First I called Rick. He had made arrangements for: a night's stay at the Yankton Inn and Convention Center, an interview with the news paper for the next morning, and a speaking engagement at the Department of Human Recourses for their Drug Rehabilitation Program.

After my call to Rick, I walked through town pulling the *Wind Dancer* behind me. The owner of the True Value hardware store came out and stopped me. He asked me where I was going. He had heard my broadcast from the day before. I explained that I had a room at the Yankton Inn and that was where I was headed. He told me that it was quite a ways there, and if I wanted to, I could store my kayak in his storeroom. I thanked him profusely.

From the hardware store, I walked to the post office to pick up my mail. In weeks past, I told Rick to tell people to write to me care of General Delivery at Yankton. This was the first time that I got mail since I had left Portland three months ago. I was looking forward to getting it. I was not disappointed.

Several people had written me, but not Ruth; I had not really expected her to write. From then on everything worked like clockwork. I walked to the inn. It was very nice. The manager Tom Biegler greeted me. I had a swim in the motel swimming pool, took a shower, had dinner, and then a driver from the Department of Human Resources picked me up for my presentation, which was to be at seven o'clock. It went very well. Afterwards I had coffee and cake with the people, and had an informal question and answer session. My program was over at nine o'clock and the driver took me back to the motel. I had a message from a newspaper reporter from Sioux Falls, South Dakota, waiting for me. He wanted to conduct an interview before I left in the morning.

Wednesday, July 8

I had breakfast at the motel and waited for the reporter. He arrived at nine and drove me to the True Value store so I could retrieve my kayak. I thanked the manager for watching over it for me. I pulled it down to the river and paddled it around while the reporter took pictures and got my story. I finally got under way at ten o'clock. I had hoped that I would get started earlier, but not to worry. I was already way ahead of my time schedule and if I didn't slow down, I would be at the Gulf of Mexico in September, which was still in the hurricane season and I didn't like that. I still had a long way to go. Now I was on my way to Ponca, Nebraska.

CHAPTER 8
MISSOURI RIVER - NEBRASKA & KANSAS

Thursday, July 9

In spite of the fact that I got a late start, I made good time and reached my goal of Ponca, Nebraska. The day was clear and quite warm. Lately the temperature had been in the low nineties, but I was still experiencing those strong southeast winds. I arrived at the city park at about six o'clock. Since the camping area was one hundred yards from the riverbank, I put the wheels under the boat and pulled it up to a fifty-foot tree to pitch my tent. I liked to keep the *Wind Dancer* nearby.

I had just finished setting up my tent when a school bus pulled into the park. It stopped, the doors swung open, and a group of girls emerged. I guessed them to be about ten years old. There must have been twenty of them. They hit the ground running and came over to where I was unloading my equipment. They were attracted to my boat and tent. The two women that were with them followed them closely. They were from the Girl Scout troop number 310 of Fremont, Nebraska. Coming across me was an unplanned diversion for them. They asked me all kinds of questions. So I gathered them around me, with their leader's permission, and told them stories of the early American explorers and contrasted their adventures with mine for about an hour.

The troop leaders gathered the girls up to complete their original intent for that day's field trip. Each girl had folded a paper boat from notebook paper and placed a small birthday cake candle in it. They took their paper boats down to the river, lit the candle, and then set them afloat. It was a mystical thing to see; what kind of good luck they would enjoy in life. I went back to my camping task.

One little girl came shyly up to me and told me she had named her boat after the *Wind Dancer*. She had copied the name off the top of the boat with a ballpoint pen and hoped it would bring me luck on my journey. That hit me where I lived, emotionally.

Okay, so I am a softy when it comes to children. We walked down to the river's edge and launched it together. I took my leave from her and went back to my tent. It was starting to get dark and I had not completed my camping routine. The two leaders gathered the children up and put them on the bus, then came over and thanked me for entertaining the girls.

All was quiet once more. I was alone in the park.

Friday, July 10

I was on my way by eight am in the morning, and by noon I arrived at the Sioux City Cameron Marina in Iowa. The marina workers allowed me to use their phone to call my partner Rick. He had lined up three interviews: two with television stations and one with a newspaper. The interviews took about three hours. When they were over, I moved on downstream and camped by the river on the Nebraska side.

Saturday, July 11

I was moving about fifty miles a day; more than double what I had planned on. I judged that the river current was now pushing me along at two miles an hour and I supplied four for a total of six miles per hour. The character of the river had changed since I entered the Missouri River in Montana. There it was narrow and wild; now it was broad and flat.

For the last couple of days I noted patches of disturbances I couldn't identify. It was just a shimmering of the water, but because of the distance and angle that I was looking at it, I couldn't tell what it was. Then it happened right in front of me.

There was a patch of water fifty to sixty feet in front of me, circular in shape and fifteen to twenty feet in diameter, which turned glassy smooth. As quick as that happened, the patch rose above the surface of the river and the edges started spilling over like an over-filled bowl, and then instantly sank down below the surface and began spinning in a clockwise rotation. By that time, the *Wind Dancer* was right in the middle of it.

The action was so violent that it threw the kayak off course and I nearly capsized. It scared the living hell out of me. I had read stories of the whirlpools in the Missouri and Mississippi rivers before, but I couldn't imagine what they were talking about or how they could form. I had encountered whirlpools on fast flowing rivers with the pools forming below the obstruction, but never in flat water on a large free-flowing river. It took me by surprise.

How dangerous was it? With the cargo compartments lending positive flotation, the kayak would not be in danger of being sucked under, but a person being thrown out without a life jacket would have a big problem. I wasn't wearing a life jacket because the weather was too hot. Could a person drown? Yes. Being pulled under in murky water, and disoriented, made it highly probable. From that time on I watched for the whirlpools and avoided them if I could, or paddled through them quickly.

That night I camped at the Decatur City Park and had to hurry to get my tent up. It looked like one of those electrical storms was brewing and there was a tornado alert posted. It looked like I was going to be in for another wild night. I pitched my tent behind a twenty-foot-high rock to give myself some protection from the wind, although I knew it would be no protection from a twister.

Live dangerously, I always say. I was right; there was a storm and a spectacular one at that. That was the third storm of that magnitude that I had gone through, and the second time I had to lay on my back and support the fiber glass rods from the inside the tent. The shrieking of the winds was nerve-racking. Any moment I expected to go flying across the countryside. There were reports of funnel clouds in the area, but I didn't see any. I was too busy holding my tent together; and besides, it was too dark to see anything.

Sunday, July 12

By morning the weather was nice and I made good time. I camped at the Wilson Island recreation area on the Iowa side of the river. It was a nice campsite but expensive. They wanted $7.50 a night. I registered as a senior citizen for the reduced rate. I fudged a year.

Monday, July 13

On this day, I only traveled twenty-five miles. I arrived at the Omaha Nebraska Marina at 11:30 AM. The marina manager allowed me to camp in her backyard. I pulled my kayak up beside my tent. The first thing I did after settling in was to call Rick and report my position. While I was making my phone call, a gentleman from the marine museum came by. It was next door to the marina. His name was Mack McCoy. At the museum they had a submarine and a World War II minelayer. Mack was a retired naval commander and the caretaker of the ship. When he saw me pull the *Wind Dancer* up from the river, he came over and invited me to look at his ship.

One thing that surprised me on that trip was how few people knew about kayaks. Back in Germany when I took up kayaking in the 1950s, almost every village had its kayak and canoe club. Here in the US, there was very little known about them.

Mack invited me over to take a look at his ship, the USS *Hazard*. I had seen many ships before in maritime museums, but I had never seen one that was as meticulously displayed as the USS *Hazard*. From stem to stern, the ship looked like it was ready to go to sea. Even the crew's quarters had the beds made up like they were ready for a skipper's white glove inspection. I was really impressed. I felt sorry for the ship. In order to get it to its present position in the park, they had to dig a channel off the river, then bury the ship up to its water line with dirt.

Talk about a ship run aground, that was the ultimate.

Tornado watch

At Omaha, Nebraska

Tuesday, July 14

I called Rick back to see what he had lined up for me. He had a two nights' complimentary stay at the Red Lion Inn, two television interviews, and one interview with the Omaha newspaper. I suspected that this journey would be the best documented journey in history.

Each of the interviews went well. I decided to stay at the marina that night. I would move to the Red Lion the following day. It gave me the chance to wash my tent. It had been collecting Missouri mud for nearly two months; they don't call the river the Big Muddy for nothing. It also gave me the opportunity to repair my kayak.

Back on one of the big lakes the wind had blown me up on the rocks and the *Wind Dancer* had sustained a four-inch crack just below the water line in the cockpit area. Every couple of days I would have to replace the duct tape. Now I could give it a permanent fix. Toward that end, I walked over to the marina repair shop and purchased some additional acetone and sand paper. I sanded the outside of the cracked area and wiped it clean with the acetone, then painted it with the epoxy and covered it with a layer fiberglass cloth. On the outside, I filled the crack with a mixture of epoxy and microfiber and smoothed it down. It had to cure for a day, and then I could sand it smooth.

My next task was to wash the tent using my plastic dishpan, liquid soap, water, and a brush that I borrowed from the marina. It needed washing badly; it was nearly black. After the job was done, I rinsed it off with a water hose and hung it over a fence. With the tent washed, I still wasn't quite finished with my laundry. I still had my clothes to wash. For this task I went to a coin-operated laundromat. While waiting for my clothes to dry, I called Chuck and Carolyn Nepodal. This couple had asked me to call them when I reached Omaha. I had met them at the park below the Big Bend Dam in South Dakota. They were happy to hear from me and invited me to spend the afternoon with them the next day.

With these tasks completed, I returned to the marina. Evening had arrived. One of the local "yachties" invited me to his boat for a drink and offered me some advice on how to proceed.

When I had first planned my route, it was my intention to go down the Mississippi River to New Orleans. This skipper suggested that I go down the Mississippi to the Ohio River then branch off onto the Tennessee River. It was a nicer river with better camping possibilities and there would be less river traffic.

Ever since I entered into the Missouri at Sioux City, Iowa, the river was like paddling a boat on the Portland freeway during rush hour, with tug boats and large, deep-draft motorboats, both commercial and pleasure. He dug out his navigation charts and we went over them. He also told me where I could get charts from Kansas City to the Mississippi River. He was right. The route more closely paralleled Desoto's route. It would cut more than two hundred miles off of my total trip. I was surprised that I missed that in my research.

It was a very productive day.

Wednesday, July 15

I left my tent and the *Wind Dancer* at the marina and moved to the Red Lion Inn. From there Chuck and Carolyn picked me up and the three of us went to Boys Town, where I met their nephew. Boys Town looked more like a college campus than an orphanage. It was originally planned that I would give a talk about my journey, but because the specific day of my arrival could not be guaranteed, they weren't able to make the arrangements. The nephew was a real pleasure. He was intelligent, well mannered, and more stylishly dressed than I was. I didn't carry a nice blazer and slacks in my kayak. The best I could do was a pair of faded blue jeans and a sweatshirt. The circumstance of his being in Boys Town was not explained to me and I didn't ask. I considered being presented to him as a role model an honor.

From there, we made our way to the restaurant where we had a marvelous dinner. The young lad and I had a lively chat about environmental matters. Since that is a subject that is very dear to my heart, I never miss a chance to make my views known to all. After our dinner, they took me back to the Red Lion Inn where I spent the rest of the evening catching up with my correspondence.

Thursday, July 16

At ten o'clock I went to the Army Corps of Engineers' office and picked up some river charts covering the area from Kansas City to the Mississippi River. The trip took me most of the morning. In the afternoon, I had another television interview, which completed the commitments Rick had setup for me. Now I could leave the next day. Chuck Huling from Charter Services picked me up and took me back to the marina where the *Wind Dancer* and my tent were.

I had enough of civilization and was anxious to get back on the water. I thanked everyone for their hospitality and said my good-byes so that I could leave early the next day.

Friday, July 17

Today was an uneventful day. I made it to mileage marker 580, about 580 miles from the Mississippi River. The heat on the river had been building ever since I reached the lower Missouri River, often reaching over a hundred degrees. The sun beating down on my back felt like a hot iron was being pressed down on me. The heat simplified making my evening meal. When I landed at night, before I did anything else, I took a can of food and I sat it on a rock in the sun. By the time I had finished the campsite chores, my food was hot enough that I didn't have to start the stove.

The day's journey was uneventful. The channel had been dredged out and the banks had been built up, making it difficult to find camping sites. Wildlife was practically nonexistent, except for a few ducks and geese.

Saturday, July 18

I made a sixty-mile run on this day. I had a mild following wind, and with the river current going in my direction, I really made good time. About the only problem I experienced was the river traffic. I had to keep a sharp eye out for the tugboats pushing barges, but they stayed mostly to the center of the channel. The boats that give me the most trouble were the big motorboats. If they stayed far enough away, I could turn into their wake without a problem. But often they would cut quite close to me; and their wake would break over the top of me and fill the cockpit full of water. It was far too hot to wear the spray skirt. I camped for the night in Brownsville, Nebraska, at the city recreation area. It wasn't an elaborate campsite, but it did have fresh water.

Sunday, July 19

I camped just below a fallen tree on a sandbar. As close as I could tell, I had traveled about fifty-three miles. I would have gone further, except I got waylaid; the river had undercut a tree standing on the bank and it toppled into the river. The tree protruded out into the river twenty to twenty-five feet. When I came paddling by, a flock of Canadian geese that had been foraging and swimming below the tree all took off, except one. That one goose appeared to be fighting something in the water right beside the tree. I saw its struggles and decided to investigate.

The goose had his head through a plastic six-pack holder which was caught on a branch of the tree. I watched for a few minutes to see if he was going to get loose. He became exhausted and quit struggling. It became apparent that he would either drown or die of starvation if I didn't get the plastic off him. I couldn't reach him from the down riverside because the current would just push me away. I paddled the kayak back up the river and maneuvered it parallel to the tree, and let the current float me back to get close enough to the goose. I took my machete and cut several branches off. All the time I was trying to get the plastic holder off his neck, he was trying to peck me.

I could have simply cut the holder off the tree and let him fly with it around his neck, but it would only be a matter of time until he would get it caught on something else. The only way I could solve his problem was to cut it off his neck. I tried breaking it, but couldn't. The machete was too large and I was afraid that I would cut his head off. So, I got my Swiss Army knife out and slid it under the plastic and cut it. When that goose got free, he took off like a rocket. I finished pulling the plastic holder off the tree and put it into the boat so some other animal wouldn't get stuck in it.

Then, I had to solve my own problem.

While I was freeing the goose, the cable that controlled the rudder got tangled on a tree limb. The kayak wouldn't move either backward or forward. I tried to pry it loose with the paddle but it wouldn't budge. The tree was too small for me to crawl out onto it, and the water was too deep and the current too swift. I was in a real dilemma. Finally, I pushed hard on the left rudder pedal. That brought the right rudder pedal far enough back so I could reach the cable and the disconnect button. I disconnected the rudder cable, which made it go slack. Then I was able to back the kayak far enough out that I could get it untangled. I maneuvered the kayak forward through the remaining branches until I got the bow out past the treetop where the river current caught the bow and pivoted it free.

Now I knew how the goose felt when it got free: elated. I paddled over to the sandbar to reconnect the ruder cable. By then I was completely saturated with perspiration. I had spent more than an hour getting that damned goose free and it was hotter than hell out there on the water. I pulled off my clothes and went for a swim. The water temperature was tepid, but it was cooler than the air temperature. After my swim I didn't feel like going any further, so I just said to hell with it and camped where I was.

Monday, July 20

I departed Nebraska and entered into Kansas. Along there, the Missouri River forms the border between Kansas and Missouri. Along the way, I met a fisherman. I asked him if he knew of a place I could camp in St. Joseph, Missouri. There were no camps or parks shown on my map. He told me to camp at his fishing club. He was going there when he finished fishing and he would tell them that I was coming. It was a nice club and the people there were very helpful. One man gave me a ride to a store, where I got supplies.

Tuesday, July 21

I was under way by seven o'clock, and again made over fifty miles, all the way to Leavenworth, Kansas. I camped at the city recreation area. It was a little expensive for me at six dollars a night, but now that I was getting into city areas, finding riverside camping sites was a problem. All along the way I spent my day dodging motorboats and barges. Ever since I encountered that pop-up whirl pool below Sioux City, Iowa, I had come upon them at least four or five times a day. They didn't frighten me anymore. If I saw one ahead of me in time, I avoided it; otherwise, I just paddled out of them as quickly as I could.

177

Wednesday, July 22

I arrived at Kansas City, Kansas, at one o'clock. When I called Rick he said that he had set up five interviews for me. I would be met at the River Queen dock by the channel 9 television news team and the photographers from the *Kansas City Times* news paper. I had a busy afternoon. Rick had arranged a two-night stay at the Roadway Inn. I left my kayak at the River Queen dock and took my clothes and toilet gear with me to the inn.

Thursday, July 23

The *Kansas City Star* and the television news channel 41 interviewed me. These two interviews took most of the day. After the interviews, the television crew came down to the river to get some footage of the *Wind Dancer* and me in action. When that was completed, I returned to the inn and did my laundry and mailed out some postcards to the people that I had promised. That list was getting longer and longer, but it was the least that I could do to repay the kindness given to me on my many stops. I had hoped that I would be able to get an early start toward St. Louis, Missouri, but that was not to be. Channel 41 wanted to do a special on my journey the next day.

Friday, July 24

I didn't get to depart Kansas City until 2:30 pm. Tom Christenson of KHSB channel 41 did a half-hour special on my journey at their studio. I still didn't like doing interviews, especially that type. When they stuck the microphone in my face, I got nervous and stammered like a blithering idiot. I debated with myself whether I should stay over another day, as I was getting such a late start, but in the end I decided to get going. I was tired of the big city and wanted to get on the water.

Chapter 9
Missouri River - Missouri

Saturday, July 25

Today is Ruth's fiftieth birthday. I wanted her to come to Kansas City so we could spend it together, but she elected to spend it with our children. She was still mad at me.

The temperature was well into the nineties and it was humid. I arrived at the Waverly City Park at four o'clock, which was a little early to quit paddling, but I was well ahead of my original schedule. I wasn't really pushing it anymore.

A fisherman stopped me on the river and told me about a really good restaurant where they served an excellent catfish dinner. So, after I parked the *Wind Dancer*, set up my tent, and took my evening swim, I picked up my water jugs and walked there. It was only two blocks away. A man and his family recognized me from the news story in the *Kansas City Times*. He came over to my table and invited me to sit with them and insisted on paying for my dinner. They told me they admired what I was doing. After dinner I returned to my tent, leaned up against a tree, and daydreamed of the days yet to come.

Sunday, July 26

The Miami Missouri City Park was at mileage marker 262. I met a fisherman on the riverbank who recommended that camping site. Though it was a little short of my goal, I decided to camp there. The next possible site was too far for me to make before nightfall, but it would make a good day's run tomorrow.

While I was busy setting up my tent, the fisherman that recommended the camping site showed up with his whole clan—even his brother and their children. They brought their newspaper clippings for me to autograph and provided a complete barbecue dinner for me to eat.

After dinner was over and I was left alone, I wished that the river was cleaner so that I could go for a swim—I now know why they call that river the Big Muddy. The temperature was hotter than hell and the perspiration had been running down my ribs all day. There wasn't any fresh water at the site to take a shower and I only had one gallon of water to last me to the next campsite, which meant that even a sponge bath was out of the question.

I went to sleep that night hot, sticky, and stinky.

Monday, July 27

I didn't get very far. Friends of the family that visited me the day before came down to see me. When they learned that I was short of water, they picked up my water jugs and took them to a nearby gas station and filled them. We had lunch together before I took off.

I missed seeing the mileage markers, so I don't know just how far I traveled. When I found a flat spot, I pulled over to the riverbank and camped. From the amount of trash laying about I could tell others had camped there before me.

I'll never be able to understand why some people leave their trash. A person would think that if they brought things with them they should pack it back out.

Previously, when I found trash at my campsite, I picked it up and took it to a trashcan. But here I couldn't do that; the volume was just too great. Whenever there was a point of land sticking out into the river, the current would form a back eddy and the trash collected in those areas. It became a vast swirling mass of garbage and filth with condoms, sanitary napkins, and disposable diapers, sometimes as wide as fifty feet in diameter. It stunk.

It was not only the trash. There was also industrial waste, such as pesticides, fertilizers, and toxic metals.

A fisherman in Kansas City told me that the Environmental Protection Agency had closed the Missouri River to all fishing from that point to the Mississippi River. What happened to all this trash? In the spring when the river reached flood stage, the water rose above the riverbanks and flushed it down into the Mississippi where it was carried down to the Gulf of Mexico.

In the Gulf, the toxic waste formed a fifty square mile dead zone where all aquatic life died...evidence that are very rapidly creating an environment where only insects, pathogens, and rodents can survive.

Is this an indicator of intelligent life on this planet? I don't think so. Who am I? I am an aging Don Quixote, jousting with the windmills of pollution, mounted on a kayak, swinging a paddle for a lance.

I felt overwhelmed.

Tuesday, July 28

I left the riverbank shortly after dawn and reached Boonville, Missouri, around four o'clock. There was a small ten-acre riverside park there. It was a little rundown but it had water and a shower, and that was a plus. After I got my tent up and had my shower, I walked into town for a hamburger. It was just too hot and muggy to cook. It was like paddling in a sauna all day. Also, going into town was cost-effective. A burger was cheaper than the freeze-dried meal that came out of the forward food locker. I saved that for when I couldn't get into a town.

Wednesday, July 29

Before I left Boonville, I did a little research to find a suitable campsite. I discovered a small town named Bonnots Mill. Reportedly, it had about a thousand people and it lay two miles up a river that was a good deal smaller than the Missouri River. I was told that the river was about a hundred feet wide and clean, so I could swim in it. When I got to Bonnots Mill, I found that there wasn't a campsite, but there was a riverside bar and restaurant. I pulled the *Wind Dancer* up on the shore and walked over to the bar, introduced myself, and asked about a place to camp. The bar owner pointed to a grove of trees on the riverbank and told me to camp there.

After I got my tent pitched, I went for a swim. It was so hot throughout the day that the water was really warm, and it was clean, which allowed me to wash up. When I emerged from the river, the bar owner came to the tent and invited me to dinner. He wanted to hear about my journey. While he was there, he looked over my equipment. He couldn't believe that I carried it all in my kayak. At dinner I asked him about the Cascade River, my next day's destination. He highly recommended it.

Thursday, July 30

I had breakfast, broke camp and once again was on my way. When I reached the Cascade River, I paddled up it a couple of miles and found the riverside park alright, and pulled the *Wind Dancer* on shore; but there was a problem. The park was posted with a "No Overnight Camping" sign. Because it was so hot and humid, I had been paddling with a pair of swimming trunks on, so I just jumped into the river. There was a family in a motorboat a few yards upriver from me having a picnic. After my swim I walked over to them and told them my tale of woe and asked if they knew of a place close by where I could camp for the night.

"Not to worry," they replied. They had a home a mile back down the river and I could spend the night with them. I got dressed, climbed back into the *Wind Dancer,* and started downriver. In a few minutes, they passed me and slowed down so I could follow them. They had a two-bedroom house on the riverbank. They tied their boat to the dock and I tied my kayak beside it and followed them up to their house. Once there, they introduced themselves to me. They were Alfred and Mary Schultz, and their ten-year-old daughter. (I forgot to place her name in my notes.)

Mary fixed us dinner, and afterwards they started loading their gear to go back to their home in town. This made me a bit nervous. Surely they weren't going to leave me alone in their home overnight? Yep! That's what happened.

When they got everything loaded, Mary came to me with the key and showed me where to hide it. She told me to take anything out of the fridge that I wanted and lock the place when I left in the morning. Imagine—someone gave me, a total stranger, the key to their house and then let me stay overnight. They left me in a state of shock.

What wonderful, trusting people there are in this world.

Friday, July 31

That morning I made breakfast from the leftover food from the night before and packed a little fresh fruit from the refrigerator. I went to my kayak and cast off. My destination was Washington, Missouri. My map didn't show a park there, but I was sure that I would find a place to camp. If I had measured the distance correctly, I could make it to the Mississippi River in two more stops. I kept the *Wind Dancer* as close to the shore as I could in order to stay away from the river traffic.

The weather was hot and humid, and as I paddled the perspiration ran down my sides, soaking my T-shirt. I had to pour lots of water down me to prevent dehydration. I was fortunate to have two full gallons of water with me, but I had a craving for a good root beer float. I promised myself when I got to town that I would get one.

I kept swinging my paddles at a steady pace, eating up the miles. There wasn't anything of interest to see along this portion of the river. There were dikes along the riverbanks, and the river traffic and the towns had displaced the wildlife. I was going to be happy to get this section of the river behind me. I hoped that the Mississippi would be better, but I had been told that it would be more of the same.

When I got to my destination, there weren't any docks or a place for me to land, but there was an eighty-foot tugboat pulled up to the riverbank. The shoreline was quite wide because of the low water level due to the drought. I landed on the rocks just downstream from the tugboat and pulled my kayak as far up on the shore as I could. I tied the painter around a rock. I picked up my paddles and walked along the shore back toward town.

As I walked past the tugboat, one of the crew called to me and waved. He asked me where I was from. I shouted back, "Oregon." Then he asked, "In that thing?" "Yep," I replied and continued. I went on into town, stopped at an A&W Root Beer stand and had my root beer float. After several inquiries, I found out there wasn't a place to camp so I return to my kayak.

As I passed by the tugboat, the crewman was still on deck.

"Where are you going?" he called to me.

"I'm going further downriver to find a place to camp, and eventually I'll make it to Florida," I replied and started on my way.

"Wait," he called, "the crew of the boat is gone so we have some empty bunks. You can stay here."

"Do you have any fresh water?" I asked.

"Sure," he said.

I returned to my kayak, picked up my two water jugs and a change of clothes, and then put the cover over the cockpit. I made sure the *Wind Dancer* was secure. Then I went on board the tug. The crewman met me and took me to the bunkroom and showed me the shower where I could wash the sweat off my body. Afterward, I put clean clothes on and went to the boats galley where we had dinner together. When our meal was over, he told me he had some work that he needed to do and to make myself at home, and then he left. The galley was in shambles with dirty dishes stacked up. It looked like no one had washed dishes in a week. Since I hadn't a thing to do, I filled the sink with hot water, found the detergent, and washed and dried all the dishes.

By the time he came back, I had them all stacked on the table. I didn't know where they went. He thanked me for washing the dishes and said I didn't need to do that. I explained that it was my practice to always leave things in better condition than I found them. He laughed and got two bottles of beer from the reefer. We sat at the table and told each other our life's adventures. Later, he told me that we would have breakfast at six am. I said good night at nine and went to my bunk.

Once again someone stepped forward and helped me out of a difficult situation.

Saturday, August 1

After breakfast that morning, I picked up my two water jugs, dirty clothes, and paddles, and returned to the *Wind Dancer*. I left the riverbank at seven AM, and right away cursed myself because I left without getting the man's name. I had been in a hurry to get started because this would be my last day on the Missouri River. I had been on this river for over 2,500 miles, and in the last two weeks, the only thing pleasant about it was the people that I had met along the way.

I thought that if Ruth kicked me out, I would just take my tent and the *Wind Dancer* and paddle the rivers of the world. I was sure to find friendly people along the way. My run down to St. Charles, Missouri, was uneventful. I paddled a little ways past town and camped under some trees. The river was too filthy to swim in and the bank was covered with litter. After I got my tent pitched, I picked up my paddles and walked into town for a hamburger and a large chocolate milkshake. I was in no mood to cook. I drug my feet during the whole operation. I was in no hurry to get back to camp. It was too depressing.

When I got back to my tent, I rolled out my pad, spread my sleeping bag open on it, and laid down completely nude. The temperature was over one hundred degrees. The sweat ran down my ribs and dripped in puddles on my sleeping bag. The next day I would be on the Mississippi River and my first stop would be St. Louis.

Chapter 10
Mississippi and Ohio rivers

Locking through

The locks on the Mississipi River

Sunday, August 2

I didn't sleep well that night, lying in a puddle of perspiration. Also, I was looking forward to an early start. I only had twenty-five miles to go and I would be out of the Missouri River. I entered the Mississippi at 12:35. The entrance was awesome. The two rivers spread out before me like a huge lake. On the last few miles of the Missouri, I was traveling in a mostly easterly direction. It was directly opposite to the mouth of the Missouri River at a place they called Camp Wood. This site was where Lewis and Clark spent the winter of 1803 to prepare for their journey up the Missouri River.

After entering into the Mississippi, my compass showed a slight southwesterly heading. Now I was going in the opposite direction. I was about ten miles north of St. Louis. My first task was to pass through a set of locks. There was a dam across the Mississippi just a short distance below the entrance of the Missouri. This was a worry for me because I didn't know the procedure. But everything worked well.

As I approached the upper doors, they swung open and I paused a minute to take a picture. The doors to the basin were massive. They closed behind me and I was floating free. The size of the basin was intimidating—it was so large it looked like it could hold a hundred barges. The pumps started, the water level dropped, and then the doors opened at the other end. I had been lowered to the level of the river below. I don't know how far the drop was; I was so full of anxiety that I didn't notice.

Right after the locks, I passed under a bridge. Immediately after the bridge, there appeared on the horizon the world famous Arch of Discovery, marking the entrance to St. Louis, Missouri. I used that arch as a navigation point and paddled toward it.

The Arch

The Arch of Discovery Saint Louis, Mo

I arrived in front of the arch at four pm. Now I did have a problem: the area in front of the arch was nothing but concrete steps leading up to a flat platform of more concrete. There was no landing. I paddled back up the river to the end of the steps and found an access road. I landed the kayak and walked up the road in search of a place to camp.

It was a Sunday and I knew I wouldn't be able to reach Rick until the next day. I returned to the *Wind Dancer* and paddled back down the river where I had seen a 150-foot fuel barge. I tossed the painter around a cleat and crawled up on deck to look for the skipper. When I found him, I told him my story and asked if I could leave my kayak there until I could find a place to stay. He was less than enthusiastic about it, but told me if I would move the kayak farther down the deck, out of their road, I could. This I did. Then I went down the riverfront a way until I found a McDonald's restaurant.

I ordered two Big Mac sandwiches and a large chocolate milk shake. I had one of those cravings again. After I ate, I went sightseeing around the shops at the base of the arch until near dark and then I returned to the barge. The skipper was gone so I asked one of the crew if I could flake out on their couch in their lounge until morning. I said that I would be out of there by first light. He laughed and said, "Go ahead"

Monday, August 3

I got off the barge at seven o'clock; I wanted to avoid the skipper. I went down to the riverfront to McDonald's for breakfast and then drifted around town a bit just killing time. I had to wait until ten o'clock to call Rick. Since I was in central time, that made it eight o'clock in Portland. One of the shopkeepers let me use her phone to make a toll-free call to Rick. I was lucky. I got him on the first ring. He was surprised to hear that I was in St. Lewis. I hadn't called him since Kansas City. He told me to hang loose, that he would call the chamber of commerce and see what he could arrange, and to call him back in a couple of hours. After two hours, I called him back. He had secured a two-night stay at the Adams Mark, one of the most expensive hotels in St. Louis. Great!

I headed back to the barge to get my gear. I looked up the skipper again and told him where I would be staying and asked if I could leave the *Wind Dancer* where it was. He said yes, if I would send him and his crew a postcard when I got to Miami, Florida. I agreed.

I went back to my kayak, picked up my clothes and sleeping bag and placed them in my tote net, slipped on the cockpit cover, picked up my paddles, and headed for the hotel. The hotel was located two blocks from the base of the arch. It was a high-rise and looked like the most luxurious hotel I had ever seen. I walked into the lobby and right away I knew I was out of my element.

They were having a convention there. The men were all dressed in business suits and the ladies in stylish dresses. I walked in dressed in a floppy sun hat, a baggy faded T-shirt, and a pair of nylon athletic pants that had been cut off below the knee. Everyone turned and stared. As I walked toward the reception desk, I was rehearsing in my mind what I was going to say. I was always embarrassed to ask for a free place to stay. When I was about five feet from the receptionist she looked up, smiled warmly, and said, "Mr. Adams, we have been expecting you. Welcome to the Adams Mark." She pushed a registration form toward me.

As I filled out the form, she told me that the manager wanted me to have dinner with him at about seven o'clock, and if I had a map of my journey with me he would like to see it. I smiled and told her that I was sorry but I didn't bring my tuxedo with me. She laughed and replied that that was alright; I would have a private table, but I should leave the paddles in the room. She called a bellboy over to show me to my room.

One thing I noted as soon as I walked through the door was that the temperature had dropped thirty-two degrees. The room was air-conditioned to sixty-eight degrees. For the past six weeks, I had been paddling in near one hundred degree temperatures; so to suddenly descend to sixty-eight was chilling.

As I closed the door I saw the room rates posted on the back of the door: one hundred and sixty-five dollars a night. If I would have had to pay for my two nights, it would have cost me nearly two months of my budget. I wondered what Rick told these people about me.

I piled my gear in the closet and leaned my paddles up in a corner. Then I stripped down and took a shower, brushed my teeth, and shaved in preparation for dinner. My formal attire for dinner was a navy blue long-sleeve shirt that I last wore for my birthday in Missoula, Montana. I also had a faded pair of blue jeans, and for a belt I used a four-foot length of rope tied around my middle in a reef knot. I had lost so much weight that my belt was too big. If people wanted to talk to me, they would have to accept me the way I was.

At seven I went to the dining room and asked for the manager. I thanked him for his interest in my journey. He introduced himself and told me his name but my hearing was bad and I didn't catch it. I was too embarrassed to have him repeat it. We ordered drinks and dinner, and while we were waiting, I showed him the map of my journey which he had asked to see.

He wanted to know why I had chosen to go south through the swamps rather than going north, the more traditional route. I explained that my route followed the one made by the seven earliest explorers and no one had tried it by kayak before. I thought it would be more interesting and I didn't want to face the traffic that I would have paddling through the big cities of the north. He was a very friendly man and seemed to have a very keen interest in my journey. He gave me his business card and asked me to send him a postcard when I got to Miami. I put the card in my pocket. I didn't discoverer that it had gone adrift until after I had left.

After dinner, I returned to my room. I had two messages waiting for me from the television station, and the newspaper wanted me to go back to the fuel barge and launch the *Wind Dancer* so they could get a picture of it and ask me some questions. I called them back and made an appointment for eight o'clock the next morning. Then I crawled into bed and pulled the covers up to my neck. I was freezing.

Tuesday, August 4

When six AM came, I got out of bed and made my way down to McDonald's for breakfast, then proceeded to the fuel barge where I was to meet the reporter and TV people. I went to the kayak, slid it off the deck into the river, climbed into the cockpit, and did a couple of laps around the barge just to get loosened up. I didn't know what they had in mind. They arrived just as they had scheduled. They called down their instructions to me, and when their shoot was completed, I hoisted the *Wind Dancer* back on deck and answered their questions about my journey. The whole procedure lasted about an hour and then they left.

I went to my room, gathered up my dirty clothes and sleeping bag, and set out to find a laundromat. I stopped by the front desk. They informed me that there was a coin-operated washer and dryer in the basement. I got a handful of quarters and continued on to the laundry room. I found it OK. I stuffed all my clothes and the sleeping bag in the washer, threw in a cup of detergent, turned the water temperature on hot, put in a couple of quarters, and pushed the go button.

Ruth would not approve of my procedure. She sorted everything out according to color and fabric. I only had one goal, and that was to get it clean and kill the odor. The washing machine needed thirty minutes and the dryer needed forty-five; that meant I would have to kill over an hour. I looked about to see what else was there.

I discovered a weight scale, a heart monitor, and a blood pressure machine. Good, I thought. I would give myself a physical. I hadn't had a doctor's physical in over twenty years. I had many friends who went regularly to doctors for physicals or whenever they caught a cold or something. Now they are all dead. Considering the old saying, "If it ain't broke, don't fix it," my attitude is, "If you ain't sick, don't see a doctor; they'll kill you." My weight was 155 pounds. I had lost thirty pounds since I left Astoria, Oregon. I had traveled 3,160 miles. Tumbling that idea in my head, I was losing ten pounds per thousand miles. And since I still had over two thousand miles to go, I probably would weigh 135 by the time I reached Florida. My resting heart rate was fifty-two beats per minute. I wasn't exactly resting; I was doing my laundry.

According to the read-out on the machine, that rate was consistent with a twenty-year-old professional athlete. That was a boost to my old ego. My blood pressure was 132 over 70. The light on the machine said that that fell within normal parameters. Since I didn't have any aches, pains, or afflictions, I felt safe declaring myself healthy. After my self-administered physical, I pulled my clothes out of the dryer, spread them out on the table, then folded and tucked them into Ziploc bags to keep them dry. I packed the filled Ziploc bags into the waterproof stuff sacks and then I returned to my room. With that task completed, I went to McDonald's for lunch.

After lunch, I drifted uptown to make some additional equipment purchases. The day before I had replenished my food stock, which wasn't much. Due to the generosity of the people along the way, I still had much of the food that I had when I left Astoria. What I wanted to buy now was insect repellent and Raid insecticide.

All along the northern states I wasn't bothered much with insects, I think because of the winds. However, now I would be moving down into the swamps of the South and would need extra protection, especially from mosquitoes and a very tiny flying insect called a "no see' um." I don't know the true name for these insects, but they are so small they are virtually invisible, hence, there common name. When they attack a person by the thousands, they can make your life miserable. I wished they had a repellent for snakes. Some of the snakes that I was likely to encounter were the rattler, cottonmouth, copperhead, and a deadly little reptile called the coral snake. I was not looking forward to finding any of them.

Another piece of equipment that I wanted to add was a weather band radio. Since I reached the Missouri River, I had been traveling at nearly twice the speed that I had estimated. So, at this point, I had been averaging thirty miles per travel day. If I continued at that speed, I was going to arrive at the Gulf of Mexico in early September; just in time to catch the last two months of the hurricane season.

Those storms were generated by a tropical depression called cyclones. When the sustained speed of the wind exceeds seventy-five miles an hour, they are called hurricanes. They got their name from the native people, Taino, who inhabited the Caribbean Islands during the time the early Spanish explorers visited these islands. The Taino worshiped a terrible wind goddess they called Hurricane.

With the trouble I had in the forty to fifty mile winds on the big northern lakes, I felt incurring a hurricane would be detrimental to my health. I purchased the insecticide and repellent at a drug store and the radio at Radio Shack. That completed my equipment. I returned to the hotel.

At five o'clock they had happy hour at the bar. During that time they served pizza along with the drinks. That was my dinner for the night. I sipped my beer, ate pizza, and sat at the bar and entertained the other guests with sea stories. At seven, I returned to my room and called Ruth to tell her I was in St. Louis and that I would be bypassing New Orleans, so we wouldn't be celebrating our wedding anniversary there. That didn't play very well. I was really digging a pit for myself.

There was one big disappointment I had with my stop at St. Louis. There was no mail. Rick had forgotten to send it.

Everything was in place for my departure the next day. I was now ready to get back on the river for my 195 miles down the Mississippi River to the Ohio.

Wednesday, August 5

I awoke early that morning, anxious to get under way. One more day in that air conditioned hotel and I would get pneumonia, which is unusual for me; most of the time I can tolerate wide swings in temperatures without a complaint. I packed up my gear, took my paddles from the corner, and went to the front desk and checked out. On my way to the fuel barge, I stopped by McDonald's for breakfast then proceeded on to the *Wind Dancer*. By eight o'clock, I had loaded my equipment in the storage lockers, slid my kayak off the deck into the river, said my good-byes, and continued my journey.

I was now paralleling Hernando de Soto's route. I wasn't finished with Lewis and Clark's journey. In 1803, Meriwether Lewis brought the equipment for the Voyage of Discovery down the Ohio River and up the Mississippi River to Camp Wood, where they prepared for their journey. From St. Louis down the Mississippi and up the Ohio, as far as Paducah, Kentucky, I would be traveling near both routes.

The Mississippi River forms the boundary between Missouri and Illinois. I planned to hug the Missouri shore. The river channel had been dredged out and the banks had been built up to protect the many towns along the way from flooding. The river level was very low because of the severe drought which forced the river traffic to stay in mid-channel. The tugboats that were plying the river were huge. They appeared to exceed eighty feet in length, and the barges they were towing were over a hundred feet. The sizes of the floats were amazing. Some were handling as many as forty-two barges. They were six barges wide and seven barges long. I asked a skipper of a fuel barge what the record number was. He told me ninety-six, handled by a single tugboat. I stayed out of their way.

I was still encountering those pop-up whirlpool phenomena's, but not as often as I did on the Missouri. While I was in St. Louis, I heard that an experienced canoeist, out on the Mississippi with two children, capsized and drowned. I wondered at the time if they had been swamped with one of those whirlpools. There was not much to see on this stretch of river; it was too built up. I was getting away from the coniferous trees, such as the evergreens, and now the native trees seem to be of the deciduous type.

I was fortunate to make it to the Jefferson County Boat Club by late afternoon. There seemed to be very few places to camp. I walked up to their clubhouse to inquire about camping there. They invited me to sleep on their couch so I wouldn't need to pitch my tent. I accepted their hospitality. They had a stove in their galley where I could cook my dinner. It made things simple for me.

After my meal, I took my equipment back to my kayak just in time to watch a thirty-six-foot sailboat drop anchor just off shore. I slipped my kayak into the water and paddled to their boat. They were Tony and Lucretia Beal from Key Largo, Florida. They were on their way upriver to St. Louis. It was nice to get to visit with a pair of sailors. Of the ten most beautiful places to live, only one will take you to the other nine: a sailboat.

When I got back to the clubhouse, I received a message from a television station located at Cape Gerideau, Illinois. They wanted to do an hour special show on my journey. It was their idea to come to my campsite at Thebes, Illinois, at six in the morning and capture my routine on video, from climbing out of my tent, having breakfast, breaking camp, and heading down the river. If I agreed to do it, I would have to find a phone somewhere along the river to make the arrangements. This journey would very likely be the most documented crossing in history.

I took down their phone number and made up my mind that if could find a phone, I would agree to the interview.

Thursday, August 6

I got up, made breakfast, and launched my kayak. When I passed Tony and Lucretia's sailboat, I called to them and waved. They were in the act of weighing anchor in preparation for their journey upriver. I turned downriver and picked up the stroke, ever mindful that I had to find a phone. I continued downriver, keeping well out of the way of the river traffic.

At noon, I stopped on the riverbank and did some stretching exercises. Sitting for hours with my legs stretched out in front of me made my legs stiff. I made my lunch and then continued downriver. At two PM, I came across a floating dry dock on the Missouri side of the river. These dry docks are used to repair the tugboats plying the river. They do this by sinking the dock down to a level that allows the tug to pull inside, and then they close the doors and pump the water out, allowing them to work on the boat just as if it was in a dry dock. It was quite an operation. I used their phone to call the television station at Cape Gerideau. They were going to come to my campsite in two days and they would videotape my morning camp routine as I prepared to get back in the river after my overnight stop. I was a little apprehensive about that. I'm not much of an actor. After the phone call was completed, I got back into the *Wind Dancer* and continued downriver for a couple more hours.

At four o'clock, I pulled the kayak up on a sandbar beside the river and camped Huckleberry Finn style for the night.

Friday, August 7

I left my sandbar not long after first light. This time I angled across the river, dodging the river traffic, to the Illinois side of the river. The television people wanted me to camp at a riverside park near the town of Thebes, Illinois. That was about twenty miles south of Cape Gerideau. It was not very far from my sandbar, so I took my time and watched my river charts to make sure I didn't bypass it.

Once I found the campsite, I pitched my tent in full view of the river so the television crew would be able to see me. Their plan was to come down the river by motorboat. I had the whole park to myself.

Usually I'm not too particular about the way I lay out my equipment, but this time I took particular care. I wanted to make a good impression so that they would think I knew what I was doing. After I got my campsite arranged the way I wanted, I took my evening swim and fixed my dinner and got everything ready for breakfast. I still had some time to kill before nightfall, so I got my river charts out to study. If things worked out right, and I wasn't held up too long, I would make it to the Ohio River the next day.

Saturday, August 8

The television shoot went without a hitch. They arrived at my campsite at five minutes to six and I was ready for them. In their instructions the day before, they told me not to look at the camera, but just to act like they weren't there. When I heard their motorboat arrive, I peeked out of my tent to see when they were all set up. Then I emerged from my tent all bleary eyed and ran down to the river and did my wake up swim, with swimsuit. Normally, I would do it in the nude. I dried off, drank a glass of Tang, and had my mucilage. Then I broke camp, packed my gear, and shoved the *Wind Dancer* into the river and picked up the stroke. I put on quite a show. The television crew followed me for about a half a mile. It was too bad I didn't get to see what they had produced.

It was only about thirty miles from there until I reached the Ohio River. There was a tower there called the Cairo Point Light. I took a picture of it for my slide program. At that point, my compass showed a northeasterly direction. I paddled for another couple of hours and camped for the night on the edge of Cairo, under a few trees. Again, the riverbank was covered with litter.

After I got my tent deployed, I walked uptown just to see what it was like and to get a meal. I found the walk along the street very depressing. It was very run-down. Many of the stores were closed. Some had broken windows and others were boarded up. The sidewalks were mostly empty of pedestrians. I went into a bar and grill and ordered a cheeseburger, a beer, and a hot fudge sundae. I had a craving again for ice cream. The place was practically deserted. I was happy to get out of there and back to my tent. I was unable to get a river chart of the Ohio River, so I wasn't exactly sure of what I would be facing. But, I did have a road map. If I had measured it right, Paducah, Kentucky, was just fifty miles from there. I secured for the night.

Sunday, August 9

I had never camped at a more depressing place, and was glad to be out of there. A few miles above Cairo, I came to a dam. It had a long line of tugboats with barges lined up to lock through. It was a very remote chance that I would get to lock through with them. Therefore, I didn't even try. The dam appeared to be only about fifty feet high so I elected to portage around it. I went over to the Kentucky side and landed just below the dam. There was no access road or path to the top of the dam, so I unloaded all my gear on the bank and carried it up to the top. Once that was done, I went to the boat and carried it up. It was quite a struggle, but I accomplished it. With that finished, I loaded everything back into the boat and slid it down the embankment into the river. That whole procedure took me about an hour. I counted myself lucky. If I had tried to lock through, it would probably have taken me a week. I continued on my way.

I paddled about five more miles up the river when disaster struck. I was paddling along the Kentucky shore about twenty feet out. The water was quite shallow and sloped up to a rocky shore, I heard the rumble of a big diesel engine, and I could tell by the sound that it was coming up fast and quite close. I glanced back over my left shoulder. There it was: a big tugboat coming up on my port side with a bone in its teeth, only twenty feet separating us. I looked back to see what its wake looked like. I was trapped.

I was too close to turn into it and take it on the bow, and too close to shore to escape it. I was going to take a bath. I didn't have the spray skirt on so I could not execute an Eskimo roll. I placed my knees into their sockets and braced myself for the impact. A virtual wall of water was coming at me like an avalanche. One second before it hit, I rolled the kayak into the wave and made a powerful drawing stroke pulling the kayak into the wave.

The wave broke over the top of me—the kayak didn't capsize, but the wave picked me up and carried me twenty feet latterly and dropped me onto a rock on shore. Then the rebounding wave carried me back into the river. I reached back into ancient maritime history and cast the worst curse that I could think of on the skipper of that tug: that he would die the most excruciating death with an unsatisfied hard on, while his mother ran up and down the riverbank howling at the moon.

When I got my wits about me, I paddled back to shore. I was sitting up to my waist in water. The cockpit was completely full. The positive flotation provided by the two storage compartments kept the kayak from sinking. When I got the bow up to the shore, I got out dripping wet. I took a hold of the grab handle and pulled it up on the rocks as far as I could. Immediately, the water started draining out of the cockpit.

There was a two-inch diameter hole in the bottom just aft of the rudder pedals. I doubled the curse that I placed on the skipper of that dammed tug. While the water was draining out of the cockpit, I removed all of my equipment from it. Since I had been able to keep the kayak from capsizing, everything was still in place. The plastic cover had protected the foodstuffs and camping gear that I stored in the plastic dishpan, which I clamped over it. My four water jugs and the plastic stuff sack that contained my toilet articles and medical supplies were still on board and in good shape. My underwater camera had been slung around my neck on a strap.

Unlike my beaching at Arlington, I hadn't lost a thing. Once the water was out of the cockpit, I used the big sponge and dried it out. Then, using a rag and a little acetone, I cleaned and dried around the hole. Acetone evaporates rapidly and carries the moisture with it. With the hole clean and dry, I pressed the shredded fiberglass back into the hole to form its original shape and covered it with three layers of duct tape. With that task completed, I turned the kayak on its side and repeated the process on the outside. With the patch completed, I loaded everything back into the *Wind Dancer* and prepared to continue on my journey.

I slid it over the rocks very cautiously because I didn't want to peel the duct tape off on the rocks. Likewise, when I climbed into the cockpit, I made sure I didn't disturb the patch with my feet. I pushed off with the paddle and took a few strokes, and then looked down at the patch for a couple of minutes to see if it was going to hold. It held. Duct tape—I love that stuff. I knew that this was just a temporary patch. Eventually, it would start to leak. Somewhere along the way I would have to find a marina where I could stay a couple of days and perform a permanent fix.

That whole process took me over an hour. I had lost an hour when I had to lift the kayak over the dam; now that hole would cost me more time. Ever since I entered into the Ohio River, I had been paddling against the current. When I left Cairo, Illinois, I had hoped to make it to Paducah, Kentucky, at the mouth of the Tennessee River. But with the delays, I was ten miles short. I had to pull over to the riverbank on the Kentucky side and camp for the night. Oh well. What the hell; I had been under way for over four months. What was one more day?

Chapter 11
Tennessee River

Monday, August 10

I left the riverbank at first light. The days were getting shorter, so I had to leave earlier in the morning in order to give myself more time to find a suitable camping site to get my tent up before dark.

I reached Paducah, Kentucky, at 2:30 pm and swung into the mouth of the Tennessee River. I stopped in Paducah and bought a few supplies before I continued. I now left the track taken by Meriwether Lewis when he brought the supplies down the Ohio River. I'm not sure where I intersected with Hernando de Soto's exploration. According to the research I did on his journey, Hernando de Soto landed somewhere near Tallahassee, Florida, in 1539 with more than six hundred men, and then preceded north crossing the Ohio River into Illinois. He then went west, crossing the Mississippi River into Missouri, looking for the fabled city of gold, El Dorado.

The Native Americans fought him all the way because of his cruelty to them. Hernando de Soto died of fever in 1542. His body was deposited in the Mississippi River. Only half of his original party had survived at that point. They made their way down the Mississippi on rafts and then continued into Mexico. What I found amazing about the early Spanish explorers was that they had introduced the horse to the Americas. By the time Lewis and Clark arrived nearly three hundred years later, the horse population had grown to the point that most of the Plains Native Americans had them.

After leaving Paducah, I continued paddling up the Tennessee River, about five miles, where I came to the dam that formed Kentucky Lake and Lake Barkley. There was a narrow neck of land separating the two lakes. As I approached the dam, I could see that there were several tugs with barges waiting to lock through. There was a boat ramp nearby so I elected to portage around the dam. When I started putting the wheels under the kayak, a fisherman came and helped me.

I asked him how far it was to the boat ramp above the dam. "Oh, it's a long way," he replied. "Okay. How far is that?" I asked. He said about two miles. I laughed and said that I had pulled the kayak from the Snake River in Idaho to the Missouri River in Montana—a total of 350 miles. "Now, *that* was a long way," I said.

He looked at me in disbelief. I put my harness on and started pulling. It was a steep hill, but I made it. I launched the *Wind Dancer* into the lake and continued my journey. After about a mile or two, I found a nice spot on the side of the lake and camped. The sun was getting low on the horizon.

Tuesday, August 11

It was still dark outside when I got up in the mornings. I fixed my breakfast inside the tent and broke camp as soon as there was enough light to see. I did that in order to make the most of the daylight hours. After paddling about five hours, I came to a very small island—no more than an acre in size. It was connected to a larger island by a causeway. They were both connected to the mainland with another causeway, which created a basin. The basin contained the Moors Resort and Marina. Good, I thought. I could stop there and repair my kayak; the water had started seeping through that morning which made me stop every few minutes and sponge it out.

I pulled the *Wind Dancer* up on the shore and then found a nice spot under some trees for my tent. Before I went any further I walked around the two causeways to the marina office to register.

The man behind the desk was Mr. Moor himself. He presented me with a registration form to fill out. When I had it completed, he asked me where my car was. I told him I didn't have one.

"How did you get here then?" he asked.

I explained that I had come in a kayak.

"This I've got to see," he said, so we went to where I had left the kayak. We chatted a while and then he left. About an hour went by when a young woman reporter showed up. She had me launch the *Wind Dancer* again so she could take some pictures. After she left, I went back to work getting my tent set up. At that point Mr. Moor's two daughters arrived. They invited me to dinner and asked for my dirty clothes so that their mother could wash them for me. I tried to talk them out of it, but they insisted. After they left, I finished setting up camp and went to their place for dinner.

Wednesday, August 12

At seven o'clock I awoke and pulled on my swimsuit. Since I was in a luxury environment I acted more civilized and wore clothes. After my swim, I shaved and went to the marina for breakfast. After breakfast I went back to camp, and two reporters and a television crew arrived. The television crew and one of the reporters were from Paducah, Kentucky, and the other was from Evansville, Indiana. That amount of publicity never entered my mind when I planned that journey.

After the reporters left, I stripped everything out of the cockpit of the kayak and put two layers of fiberglass on the inside over a hole. I let that cure for a couple of hours then mixed a small batch of epoxy, about a half a cup full, and mixed in a few spoons full of microfiber, creating a thick paste.

I worked into that into the pulverized fiberglass on the outside and smoothed it down with my fingers. By morning it would be hard enough to sand.

It was then time for me to go back to the Moors' for dinner and pick up my laundry. Poor Mrs. Moor; one of the items in my laundry was my sun hat. When it came out of the dryer the whole top of the hat had disintegrated. Over four months of wind, rain, and searing heat had weakened the cloth so much that it just fell apart.

I told her not to worry about it. I had a baseball cap I could wear, and down the way I'd buy a new one. That wasn't good enough for her. She wanted me to take one of her son's hats. I didn't want to argue with her. I've never been good at arguing with a woman; I lose every time.

After dinner I gathered up my laundry and bid them a good night. They invited me for a waffle breakfast the next morning. They guessed my weakness. I could never refuse a waffle.

Thursday, August 13

The first thing I did when I got up that morning was sand down the fiberglass patch job and check it out for soundness. It appeared to be strong enough to withstand the rigors of travel. Then I broke down my tent and packed. I was ready to continue my journey.

At seven o'clock I made my way back up to the Moors' for breakfast. Afterwards, they gave me some fresh fruit and filled my water jugs. They warned me not to camp on the east side of the lake because it was badly infested with ticks which carried the often fatal Lyme disease. They walked back with me to the *Wind Dancer* and waved as I left.

I got off to a rather late start. It was nearly eleven o'clock before I cleared the marina. The Kentucky Lake was another of those 180-mile reservoirs. I'd be on it for a few days. I camped that night on Pierce Point. I had only made seventeen miles.

Friday, August 14

I pushed myself out of my lethargy and made thirty miles that day. The water was clear and the forest on the lakeshore was lush. It was a pleasant place to paddle. I camped at Paris Point State Park, which was very clean. What was surprising was that it was virtually empty. It appeared I had it all to myself. After I pitched my tent and got my camping chores done, I went for a swim and washed the perspiration off. It felt good to be clean after a hard day's paddle. Then I prepared my evening meal and settled in for the night.

Saturday, August 15

I was really happy that the yacht captain in Omaha, Nebraska, recommended that I change my route to the Tombigbee Waterway. Actually, they called it the Ten Tom because it included the Tennessee River. The small towns along the way weren't on the riverbanks. They were back a few miles to escape the flooding.

I camped on a small sand island near the National Bedford State Park. Nearby, was a group of Tennessee River folk in what I judged to be twenty-four-foot pontoon boats. The boats were quite popular on the river. The group called themselves the Tennessee River Rats.

No sooner had I landed and started to set up my tent, when one of them came over to my location with a beer. He asked me where I was from and where I was going. I told him my story. He insisted that I come and join their fish fry; they where cooking catfish fillets and what they called hush puppies. They fried the fish in a beer batter. I asked them what a hush puppy was. They said they were made from a thick batter of corn meal, a little flour for a binder, egg, chopped onion, garlic, green pepper, and beer. After it was mixed, they formed a ball about the size of a golf ball and deep fried it to a golden brown. The combination of the two was delicious.

I asked how it became known as a hush puppy. The woman cooking them said that the woman who developed the recipe was cooking a batch when a puppy she had in her kitchen started barking. She threw one to him and shouted, "Hush puppy!" The dog quit barking, and from that time on they have been known as hush puppies.

Was that believable? Anyway, I had a good time. After about two hours they packed up their gear and buzzed off down the river. Before they left, one of the men came over to me and gave me a warning about the aggressive behavior of the cottonmouth snake. He told me that I could tell when the snakes were around because they had a very bad smell. I told him that if the snakes got close enough that I could smell them, they were already too damn close. He laughed and left.

I returned to my tent and zipped it up tight.

Sunday, August 16

Lately, I'd been finding very nice islands to camp on. That day I was on Dennison Island. When I first arrived, there were two families in their pontoon boats. I didn't encroach upon the peace and tranquility of their evening. They soon left and it was quiet. I did my usual camping routine and turned in for the night.

Monday, August 17

I made it to the Clifton Marina. Getting there was quite an ordeal. At three o'clock in the afternoon, I got caught in a hellish electrical storm; high winds and sheets of rain were accompanied by great jagged bolts of lightning and claps of thunder that were deafening. Up ahead, I saw a tugboat tied up to a dock. I could see someone in the wheelhouse. I paddled up beside it and tapped on the hull with my paddle. The skipper stuck his head out of the window and his mouth fell open in disbelief when he saw me sitting in the *Wind Dancer* below his boat.

I asked him where the marina was. He told me it was on the left, up the river about a half a mile. Then he asked if water could get into the boat if I tipped over. "The trick is not to tip over," I replied. I didn't want to take the time to tell him about the Eskimo roll.

I resumed paddling. In a few minutes, I found the marina and pulled into a covered slip. Picking up my paddles and taking them with me, I ventured up the dock and ramp to a twelve-by-twenty-four building that was being used as an office. As soon as I opened the door, my nostrils detected the aroma of chili bean soup and fresh baked corn bread. My mouth watered.

A man and woman in the office introduced themselves as the managers. I told them about my journey and that I had parked my kayak in one of their covered slips. I asked if I could pitch my tent on their property. They told me that they had a twenty-four-foot trailer house out back, and for twenty bucks I could rent it for the night and I wouldn't have to pitch my tent. I said that if they would throw in a bowl of their chili and a slab of corn bread they'd have a deal.

They laughed and served me up a large bowl of soup topped with chopped onions and cheese. Since my stomach thought my throat had been cut from the lack of food during the day, it tasted like a banquet. The manager got the keys to the trailer and we went to it. I told him I'd be on my way at first light. He asked me to stop by the office and have coffee and a cinnamon roll before I left. I asked, "Is that included?" He smiled and said sure. I was on a tight budget you know. I retired for the night.

Tuesday, August 18

I returned the key to the office, had a couple of cups of coffee and a roll, and continued my journey. At two pm, I got caught in another of those electrical storms. This storm was even worse than the one the day before. Not only was there wind, rain, lightening, and thunder, I was also being pelted with chunks of ice. As quickly as I could I made it to shore beside a blown down tree, I jerked my ground tarp out of the kayak and draped it over the roots of the tree and crawled under it to escape the hail. I placed my life jacket under my head and dozed off to sleep for a half an hour. After the hail stopped, I continued on my way. I camped for the night at the Savanna City Park in Tennessee.

Wednesday, August 19

I camped that day at the Green Water Marina access area. The area was a mess with litter. It was depressing. After the beautiful Kentucky Lake and the little islands on the Tennessee River, that was really a letdown.

I locked through the Pickwick Dam and Lock. That put me into the Pickwick Lake. Just a couple of miles further, I passed through another lock into Yellow Creek, leaving the Tennessee River behind. I paddled through Kentucky and Tennessee and entered into the northeast corner of Mississippi. Yellow Creek was the beginning of the Tombigbee Waterway.

The government had turned the creek into a channel, in order to take the heavy traffic off of the Mississippi. But it hadn't been successful, because it couldn't handle the large tugs and barges. So, only the smaller floats and the pleasure yachts used it now. They tied up at lock E Public Access Area, just above each set of locks, where the tugboats and their tows tied up while they waited to lock through a wide basin. I reached the area in the late afternoon, so I had to camp on the shore so that I could lock through first thing in the morning. I often had to wait to get through.

Thursday, August 20

I got through the lock early and made forty miles and paddled fourteen hours. I met a fisherman who explained how

I could find a place to camp for the night. It was dark when I arrived at a campsite and set up my tent. After I had been in bed for a couple of hours, I saw a light being shown on my tent. I got up to investigate. It was a sheriff looking for me. The fisherman I met earlier in the day had told him to find me and give me a ten-pound watermelon. I thanked the sheriff for bringing it to me. After he left, I stood there wondering what the hell to do with the melon. I took my machete and cut a big slice out and ate as much as I could, then carried the rest over to a trashcan and disposed of it. I hated to do that, but there was just no way I could carry it with me.

Friday, August 21

I reached Smithville Marina just at dark. I was held up at lock E for two hours. But I wasn't upset with the delay because I had a nice visit with the captain of a motor yacht going to Florida. And the lockmaster gave me a cup of coffee while I waited. Also, I solved a mystery that had been bugging me for a couple of weeks.

Ever since I had entered the Tennessee River, whenever I came to a downed tree at the river's edge, I'd see a splash, and few seconds later I'd see a reptilian head sticking above the surface of the water. But it would disappear before I could get close enough to identify what it was.

I asked several fishermen about it, but they didn't know what I was talking about. While I was waiting for the motor yacht to clear, I wondered down to the lower end of the lock and looked straight down into a pool of water and saw a half dozen turtles swimming. That was the answer to my mystery. The turtles would sun themselves on the logs and when they heard me coming, they would dive in the water and then raise their heads when I came by. Why didn't I think of that sooner?

As soon as I reached Smithville Marina, I walked up the ramp to the office to see what arrangements I could make for the night. My arrival had been observed. As soon as I got in the building, I played the twenty-questions game with the guy behind the counter: what, where, when, how, and so forth. The tiny *Wind Dancer* attracted more attention than a one hundred-foot luxury yacht. Or, it could have been my age. No one expects an old bearded man to show up at a marina in a kayak.

I answered all his questions and then asked if I could pitch my tent on his dock. He suggested that I roll out my sleeping pad on the floor of his office. I accepted. He also called the local television station to report the story. That was fine with me. I needed to lay over a day to do some repairs to the *Wind Dancer*. When the skipper of the motor yacht gunned his engines to take off, the prop's wash sent the *Wind Dancer* into the wall of the lock, fracturing the hull just below the waterline. I was sure glad that I had my fiberglass repair kit with me.

Saturday, August 22

I lay over to do my repair work and wash my clothes and sleeping bag. The television people came out and did their story. Afterward, I asked Jesse Cox, the marina owner, where the closest supermarket was. He told me it was about four miles away. I got my tote net and prepared to walk to get a few more supplies. Jesse stopped me. He gave me the keys to his car and told me to drive. I was amazed. People had given me their home, their kid's hats, and some had even given me their kid's bed for the night. Now, Jesse was letting me, a total stranger, use his car.

When I got back from shopping, there was a message for me from the television station. Their editing machine had ruined the footage they had taken and they asked if they could do it again the next day. Why not? I thought. I was already over a month ahead of schedule. I would take a bit of rest and write some postcards out to the people I had promised to keep in touch with.

Sunday, August 23

Everything worked out well that day. I mailed out my correspondence and had a picnic lunch with Mr. and Mrs. Cox. At three pm, the young fellow from the television station came and re-shot the story. I paddled my kayak around a bit for a little action footage—something I didn't do the day before because I had just repaired it.

Later in the evening, Mrs. Cox brought me a catfish and hush puppy dinner. She also verified the story I was told by the Tennessee lady at the fish fry. She told me it was true. I spent the rest of the evening helping Jesse with the chores around the marina.

My journal was up to date, postcards were mailed, and I had a dry kayak again. I had a good feeling about everything.

Monday, August 24

I camped at Morgan's Landing, two miles from the Aberdeen lock. I had a nice stay at Smithville, but I was glad to be under way again. I'm now 355 miles from Mobile Bay. I wanted to be there by the fifth of September. But it didn't look like I was going to make it. I was having trouble matching campsites with thirty-mile days. Also, locking through the locks was holding me up.

That morning I made a real boondoggle. I missed the entrance to the lock. When I paddled up, I had my eyes focused on the dam and I paddled right past the entrance to the lock. I felt very foolish. Jesse the marina owner had called the lockmaster on his VHF radio and arranged for me to lock through without a delay, but I blew it. The lockmasters had a good laugh when I told them what happened.

Once I got through the lock, I made good time. When I reached the Aberdeen lock, a reporter from Aberdeen met me. It was my guess that either Jesse or the lockmaster had called her. When I locked through lock "A" that morning, the lockmaster,

Clifford Smith, invited me up to the control room for coffee and explained to me how the locks worked.

As I paddled my way down the river, I spotted two fawns playing on the bank of the river. They stopped and watched me paddle by before they scampered away. The forest along the riverbanks now had that subtropical jungle look. The short bushes looked like miniature palm trees and the tall cypresses were covered with what the locals called Spanish moss.

I asked a fisherman why it was called Spanish moss. I was told that in the early days of Spanish exploration, a grandee wearing a beard raped and murdered a Native American girl. The Native Americans caught him and hung him on a tree. His beard took to the tree and has remained ever since.

Was that grandee part of de Soto's expedition? My research showed that they were very cruel to the natives. They made slaves out of them, raped the women, and murdered at will. I tumbled the information in my head. Logic told me that those trees had moss on them long before the Spanish came, and most probably before the Native Americans arrived, but it made an interesting story.

In that area, I saw my first white egrets of the journey. There would probably be more as I work my way south.

Tuesday, August 25

I got off to a nice start that day. I only had one lock to go through and it was the lock at Columbus, Mississippi. Again, I was held up. This time, television station 4 wanted to watch me lock through. Also, their newspaper reporter got lost. I had to wait two hours for him. The delays put me two days behind schedule. I had wanted to be in Demopolis, Alabama, on Thursday. Now, it looked like I wouldn't make it until Saturday.

That night I camped on the lawn of the Rueben Fish House. The lockmaster at Columbus told me to stop there for a catfish dinner; all you could eat for $9.50. It was excellent. When I paid, I asked the manager if there was someplace I could camp for the night. It was getting dark. He said sure, on his front lawn above the dock.

Wednesday, August 26

Since there was a shopping mall near the fish house and my arrival in Demopolis was delayed until Monday, I decided to get my supplies now. That meant that when I got to Demopolis, all I'd have to do was pick up my mail and then keep on going. I did my shopping and washed my clothes. I packed everything up except my tent, the air mattress, and sleeping bag. The next day I'd continue my journey.

Thursday, August 27

I camped at Cochran's Park by mile marker 295. It was the cleanest and nicest campsite I had encountered on the trip, and surprisingly only a few people were there. I left the Rubens Fish House at 6:30 in the morning and got to the locks at 2:30 that afternoon. Then I paddled another ten miles to Epes. I had made thirty-five miles.

I reached the campsite just in time. I barely got my tent up when one of those violent electrical storms broke. I had to prepare my dinner inside my tent. That's when I made a big mistake. Usually I took my empty food can and put it back into the Ziploc bag and deposited it into the nearest trashcan, or I'd put it back into the storage compartment to dispose of it later. This time, I just pitched it out the front of my tent to be picked up later.

After the storm abated, I left the tent to go to the washroom and stooped to pick up the empty can. Immediately my arm, from my hand to my elbow, burned like I had stuck it into a fire. Fire ants! They're tiny little ants, less than a quarter of an inch in length; fire ants are vicious biters. I dropped the can and decided that I'd leave it there until morning when I could see. The next morning I picked up the can with a stick and deposited it in a trashcan.

Friday, August 28

I left my campsite at first light and made good time to the Gainesville Locks. I got there just as another storm broke. I beached my kayak and went into the lockmasters control room until the storm was over, and then locked through. I camped about a half a mile away at the lower dam access area. I had made thirty miles. Then, I discovered another malady.

Several days earlier, I saw a little black dot on the back of my left hand. Some flying insect had bitten me. What was odd about this insect bite was that when a fly or mosquito bit me, it would leave a little red mark, and in a few hours it would disappear. I usually have a natural immunity to insect bites, but not this time! Now I had two marks on my left hand and one on my right hand. The bite I got first was as big as a dime. It was clear I had to do something about it. I got out my Swiss Army knife, sterilized the blade, and dug the black matter out of it. At the same time, I dug the two smaller ones out, and then worked some Neosporin into the wounds. From then on, I kept a lookout for the bites. I've never discovered what had been biting me.

Saturday, August 29

At river slough mile marker 230, I camped on the riverbank. I found a spot that I could clear with my machete.

I had quite a struggle with those little fire ants. It seems that they were waiting on the shore for me. They immediately set up a train into my storage lockers. I didn't know why. All of my food was either in cans or Ziploc bags. I tried putting my kayak up on blocks and spraying the blocks with insect repellent, but nothing seemed to stop them. Fishermen had told me that their survival instincts were so strong that in times of floods they would form a ball around their queen as big as a bowling ball and float to a new location. While the outer layer died, the inner ants survived.

I had to add another task to my morning departure. I emptied everything out of my kayak, sprayed it with insecticide, and then wiped all the ants out. That didn't do a whole lot of good though. By the time I got everything loaded, they were back.

I added three additional tasks to my evening camping routine. As soon as I got my tent up and retreated inside, I zipped it up, held my breath, and sprayed the inside with insecticide. I did it to kill any flying insects that managed to slip in with me. It was my feeling that de Soto died of malaria. I didn't want that to happen to me. While I ate my evening meal, I listened to my weather band radio. That prepared me physiologically for what would come, weather-wise, the following day. I had completed thirty-five miles that day.

Sunday, August 30

This was mine and Ruth's twenty-fifth wedding anniversary. I wrote her a letter that I'd sign on board for another twenty-five years if she would like. Unfortunately, because of this trip, another twenty-five years seemed unlikely. Being Sunday, I wasn't able to get my mail until the next day. I talked to some local people about making a stop in Mobile, Alabama. I was told that it was on the west side of the bay. That would be twenty miles out of my way, making a combined distance of forty miles. Therefore, I decided to bypass Mobile.

These small towns have some strange laws. You couldn't buy alcohol on Sunday unless you bought it at a private club. The bars called themselves a club. You could join for a dollar a day, or you could pay ten dollars for a whole year. On Sunday, the town was dead. I walked a couple of blocks without seeing a single person. A few cars drove by, but not a single store was open. I stayed overnight in a motel so I could get under way as soon as possible.

Monday, August 31

I had breakfast at seven; I had bacon, eggs, and grits. I wanted to try a typical Southern cuisine. After breakfast, my first stop was the chamber of commerce where I acquired a map of Alabama. Then I proceeded to the post office. Rick had come through like a champ. It was nice to hear from everyone.

I returned to the yacht basin to continue my journey, but I was told that the local newspaper wanted my story, so I waited for them to arrive. I finally got under way at 11:30. The lock was waiting for me and I was able to get right through without a problem. I camped that night on the riverbank, had my evening meal, and consulted my map for the next day's run. It was getting increasingly difficult to pick campsites. I was 197 miles from Mobile Bay.

Tuesday, September 1

All that day there was a light, warm rain. It didn't bother me. The rain wasn't a problem unless it was accompanied with heavy winds and/or lightning. Those tiny fire ants still plagued me though. There was no way for me to keep them out of my kayak.

Wednesday, September 2

The towns were getting farther and farther apart as I got deeper and deeper into the swamp. The vegetation was definitely getting subtropical. The low-lying bushes and ferns looked like miniature palm trees and the cypress trees were tall and hairy with Spanish moss. The white egrets were now quite numerous.

I camped on a sandbar. It was much safer because it was easier for me to spot snakes. Getting bitten while down in those swamps would have ruined my whole day.

Thursday, September 3

That day I passed through the Coffeeville Locks. I was caught by another of those severe electrical storms again. I pulled the *Wind Dancer* up above the locks and went into the control room and waited it out. When the storm was over, I returned to the kayak and locked through. It was too late in the day to go any further, so I camped for the night in a small park below the dam. That was the last set of locks I'd have to go through on the Tombigbee Waterway.

I was now 116 miles from Mobile Bay. In about forty miles, I'd be entering into the second most dangerous section of my journey: a vast swamp, sixty miles long and forty miles wide with no campsites noted on my maps. It was going to be catch-as-catch-can. I was not looking forward to it.

Friday, September 4

As I paddled down the river, a tugboat skipper called out that there was a woman waiting for me under the railroad bridge at Jackson, Alabama. I waved back that I understood and continued paddling. Sure enough, when I got there, she was under the bridge. She was a reporter from the newspaper at Jackson. She'd been told by another reporter that I would be passing by her way. She interviewed me there on the riverbank as I battled the ants who wanted to take possession of the *Wind Dancer*. After the interview, I camped in the same spot. It was too late to go further.

Saturday, September 5

After leaving my campsite under the railroad bridge at Jackson, I continued paddling down the river. I was getting ever deeper into a virtual jungle. I wasn't happy about my situation at all. But luck was with me one more time. At about five o'clock, I met a fisherman in a motorboat. I asked him where I could camp for the night. He told me to follow him. He led me to what he called a fish camp. It was a rustic wooden shack with half a dozen wooden docks. He told me to leave my kayak there and he would take me home with him to Eight Mile. (That was the name of the town.) He wanted his mother and father to meet me. He said that I could sleep in a bed that night and he would bring me back to the *Wind Dancer* in the morning. That sounded a hell of a lot better than sleeping with the snakes, so I accepted his hospitality.

Sunday, September 6

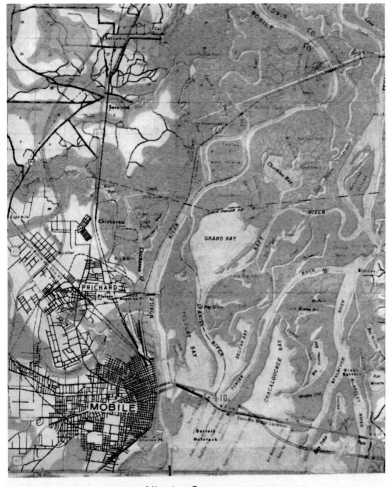

Aligator Swamp

I got lost somewhere in the Big Delta swamp. Was I really lost? Well, not really. I knew I was about thirty miles north of Mobile Bay, the center of the Mobile Big Delta Swamp. It was at this point, a little over sixty miles below Coffeeville, where the Alabama River merges with the Tombigbee. The two rivers spilled into dozens of smaller rivers, creeks, and bayous that meander through the swamp, forming countless small lakes and ponds filled with islands of heavy vegetation. I missed the main shipping channel when I made a wrong turn and got into a bayou that dead-ended in a pond about the size of a football field, filled with a number of small islands like a maze. I couldn't find a way out.

It was getting late in the afternoon so I looked for a place to camp. It was clear that I wasn't going to make it to Mobile Bay before dark. I'd take a few strokes and then let the kayak drift as I looked for someplace to camp. Ahead, I saw what I thought was a piece of bark floating on the surface of the pond. KAPOW!

The water under the *Wind Dancer* literally exploded. A three-foot section of scaly tail slammed into the side of my kayak, nearly turning me over. I stabilized the kayak with a brace. The suddenness of the encounter scared the living hell out of me. My kayak had drifted across the back of an alligator. He must have been close to eight feet in length. Fisherman had warned me that alligators were in here, but up to that time I hadn't seen any.

Once I got my wits back, I tried following it. I had my camera on a strap around my neck and I wanted to take a picture for my slide program. But the gator wouldn't pose for me. Every time I'd get close enough to take the picture, he would dive. Finally, he hid in a mass of water lilies and I gave up. Besides, I'd wasted about fifteen minutes in the quest, and in another three hours I'd be running out of daylight. The thought of floating around all night in that snake- and alligator-infested swamp was not high on my list of priorities.

I continued my search for a camping site. I spotted two small islands heavily covered with mangrove bushes. The islands were about five feet in diameter and separated by a two-foot gap. The mangrove bushes were seven to eight feet tall. That gave me a brilliant idea: if I couldn't find a campsite, I could create one. I circled the two islands while pounding on them with my paddles to discourage any tree-climbing reptiles. Ophidiophobia? Okay, I have it.

With my inspection complete, I paddled a little way out into the pond, then turned, pointed the kayak toward the gap between the two islands, brought the *Wind Dancer* up to battle speed, and headed it into the gap between the two islands, ramming it in as far as I could. I took my paddles apart and stored them inside the kayak.

My next act was to brace my knees in their pads, then reach out and grasp the mangrove branches; I forced the kayak further into the gap, wedging it in as tight as I could. Next, I took out my machete and chopped the mangrove trees down at a level below that of the top of the kayak. I piled the shorter branches beside the kayak up to the level of the top. The longer branches I laid across the kayak with the ends on the two islands anchored between the stubs. I created a platform.

With that done, I crawled forward to the food compartment and got a packet of food, the cabin portion of my tent, and the fiberglass rods. I set up the tent so that it aligned fore and aft with the kayak. That allowed me to get to the forward compartment of the kayak through the back window and the aft compartment through the door. Then I lashed the tent to the platform with some fish line. After that, I crawled out the back window and got my air mattress. The weather was still warm enough that I didn't bother with the sleeping bag. I blew up the air mattress as tight as I could and laid it across the tent floor. I zipped up the tent and sprayed it with the insecticide.

Voilà! I was ready to settle in for the night. It was already getting dark. Was I comfortable? Hell, no. That platform had more lumps and sags than you could imagine. Was I secure? Again, the answer was an emphatic no. The mesh screen would keep the insects and the snakes out, but that alligator worried me. I was less than fifty yards from where I ran over him. I didn't know if that alligator would think of that tent as a barrier or a napkin.

Swamp

An impenetrable swamp

Monday, September 7

It's obvious that I survived the night. But it wasn't pleasant. Don't ever let anyone tell you that nighttime in a Southern swamp is quiet. There was constant sound all night long. Owls hooted, birds flitted from branch to branch, and there were splashes from aquatic animals like possums, raccoons, and an animal that looked like a cross between a muskrat and a beaver called a neutrino. I'd hear a sound, sit bolt upright, and grab my machete ready to do battle with an alligator.

When morning came, I broke camp as soon as I had enough light to see. I still had to find a way out of that swamp. Breaking camp was as much work as building it. The kayak had settled into the mud and stuck fast. I took two of the poles that I had cut for the platform and, rocking the kayak side to side, I was able to get it to come loose. Once free, I started exploring the perimeter of the pond to find the opening. Logic told me that I had gotten in there, so there had to be away out. I avoided the area where I ran over the gator the night before.

After several tries and disappointments, I emerged into a stream that had some current to it. From my map, I identified it as the Tenshaw. It would lead me to the Blakely and Apalachee rivers. Both of the rivers would lead me to the head of Mobile Bay on the east side. I had lucked out again and none too soon. I was running low on water. I didn't dare try purifying that evil looking brew that I had paddled on last night.

I reflected back over the terrain I had passed through over the last five months. The Pacific Northwest with its rolling hills topped with lava flows and sides covered with trees, and the spicy aroma of the newly opened leaves. Then mountain states followed, with wild flowers growing out of the cliffs and the raptors circling overhead. The scenic Missouri River had wild roses growing on the banks and flocks of great white pelicans.

Down here in the swamps, there was a different style of beauty, with tall cypress trees, hairy with Spanish moss and surrounded with palm ferns, and clumps of mangrove bushes. White egrets graced their branches. The aroma of the swamps was a pungent smell of decaying vegetation, which wasn't unpleasant. It was the primeval smell of evolution. Many men my age count their vast wealth or political power as success. My greatest achievement was adventure.

I came upon the Tenshaw River at eleven am. It was two pm when I looked up and saw the interstate bridges across the head of the Mobile Bay. In another hour, I'd be at my destination,

Daphne, Alabama, on the east side of Mobile Bay. I reached the city park at three o'clock and set up camp. There was a couple getting ready to go out on the bay in their canoe. They appeared to be in their late thirties.

When I came in, the couple stopped what they were doing and came over to me. They were very friendly and wanted to know where I came from. So, I explained what I was doing. The guy was Roy and his girl friend was Carol. After I explained my trip, Roy talked me into taking my tent down and going home with him to his house. His plan was that I should stay with him a couple of days so he could show me the sights around town. I'd certainly enjoyed swings of fortune in two days, going from sleeping perched on a platform in a swamp fearful of being eaten by an alligator, to sleeping in luxury in a bed. I accepted his invitation.

Tuesday, September 8

Roy and I had breakfast at his house. He called two newspapers and the local television station. They were going to come out the next day and interview us. Roy had decided to go with me part way as a buddy boat in his canoe. That would be a new experience for me. I had never traveled with anyone before. After his phone calls, I called Rick in Portland and told him where I was and let him know that the next day I'd be heading for Pensacola, Florida. Then Roy and I proceeded on our sightseeing trip to Mobile City. We visited the marine museum and the battleship *Alabama*. From there we visited some of the historic plantations, and then returned to the house.

Wednesday, September 9

We didn't go very far that day; we got off to a late start. Two newspapers and the television station met us down at the Daphne City Park to do their interview. Afterward, we started paddling. We were beating into a southeast wind and only made about ten miles. We faced heavy chop and headwinds. We were still in the Mobile Bay, so we camped for the night at Mullet Point.

Thursday, September 10

I got off to an early start. I left Roy behind. He had more gear than I so it took him longer to get started. He had a back-up for every piece of equipment he had, and he had back-ups for his back-ups. He called himself Redundant Roy. Another problem was that he couldn't keep up with me when he paddled, but he had a two and a half hp Evinrude engine. When he was under power, I couldn't keep up with him. And I couldn't stand the noise of that damn engine. It frightened the birds. So I just left. He could catch up later.

It took Roy about four hours to catch up. Then he passed me. We stopped at a marina for the night. We went into the restaurant for dinner and when I went to pay our bill, the manager said the dinner was on the house. She had seen me on the news the night before.

We were in the Florida Intracoastal Waterway at that point. I had completed the portion of the journey that paralleled the journey of Hernando de Soto, and now I was taking up the one made by Narváez and de Vaca.

The next day I'd enter into the state I'd been looking for: Florida.

CHAPTER 12
FLORIDA INTRACOASTAL WATERWAYS NORTH AND WEST

Friday, September 11

I left the Bear Point Marina around seven o'clock. Roy was still getting his gear loaded up. I wanted to get to Pensacola Naval Air Station before dark. That again was one of my major supply points. Since I had been in the military, I felt I could get a place to stay in one of their guest accommodations.

As I approached the Florida state line, a trio of bottlenose dolphins picked me up. They acted as an escort for nearly an hour. One took the lead and the other two positioned themselves on either side of the *Wind Dancer*. But when I got closer to Pensacola, they left me. I guess they thought I was close enough that I could find my own way. Soon after that, I heard the buzz of an out-board motor. Roy had caught up with me.

When Roy came alongside, he turned his engine off and tried to paddle along with me, but he kept falling behind. Finally, he gave up and fired up his engine again. He told me he would find us a place to stay and would meet me at the marina. I agreed that was a good idea. I was happy to get the noise of that engine out of my head. I continued on my way.

Just as I reached the entrance to the Pensacola marina, six of the Blue Angels swept over me making their approach for landing. That was a thrilling sight.

When I pulled into the Sherman Cove Marina, Roy was there with Diane Shepherd, the base civil affairs officer. She arranged for the news media for the following day. Jokingly, I told her how nice it was that the Blue Angels had honored me with a flyby as I entered the marina. She got a big kick out of it. I had wanted to get an early start the next morning, but because of all the media interviews—newspaper, television, radio—I realized that it wasn't going to happen. Since I needed some supplies, such as sea charts for the rest of my journey and reading glasses to replace to ones that went over the side in the Mobile Bay, I decided to make the most of the layover. That night we stayed at the navy lodge. But not for free. It cost me fifty dollars!

Saturday, September 12

When morning came, we had breakfast at the base cafeteria and then proceeded to town where I bought a cheap pair of reading glasses. My next purchase was not so cheap. My sea charts cost seventy-five dollars. But, they were a complete set covering the entire east coast of Florida, complete with a waterproof case. The maps were expensive, but I thought they would be worthwhile.

When I got back to the navy lodge, I had a message. The commander of the Blue Angels invited Roy and me over to their headquarters for a visit. Diane had called him and reported my comments about their flyover. He sent a staff car over and picked us up. We spent over two hours with the crew. They showed us videos of their training and posed us by one of their planes and took some photos. They also gave me an autographed poster, which they put it in a mailer and mailed off to Ruth. Afterward, they took us back to the lodge.

By then, Roy's girlfriend, Carol, arrived with the trailer. We loaded his canoe and said good-bye. They were going back to Daphne. Roy mentioned that he would probably meet me somewhere along the way and go with me the rest of the journey. I thought the probability was remote so I didn't voice any opposition to it. I felt guilty for my lack of enthusiasm. He had been so hospitable and helped me so much. There wasn't anything wrong with the way he traveled; it was just so different than mine.

After they left, I checked out and moved my stuff down to the marina. This stop had been the most expensive stop on my whole journey; with the cost of my charts, glasses, food, and lodging, it came to over two hundred dollars. It was a whole month's budget in one day. It didn't bother me though. Because of people's kindness along the way, I had built up a surplus of money. I spread my air mattress and sleeping bag under one of the covered slips and bedded down for the night. I wanted to get an early start the next day.

Sunday, September 13

When I awoke that morning, I prepared my breakfast under the roof of the covered slip, then packed everything into the *Wind Dancer*, slipped into the cockpit, and began paddling. After about a mile, I passed under the nose of a huge aircraft carrier and entered into the Pensacola Bay. I crossed the bay and found the entrance into the Intracoastal Waterway (ICW).

The Intracoastal Waterway appeared to be a wide channel with a lot of bays filled with reeds and different species of aquatic birds. At noon I pulled over to the shore and prepared my snack, then continued my journey. That was a sharp contrast to paddling the swamp of Mobile's big delta. The sea charts I purchased were a great help. It made it much easier to locate and identify the features of the waterways. Santa Rosa Island is a long narrow island that nearly encloses Pensacola Bay and extends all the way to Choctawhatchee Bay. It forms the south shore of the Intracoastal Waterway. It is quite nice with a broad sandy beach. Since the site was surrounded by salt water, and had no snakes, I camped for the night.

Monday, September 14

I had a good trek this day. I was back in stride. There were few distractions along the route and the water traffic was light; only an occasional pleasure yacht and fishing vessel, mostly shrimp boats. A person really had to watch their navigation along that area. The channels between the islands were quite narrow. If you made a wrong turn, you would wind up in the Gulf of Mexico. And the winds could sweep you out to sea.

Late in the afternoon, I pulled into the coast guard station to find out if I could camp on their beach. I could see on the charts that I was approaching a wide bay named Choctawhatchee Bay. The duty officer had tracked my arrival. He came down to the beach when I pulled up. He wanted to know what I was doing. I introduced myself, told him a short version of my journey, and asked him if I could camp for the night on his beach.

He invited me into the station and assigned me a bunk and bedding. I didn't even need to break out my sleeping bag. He told me I could have my meals with the crew and he showed me where the shower was.

When I planned this journey, it was going to be totally on my own. I figured I would lock my kayak to tree, go to a store to resupply, and go my way. But because of Rick's contacts with the chamber of commerce along the way and peoples' curiosity about my journey, I had a constant willing support team. It was better than anything I could have had imagined.

After my shower, I went to dinner. The rest of the evening I spent visiting with the crew. Their mission was to rescue boaters that got themselves in trouble in the gulf, and to stop drug smuggling. That evening they had to go out and rescue two people that had capsized a catamaran. At ten, I retired for the night.

Tuesday, September 15

I arose at five in the morning and had breakfast with the coast guard crew. Since I didn't have my usual morning chores, I got off to an early start. I crossed the Choctawhatchee Bay and entered into a channel that connected to the West Bay. That would put me in Panama City, which was this day's destination. I was making good progress. By mid-afternoon, I arrived and started looking for a likely place to camp.

The area was a built-up area and there was no designated camping area. There were a lot of bayous leading inland, but they had private homes built near the shores. I paddled slowly along the shore until I came to a point of land protruding out into the bay at the head of a bayou. It was not posted and it looked like it would be a good campsite.

As I made my approach, two young men, who appeared to be in their early twenties, came toward me in an inboard runabout motorboat. I hailed them and asked if they thought anyone would mind if I camped there for the night. They told me no. It would be fine; no one would complain. They lived just across the bayou. They asked the usual questions of where I was from and what I was doing. Then they pulled their boat into a boathouse across from me. I drug my kayak up on shore and proceeded to set up my tent.

In about an hour, the two young men were back. One of them told me that his mother and father were gone for the evening and they had cooked up a large pot of spaghetti and meatballs. They would trade me a plate of spaghetti and a glass of Chianti if I would tell them the story of my journey. I laughed and told them they had a deal.

The warmth of their hospitality only exceeded the beauty of their home. I had a plate of delicious spaghetti and several glasses of wine. Later, his mother and father came home and I was introduced to them, Dr. and Mrs. John Lueth Wambo. It was a very nice family and a very enjoyable evening.

Wednesday, September 16

I awoke that morning with a hail from Dr. Wambo. "Hey, Karl," he shouted across the bayou, "where's your kayak?" I thought he was playing a joke on me. I popped my head out of my tent and looked where I had placed it the night before. My beloved *Wind Dancer* was gone. I had committed the ultimate sin for a sailor: I hadn't placed my kayak above the tide line, and I hadn't tied it off. That task was something I had never failed to do before.

I had been handling boats for over fifty years without something like that happening. (I was tempted to not report this in my journal). Dr. Wambo told me to stand by; he would get his boat, pick me up and we would go look for it. He returned to his house, called his office, told them he would be late, then came and got me. We went to the end of the bayou. The *Wind Dancer* wasn't there. We searched the bay hoping that we would come across it floating out there, but no luck. We returned to his house and he called the sheriff's water and harbor patrol. They told him they would check around and call him back. Dr. Wambo went to his office. There was nothing more he could do.

I stayed at his house, pacing the floor, absolutely sick with apprehension and occasionally feeling the side of my head to see if long donkey ears were protruding from it. I just couldn't make myself believe what I had done!

After two hours, Mrs. Wambo received a phone call from the sheriff. My kayak had been found. A guy had gone out fishing before he went to work and had found the kayak floating in the middle of the bay. He towed it to a water treatment plant where he worked, and reported it to the Sheriff's office. The sheriff sent a patrol car over to pick me up and take me over to the kayak. I thanked both the fisherman and the patrol officer, slipped into the cockpit, and paddled back to my tent.

By the time I arrived, a newspaper reporter was there to get the story. Explaining what happened was the most embarrassing and humiliating experience of my life, but it had to be done. That evening Dr. Wambo gave me a book of Florida maps and made me promise that when I reached Miami I would send him a postcard, so he would know that I had made it alright. Maybe he thought I was getting a little senile. No wonder; I was beginning to think so myself.

Thursday, September 17

The fall equinox was approaching, which meant that the sun was taking longer to lift above the horizon. Since I normally woke between 4:30 and 5:00 am, it was still quite dark outside. I lay in bed with my battery-powered razor and shaved by feel. Then I donned my headlamp to complete my morning chores. This made it possible for me to begin my day's journey as soon as it was light enough to see. My days were getting shorter and shorter. I had to use every bit of available light to gain the distance I needed before I had to camp for the night.

When I checked my chart the night before, I was unable to pick a designated campsite, so I would have to find whatever I could. The ditch, as the locals called it, was a channel that connected the east bay with Lake Wimico.

Down inside the channel, I was protected from the onshore wind. The channel was well below the bank and the trees offered good protection. I paddled steadily all day, pausing only briefly at noon to eat my lunch. I passed through the lake before I decided to stop for the night. I pulled the kayak up on the bank and placed it on top of two logs well above the water line. I tied it off securely. I was still very badly shaken by my loss the night before. I had to climb about twenty feet up the bank before I found a flat spot big enough for me to pitch my tent.

Friday, September 18

I got off to a quick start and was making good time. A few miles from Apalachicola Bay, a motor yacht going west stopped and gave me the news that Roy, the man I met at Daphne, Alabama, was there waiting for me.

I received this news with mixed emotions. The trek with Roy from Mobile Bay to Pensacola was less than stellar. I hoped things would be better this time. Maybe it would work out for the best. Soon, I would be leaving Apalachicola behind. I would have two hundred miles of open coastline; no waterway to follow. Another boat would be an asset—if we could stay together. I had a sinking feeling that this would not be a fun adventure, but there was nothing I could do about it now. I was committed. I had to grin and bare it.

It wasn't Roy's fault. I didn't like that outboard engine and I didn't trust his canoe in open water. As far as I could see, it didn't have any positive flotation, and the way it was loaded, if it got swamped, it would go down like an anchor. I had the feeling that I was about to have the head of an albatross put around my neck.

I reached Apalachicola City at 12:30 pm. I found Roy at the city park. He had talked to the newspaper and they wanted me to come to their office and give them my story, which I did. Apalachicola was a small town with a population of about two thousand. I talked to the newspaper publisher himself, which was a lucky break.

The publisher was a history enthusiast of that area. We discussed at length the Panfilo de Narváez and Álvar Núñez Cabeza de Vaca, treasurer for the expedition. Their supply ships did not come to them so they had to make boats from timber found there in Florida. They were forced to kill their horses for food and skinned their legs to make water sacks. Many of the men died of hunger, others died from drinking salt water because the water sacks rotted. Two of their boats were swept out to sea, which included the Narváez. The two boats were never seen again. In the end, only four men survived: Vaca, his Moroccan slave, Estevan, and two others.

I was having much better luck. I planned to leave the next day.

Saturday, September 19

A storm came up during the night. High winds churned up the bay and it was raining. There were no protective barrier islands, so I decided to lay over another day. I was nearing my final destination. As near as I could calculate, the distance from here to Miami was just about eight hundred miles away. There was no need to take chances.

A gentleman by the name of Tom Grey saw our two boats in the park and he came over to talk to us. When he learned what we were doing, he invited us to his house to spend the night so we wouldn't be out in the rain. He fixed us a chicken dinner and we spent the evening talking about the journey. Before night fell, I went back to the boat and packed it up to be ready to go in the morning.

Sunday, September 20

After sunup, we left Apalachicola Bay and entered St. George Sound. St. George Island was still protecting us. It was a little windy and a light rain was falling. Roy went on ahead to find a campsite. I didn't like that arrangement, but I hadn't thought of a way to let him know. It was especially bad because he didn't have charts of his own, so I had let him use mine. When I had given him my charts, I thought that we would be staying together. I really could have used them.

At five o'clock, I saw his boat pulled up on shore by the Island View Motel at Carrabelle. Roy had arranged for us to camp there for the night. They had given us a key to one of their empty units so we could take a shower.

Monday, September 21

The first stroke of the day hit the water at seven. Roy was staying back again. He wanted to shift some of his gear around and boil some eggs that he thought were going to spoil. At ten, I began to worry about him. The wind had piped up and I had to go ashore and install my spray skirt. The waves had been breaking over the top of me.

At noon, I beached the kayak and found a store and called back to the motel. I was afraid that Roy had gotten swamped and thought I might have to report him missing. The people at the motel told me that Roy hadn't left until ten. By the time I got back to my boat, Roy had made it to my location. He said that he had had trouble with the waves. He had to go ashore and cover his boat with a tarp. After he joined me, we continued on our way until we reached Shell Point. We camped overnight at the marina.

Tuesday, September 22

Again, I left before Roy, but in short order, he caught up. We didn't get very far. I had paddled about five miles when Roy's engine quit. We couldn't get it started so we returned to the marina. Roy took the engine apart and tried to fix it, but it still wouldn't start. By then it was dark. We had to stay there another night.

That is why I liked my body power; it wasn't very pretty, but it was functional and it never broke down. Well, hardly ever.

Wednesday, September 23

Roy took his engine into Tallahassee to either get it fixed, or get a new one. Florida had more insects than any state yet, especially that time of year. There is an insect that they called the love bug. They were mating and flying around, coupled together by the millions. They landed on my white tent for some reason or another, turning it absolutely black. They even flew in clouds over the water making it hard for a person to breathe.

The ants got into everything, and even though I covered my hands with insect repellent, the backs of them were beginning to look like raw hamburger paddies from digging those black bites out. I had not discovered what was doing it.

I would be glad when I was out of there. I made up my mind that I was going to leave the next day—with or without Roy. I was about a week behind where I thought I would be when I left Mobile Bay. The local television station and newspaper came out in the evening and interviewed me about my journey. The marina manager had called and told them about me.

Thursday, September 24

Roy called. He had bought a new out-board motor and would be back to the marina that afternoon. That meant that I would be held up another day. I took a shower, washed my clothes, and wrote some postcards out to my friends and family. If things worked out the way I wanted them to, I would be working up the west coast of the main Florida peninsula, and in six days I would be in the west coast Intracoastal Waterway. That was a happy thought.

Friday, September 25

I cleared the marina at seven o'clock and headed south by southwest. We studied the charts the night before and picked Rock Island as our next campsite. Rock Island wasn't the best selection; I had to go further, but the next possible campsite was just too far. The depth of the Gulf at this point was very shallow. I noticed a type of jellyfish that I had never seen before. For want of a better name, I called them canon ball jellyfish. They were round, and appeared to be quite solid. They ranged in size from a softball to nearly the size of a bowling ball. They didn't seem to have any means of locomotion; they didn't have an outer fringe of tentacles to drive them along. They just seemed to float, suspended above the bottom of the bay which was no more than four or five feet of depth. While I was at the marina, I had talked to a shrimp boat skipper about these jellyfish. He told me they were a real problem for shrimp fisherman because they would fill their nets and were difficult to get rid of.

Roy caught up with me at two o'clock. We made Rock Island at 4:45 pm and pitched our tents. The fly population was horrendous; millions of what looked like houseflies, but their bite was vicious. We had to get our tent up as quickly as we could, spray the inside with insecticide, and cover ourselves with repellent. We also had to prepare our meals inside the tent.

We had camped on the west end of the island. I ventured out to watch the setting sun. It was worth the insect bites. The setting sun was spectacular.

Saturday, September 26

We left Rock Island at eight am. That was a little late for me, but since I had been having trouble navigating without my charts, I wanted Roy to stay with me. Our destination was the Steinhatchee River that flowed into Deadman's Bay. It had an ominous ring to it. The Ideal Fish Camp was listed as being located there. The entire coastline was swamp, except where a river flowed in. We had to paddle up the river a ways to find a place to camp. The managers at the campsite were really nice and allowed us to camp on their property and use their showers.

Sunday, September 27

Once again I had to leave before Roy. I needed to leave as soon as it got daylight so as to have enough light to find the next campsite. Roy was supposed to catch up with me before I reached the entrance of the Suwannee River. During the day, there was no place to land so I had to eat my noon lunch in the cockpit.

Shortly after noon, I was paddling in about four feet of water when I noticed a rather large fish was following me. Then it rose up to the surface right next to my kayak. It was about half the length of the *Wind Dancer,* and it was a hammerhead shark. I had read that the gray nurse and the great white sharks were dangerous, but I couldn't remember anything about the hammerhead. But he was sure big and ugly.

I tried paddling away from him, but he followed and it looked like he was getting more excited. At that point, I tried another strategy. I stayed, still hoping he would just go away. That didn't work either. He started bumping the kayak with his nose; I guess to see if it was tender enough to bite. This guy was definitely making me nervous. It was time for me to try something else.

I shifted my hand on my paddles so that my left hand was next to the blade while my right hand was at the center of the paddle, then I lifted the paddle high over my head. I waited until the shark made his next pass, and then as he turned to swim away from the kayak, I brought the flat of the blade down as hard as I could just above his head.

KASPLAT! He took off like a rocket in one direction and I in the other. I think I broke the record for a quarter-mile sprint for a kayak before I ran out of steam. I kept paddling; and looked around and didn't see him anymore

When I reached the harbor, Roy wasn't there. I had studied the charts the night before and I knew I was in the right area, but I wasn't sure of the correct entrance. While I was studying the situation, a coast guard boat came in so I followed it thinking it would lead me to the right spot. It didn't.

Its dock was at a place called Salt Creek, which was west of the village of Suwannee. I found a place under a tree where I could pull my kayak up. Nearby, there was a footpath leading into the village; I walked there and found a fish camp, Moore's Suwannee Marina and Fish Camp, owned and operated by Charlie and Tammy Moore. It was dark by the time I got there.

I told Charlie and Tammy my tale of woe—I had lost my partner Roy. They got out two boats with searchlights and went looking for him. No luck. Finally a fisherman came by and said that he had seen Roy at another campsite. Charlie and Tammy allowed me to sleep on a couch in their office so I wouldn't have to go back and pitch a tent.

Monday, September 28

I joined Roy at Millers Campground. I found a channel from Salt Creek that led over to the Suwannee River where the campground was located. I had to wait for Roy to get ready. We had some open water to navigate and I needed access to my charts. We finally cleared his campsite at 7:30 am.

We paddled up the Suwannee River a short distance because there was a channel which led over to a bay farther to the southeast, which was a more direct route. It was there on the Suwannee that I saw my first manatee.

I have heard that these mammals were believed to have created the legend of the mermaids. How ancient sailors could see these creatures as beautiful women was beyond me. It just goes to show you what an imagination sailors have.

The relationship between me and Roy was a little cool. I had a few unkind words to say to him about his inability to stay with me. It was my own damn fault. I knew from the beginning that our two boats weren't compatible. It was never a good idea to pair up with a stranger on a cruise, either by kayak or sailboat, for any length of time.

As sweet and lovable as I am, I had never been able to find anyone that could handle me for any length of time. On this day Roy would paddle until I got about a quarter of a mile ahead of him, then he would fire up his engine and get about that far ahead of me, then he would paddle until once again I passed him. I didn't know how long this would last.

At about 1:30 pm, we came in sight of the resort area of Cedar Keys. We went in and made some food purchases and I filled my water jugs, after which we continued over to Atseno Otis Key, which is a deserted island with a nice beach that would be a good jumping-off point to reach the mainland the following day. We camped there for the night, but before I could pitch my tent I had to do a little repair work on it. One of the fiberglass rods had finally shattered completely. Using a section of a broken whip radio antenna that Roy had, and a piece of copper tubing which I crimped on the end of the antenna to get the right length, it worked. My poor tent had to last me at least three more weeks. It was getting a little ragged.

Cedar Keys

Cedar Keys off the West coast of Florida

I studied my charts that night. It was about twenty miles of open water between our islands across to Waccasassa Bay and then on to the Crystal River on the mainland. If I steered a 120-degree heading, I could hit it right on the head. My anger at Roy had subsided a little, so I decided to ease up on him. I wanted to get an early start. My worst fear was that I could get caught in a squall. The weather forecast for the following day was clear and calm. I told Roy I was going to leave before daylight, and that he could leave when he wanted to. I said there was a nuclear power plant at Crystal River and we would camp somewhere south of that power plant the next night. I left a snack out for my breakfast and packed everything else up, except my tent, air mattress, and sleeping bag, and retired for the night.

Tuesday, September 29

I don't know what time it was, but it was still dark outside when I ate my breakfast, broke camp, and packed the kayak. I drug it down to the beach and launched. The sky was filled with a million stars. The morning was still, with a promise of a good day. Since we had camped on the west side of the island, I had to swing around before I could pick up my desired heading. After paddling about thirty minutes, a faint pink glow appeared on the horizon ahead of me. I paused in my paddling to take a picture.

A few more minutes passed and the rising sun balanced itself on the eastern horizon.

Sun Rise

Sunrise over the Gulf of Mexico

It was such a beautiful sight, I stopped paddling to watch. As I sat there transfixed by the beauty of it, a string of Florida brown pelicans flying in a single file from north to south flew right through the center of it. I made a mad grab for my camera to get the picture, a picture that would be the picture of a lifetime. But, by the time I got my camera up to my eye, they were gone. But I took the picture anyway, getting the bow of the *Wind Dancer* in the picture to testify that I had observed the rising sun above the Gulf of Mexico.

About noon I stopped paddling for a while and ate my midday snack. The winds were calm, and I couldn't have picked a better day to make that crossing. I had been apprehensive about it for many days and now I was about to put my worries behind me. I paddled about an hour longer when I had four more visitors. A pod of dolphins joined me. I must say they were a hell of a lot more welcome than that damn hammerhead shark from a couple of days ago. They played around the boat for about fifteen minutes and then got bored and left me. I guess I wasn't fast enough for them.

About four o'clock I heard the buzzing of an outboard motor. Roy had caught up to me. We took up the same pattern of travel that we had the day before. He would paddle with me for a while, and when he fell behind, he'd catch up with his engine. This didn't last long though. At 5:30 pm, we reached a very nice campground just south of Crystal River. The strange thing was that it was deserted. Florida people must not be much on camping. It had toilets and an outdoor fresh water shower. There was no hot water, but who needs it? Being able to have a shower after a hard day's paddle is a shear luxury. We camped for the night.

Wednesday, September 30

We left Crystal River at eight. Roy stayed with me much the same way we had been doing the past few days. We were getting closer and closer to the ICW (Intracoastal Waterway) and it was becoming increasingly difficult to find camping sites. We found one at the Bay Port County Park at 6:30. We were lucky to get our tents up before dark. For the past few days I had been keeping my fingers crossed. The national weather radio service had been predicting a weather front coming in. I wanted to get into the ICW before it hit.

Thursday, October 1

I woke up to a light rain. The cold front had finally arrived. I got up, had my breakfast, packed up, and got under way as quickly as I could. At about 6:30, I headed toward Tarpon Springs. I had to leave without Roy again. He just couldn't get moving in the mornings.

During the day, the weather worsened. I was hit by one squall after another, but not any of the squalls were as bad as the ones that I had encountered in the northern states. Again Roy hadn't caught up with me. I had to navigate with a road map and a Florida county map which didn't tell me a damn thing about the coastline. I got trapped behind peninsulas and paddled around islands that with the correct maps, I could have gone between. I was as angry as hell. Roy had my navigation charts again.

In spite of my problems, I punched right through the squalls and reached Tarpon Springs at five o'clock. I found a city park with a shower. I looked out into the harbor and recognized a sailboat belonging to Steve and Lajune Neal. I had met them in Apalachicola. They had also met Roy.

Before I set up camp, I paddled out to their boat. I told them that he was missing and that he was supposed to meet me here. Steve suggested that we take his dingy and go out and look for Roy. After an hour, we gave up when we couldn't find him. We went into Tarpon Springs for dinner. Tarpon Springs is a quaint little Greek fishing village that somehow got plucked out of Greece and transplanted on the west coast of Florida. It was the most authentic Greece village I had ever seen; it had Greek restaurants, pastry shops, and shops with natural sponges in piles on the sidewalk. I was really impressed. I made up my mind that someday I would bring Ruth to see it.

When we got back to their boat, Roy was still nowhere to be seen. Lajune and Steve invited me to stay on their boat so I wouldn't have to pitch my tent.

Friday, October 2

That morning I waited four hours at Steve's boat for Roy. When he didn't show up, I asked Steve to call the marina on his VHF radio and tell them that if Roy showed up to tell him that I had gone on. I just couldn't wait any longer.

When eleven o'clock came around and he didn't show up, I got worried about him and went to a Coast Guard station and reported him missing. I was afraid that he had gotten caught in one of those squalls and swamped. After that I called Rick in Portland to tell him where I was and to ask him to try to find a place for me to stay.

Rick told me that Roy had called him and said he had gone into a marina and camped because of the storms. So, I continued on my way. I wanted to make St. Petersburg before nightfall. Under the circumstances, I had a hell of a time finding the entrance to the waterway, but I succeeded. Roy had my maps.

Around four o'clock, I stopped at a marina and asked where I could find a place to stay for the night; I was in an area that offered no place to camp. They told me the location of a motel and I continued on my way. After about an hour, a big Chris-Craft motorboat pulled up and hailed me. The captain had a message from Roy. He said that Roy was about four miles behind me and wanted me to wait for him.

The skipper of the boat was Bill Shaffer, a real nice gentleman. I asked him what time it was because my watch had quit. I told him there was something about my body chemistry that ate watches. That was the fourth watch that had quit on me this trip. Bill pulled his watch off and handed it to me. I told him I didn't want his watch, I just wanted to know what time it was. He laughed and said I could keep it. Bill pointed me to a Mc Donald's and said he would buy me a hamburger and a cup of coffee, then he and his friend would find Roy. That sounded like a real winner to me. It would give me a chance to call Rick again.

I didn't get Rick, but I did reach his father. He told me that Roy and I were booked for the following night at the Trade Wind Hotel, which was located right on the Tampa Bay shore. By the time I finished the call, Bill was back with Roy. It was decided—without too much input from me—that we would take the two boats over to Bill's house. Bill had three slips in front of his home, which was right on a channel. Roy and I would stay overnight with Karl Weisser, the other fellow that was helping us. The two of them were at the marina where Roy had inquired about me. So, everything worked out just fine. The next day we would move to the Trade Wind.

Saturday, October 3

That morning I got Karl and Roy up at 6:30 AM. We were invited to Bill Schaffer's home for coffee, and then we were all going out into the gulf, me in the *Wind Dancer* and the others in a boat. Brad Billings, the public relations man for the Trade Winds, had arranged for the news media to witness my arrival at the hotel at 10:00 AM. So that's the way I played it.

I landed on their beach right on time, but the news people didn't arrive until an hour later. So I paddled around out in the bay, waiting for them. I wondered if the Native Americans had staged an arrival for the Narváez landing...probably not. A shower of arrows probably greeted him. I made my landing, the photographer took my picture, and I was interviewed. Of course, that drew a crowd of spectators.

When it was over, they gave us a room and treated us to lunch at the Flying Bridge Restaurant. That night, one of the spectators called the room and took us out to a seafood dinner. It was a very luxurious hotel—$250 a night. It was lucky for me that it was complementary. I could never have afforded to stay there otherwise.

At nine that night, Ruth called. She was booking her flight to Miami for the thirteenth. I sure hoped that she wouldn't bring her meat cleaver. She had been threatening to part my hair with it for years.

Sunday, October 4

With all the hoopla the day before, I didn't get everything done that I needed to do, so it was necessary for me to lay over a day. This was getting hairy.

Ruth would be getting into Miami in ten more days and I had over four hundred miles to go. But it couldn't be helped. There were two other items of interest that were making me nervous. One, of immediate concern, was a weather front to the southwest that would be pulling northeasterly winds across the bay the next day. And the second, one thousand miles to the southeast of the Caribbean was a tropical low-pressure system building. It was traveling at a rate of two hundred miles a day on a northwesterly course. Believing in "Murphy's Law", I knew that the tropical depression would become a hurricane and hit the tip of Florida just as I got there.

That morning when we went to breakfast, another of the spectators picked up the bill. We were still getting the royal treatment. The rest of the day I completed getting my supplies. The next day the journey would continue.

Monday, October 5

I went down to the *Wind Dancer* to launch and go across the Bay. When I arrived, Roy informed me he wasn't going with me. Roy knew that I was pissed about the way things were going. I didn't understand why he wanted to go with me in the first place. I guessed he was just along for the ride. The stress of worrying about him had me wound up tighter than an eight-day clock. I was sorry we weren't parting friends. I really owed him for his hospitality at Mobile Bay. I got my charts packed up and left.

I had my spray skirt on, my life jacket, and an inflatable bladder fastened to my right paddle blade to help me stabilize. There was a twenty-knot gale blowing which kicked up three to five feet of breaking seas. I was really getting hammered. Maybe Roy realized he wouldn't have been able to make it. I was thankful that he hadn't tried it.

Twice, I nearly broached. I decided to change tactics. Instead of quartering it, I swung the bow dead into the wind and retracted the rudder. I paddled just hard enough to control the kayak and punch through the incoming waves on a northeasterly course. The ICW was in the southeastern corner of the bay. The wind pushed me right into the entrance. I tried this technique in one of the big lakes up in North Dakota and it worked, and it worked again here.

It took me three hours to make the seven-mile trip across the bay; the most dangerous seven miles of my journey. Once inside the waterway, the waves were reduced to rough chop, but they were easier to manage.

With the wind behind me, I made good time. I continued and crossed the Sarasota Bay. It was believed to be the staging area of both Narváez and de Soto's expeditions. That left me only the large bay at Port Charlotte. I made good time in spite of the rough water and high wind. I covered a little more than forty-five miles. I camped for the night at Stock Way Point at mileage marker seventy on the ICW. That was a good campsite with a marina and a restaurant nearby. I was getting short of food, but I didn't want to stock more. There were few stores close to shore where I could shop. It was cheaper to eat at restaurants than shop.

Tuesday, October 6

After I left Stock Way Point, I had paddled a few miles when I met a gentleman out rowing a racing shell. That was the first rowboat I had encountered on my trip. I had seen two white water kayaks and five canoes, but this was the first rowboat. He hailed me, so I stopped to chat. His name was Phil Moore; he lived on the water.

Phil invited me to follow him home and have breakfast with him. When someone offers a meal, I stop. While I was there, he asked me to stop at Venus for an interview with the newspaper. He called them and they explained where I should land. They would meet me on the waterway. Am I a publicity hound? I guess so. The stop cost me about four hours. Therefore, I only made about thirty miles. I found a campsite beside a bridge where there was a boat ramp. The road noise was bad, but I had camped at worse places.

Wednesday, October 7

I left the boat ramp as soon as it was light enough for me to see. I paddled across Charlotte Harbor and into the ICW. Ruth and I had visited there in 1985. She liked the area very much, especially the city of Boca Grande. I paddled under the very bridge that we had driven over on that trip. I camped that night on a romantic little island called South Bank Key, located at the north end of Sanibel Island. I set up camp early in the afternoon . After I got my tent up, I went for a swim. The water was nice but salty. I used a little of my fresh water to sponge off the salt water, then I fixed my evening meal.

Now I had a decision to make. My original plan was to follow Ponce de Leon's route around the tip of Florida. From the map of his journey, this seemed to be near the place where he received the Seminole arrow that killed him. But now I had to reassess my plan, which was hard for me to do because once I set a program, virtually nothing could change me. However, since I left St. Petersburg, I had been monitoring the approach of the tropical storm brewing in the Atlantic. It was still on track with the Caribbean. It packed sustained winds exceeding seventy-five miles an hour, and had been upgraded to a category one hurricane. It was three days from Cuba; one more day and it could hit the southern tip of Florida.

The southern tip of Florida is one massive swamp with thousands of mangrove islands. There is only one town in two hundred miles. To paddle through that area on a good day would be life threatening; in a hurricane it would be detrimental to my health. People had told me that I had more guts than brains, but I'm not suicidal. I was on a collision course with Hurricane Floyd.

South Bank Key was just ten miles west of the mouth of the Caloosahatchee River. It is part of the ICW to Lake Okeechobee and St. Lucie channel, which come out at Stuart on the east coast. At that point I would intersect Ponce de Leon's route. According to my map of his journey, he had landed somewhere just north of what is now St. Augustine. I could turn south and still travel a hundred miles of his route to Miami. The next day I would head to Fort Myers and the Caloosahatchee River. I would race Floyd to Stuart. If I really pushed, I could reach there by the tenth of October. That is the day my calculations predicted it would hit. I would find shelter and ride it out.

As I made my approach to the key, I was paddling in about four feet of water. The water was crystal clear. I happened to look over the side and I was fortunate to see four small Manta rays, only twelve to eighteen inches from wing tip to wing tip, swimming in single file. A few minutes later, I saw one a little larger. It was two to three feet from tip to tip, light gray in color with spots like a leopard. I am fascinated by wildlife.

CHAPTER 13
FLORIDA INTRACOASTAL WATERWAY - EAST

Thursday, October 8

When I arrived at Mileage Marker 130 on the Okeechobee Waterway, the South Bank Key was uninhabited except for the sea birds and me. The call of the gulls awoke me that morning. I quickly broke camp and headed across the bay to the mouth of the Caloosahatchee River. It's called the Okeechobee Waterway. I pushed right by the city of Fort Myers. Six miles east of Fort Myers, I pulled into a marina on the north side of the river. I wanted to get more supplies before I continued.

I checked with the marina manager for the location of the nearest store. She had watched me paddle in. She told me she had never seen a craft like that on the waterway before and wanted to know where I was from. I gave her a rundown of my journey, and then departed to look for the store she had given me the direction to. When I returned to the marina the manager asked me to wait. She had called the two television stations at Fort Myers and they were sending a team out to get my story. While I waited, I got into a conversation with the skipper of a sixty-five-foot motor yacht that was moored there.

I stopped there at about three PM, and by the time the interview was over, it was nearly five o'clock. I was rather amused at the way the interview was conducted. The reporter was a young fellow; I guessed in his mid twenties. He asked me to let him paddle the kayak. While he paddled around, he demonstrated to his camera crew what I told him about the *Wind Dancer*. He had quite a time with it.

By the time the interview was over, it was too late for me to go on. The skipper of the motor yacht invited me to stay overnight on his boat. I readily accepted. The next possible campsite was at LaBelle which was over thirty miles away. Now that would be my destination for the next day. My Okeechobee Waterway charts were marked off in five-mile increments starting from Stuart. Since I was at mileage 130, I would have to make over forty miles a day over the next three days in order to beat Floyd to Stuart. That was a tall order.

Friday, October 9

I left the yacht at six in the morning and had breakfast at a little Greek restaurant near the marina, then got underway as quickly as I could. The weather was still quite nice at that point, but I knew it was about to change. When I entered the channel, it was quite narrow. The trees on either side hung their branches over the water. That is where I observed the strangest bird I had ever seen. It roosted on the branches that overhung the canal at a height of fifteen to twenty feet. It had a small squat body, not much larger than a wood duck. Its feet were webbed and the legs were short, but it had a long neck like a heron. As it sat on a branch, it would weave its head from side to side like a snake. In fact, when I first saw one that is what I thought it was. But as I watched, I saw that it was a bird. It blended in with the trees, so I really couldn't tell what color it was. Since I didn't have my binoculars with me, I couldn't inspect it. It didn't dive like a gannet or pelican. When I got within fifty feet, it would cast itself off the branch and seemingly just fall into the water. Immediately upon hitting the water, it disappeared. It was an underwater swimmer. I never did see it fly. Obviously it could, otherwise it wouldn't get that high in the trees.

About dark, I reached La Belle. I found a riverside park and camped for the night.

Saturday, October 10

During the night, I had the first negative encounter with the local population; although, at the time I didn't know the nature of the problem. After dark had set in and I was in my sleeping bag, I kept hearing and feeling a heavy object hit my tent. I would get up and look out to see what was happening but I didn't see anything. I would lie back down and in a few minutes it would happen again. This went on until long after midnight and then it stopped.

When morning came and I started to tear down my tent, I realized what had happened. Just behind my tent site was a twenty-foot embankment and a parking lot. Some rowdies had parked up there drinking beer. They had used my tent as a target for their empty beer bottles. After I got my tent and gear all packed away, I picked up the empties and put them in the trashcan. There must have been twenty bottles. I didn't want people to think I was responsible for all those empties.

As soon as I completed the task, I continued my journey. The weather, which had been quite nice, had changed. The sky was dark and ominous and I was being battered by high winds and rainsqualls. Between mileage markers 95 and 90, I passed through a set of locks. Fortunately, I was alone on the canal so I didn't have to wait for anyone. I guess I was the only one dumb enough to be out on a day like that.

I entered into the Okeechobee Lake at Moore Haven. The canal continued around the southern rim of the lake. It was quite beautiful. The banks were lined with alligators and exotic birds. It looked like a jungle river. I wished the weather had been a little better so I could enjoy it more. But I had to push on as fast as I could if I wanted to get across that lake before the hurricane hit. It looked like it was gaining on me.

I reached Clewiston at mileage marker 65 just as it was getting dark. I had really cut it close. I found a regular campground that had a fee to camp, but no one was there to take my money, so I just found a high spot to pitch my tent. They had forecast heavy rains for that night. I had a hell of a time getting my tent up in the high winds. I got it up all right, but my little tent was taking a beating. That night I fixed my evening meal inside the tent.

Sunday, October 11

I arose early, broke camp, and left Clewiston before daylight. During the night, the weather had dumped four inches of rain on me. I was surprised that the tent kept me dry. I followed the rim canal until it emerged into the lake about fifteen miles from the entrance to the St. Lucie Canal. That put me in the open lake. I had to paddle like hell to make any headway at all. I was within a mile of a marina at Pahokee. I could see it in the distance but it took me over an hour to get there. I reached it at two pm, which was too early to quit; I was still twelve miles from my destination for the day. I took out my road map and found that Highway 441 followed the edge of the lake. It was time for me to put the wheels under the kayak and continue my journey by land.

Twenty-five knots of wind hit my chest and stopped me cold. Then came the rain; it driven by the high winds in sheets so heavy I could hardly see. I didn't even try to keep dry. I just kept sloshing along, not even bothering to avoid the deep puddles. My goal was the Cypress Lodge, which I was told was at the entrance to the St. Lucie Canal. I was hoping they would have a vacant room. I walked on, pulling the kayak behind me.

A car pulled up beside me; inside the car were Ed and Shirley Warner. They asked me if they could tow my kayak behind their car and invited me to spend the night with them. They lived at Canal Point, just a mile from the entrance to the canal. I declined their offer of the tow but accepted the night's stay. They told me they knew there had to be a story connected with a man pulling a kayak down a road in weather like that. They drove off and I continued down the road.

After thirty minutes, I met a young boy on a bicycle. He was their son. They sent him back to guide me to their home.

A hot shower, dry clothes, and a bowl of clam chowder improved my outlook immensely. The Warners put me up in their motor home which was parked behind their house. I was one day ahead of Floyd. I wondered when my luck was going to run out.

Monday, October 12

I left Ed and Shirley's home at six that morning. They accompanied me to the ramp leading down into the canal, thus avoiding the lock. The high banks on either side of the ditch protected me somewhat from the high winds, but I was still being subjected to the heavy rains. Hurricane Floyd had stalled over Cuba, so it might give me another day before it hit. I was still in the race to Stuart. If I could make it there before nightfall, I would be able to find shelter.

There were several alligators along the banks, but they seemed to be afraid of the *Wind Dancer*. At least, they didn't bother me. The exotic birds hunkered down in the trees and didn't fly when I came by. Even the serpent bird stayed put. I increased my stroke to sixty to seventy strokes per minute and tucked my head down. I covered the forty miles in record time.

I arrived in Stuart in the late afternoon. I was held up at the locks for fifteen minutes. They dropped me down a few feet, and when the gates opened, I emerged into the harbor. I paddled a short distance until I was clear of the gates and paused a minute to get my bearings. Immediately, I was hailed by what appeared to be a forty-foot motor yacht. John and Mary Andrew, an elderly couple (my age), had brought their boat down to the harbor to watch the yachts exit the locks to escape the hurricane. They were surprised to see my tiny, peanut-sized craft come out. They asked me where I came from. They stared at me in disbelief when I told them that I had come from the Pacific coast and had crossed the continent in 198 days.

I was impatient to get under way because I needed to find a place to stay for the night. I asked them if there was a hotel nearby where I could hole up until the storm passed. I still had to go another hundred miles to Miami. They told me to follow them. Their home was on the old St. Lucie River channel just a mile from where they were anchored.

All across the continent I had bragged about making the crossing without a support team, but the truth was, the whole blessed country had turned out to be my support team. With Rick back in Portland, and the kindness and generosity of the people along the way, I was cared for and pampered more than if I had had an organized support team. I hadn't thought about that before.

I followed them over to their home, pulled my kayak up into their yard, and secured it as best as I could. We spent the rest of the afternoon putting up sheets of plywood over his windows. I could tell they had been through hurricanes before. The sheets of plywood had that well-used look.

In the evening after dinner, John brought out a large map of United States and a marking pen and asked me to me to mark the route I followed and write down the waterways I used. He was very interested in my journey. The rest of the evening, we watched the weather broadcasts to see what Hurricane Floyd was going to do. I turned in for the night. I wanted to get an early start the following day if it was possible.

Tuesday, October 13

I got up at six am as quietly as I could. I didn't want to wake John and Mary. I didn't even turn on my weather radio. I looked out the window. The wind was blowing hard and the rain was still coming down, but no worse than what I had handled before. So I went for it. I was determined to get as far as I could. Nothing, not even a hurricane, can stop old Captain Karl from his destination.

I paddled all day, keeping as close to the west side of the ICW as I could. I was paralleling the course taken by Ponce de Leon as he sailed south when he left what is now St. Augustine, and I would be until I reached Miami. Because of the storm, there was very little boat traffic. That was a blessing. Those damn Florida cigarette boats were a pain in the ass. Most of them would slow down or move far enough that their wake wouldn't bother me, but others would come blasting by so close that they would nearly capsize me. All I could do was brace and curse.

I made about forty-five miles passing North Palm Bay and reached Peanut Island. There was a campsite there. It was a little soggy, but I could manage. My poor tent was a basket case. It was still sopping wet from the soaking it got at Clewiston. But it kept the wind out and the rain off my head.

Floyd had passed Miami and headed for the Bahamas, but there were still plenty of backlashes from it. I was thinking at the time that this would be my last campout. If I could arrange it, I would try to find a motel for the night the next day. I had enough funds left over and I could afford it.

Wednesday, October 14

I was awake at five o'clock. I sat cross-legged on my sleeping bag and fixed my breakfast.

Around midnight, I had heard vandals breaking into my kayak. I got up to investigate. Two raccoons were ransacking it. I chased them away, but they soon came back. They took out my toilet kit and squeezed out my toothpaste, the damn little rascals. I got up and threw some rocks at them. They finally took the hint and left. After I finished my breakfast, I tore down my tent and stuffed it into a nearby trashcan. It was in shambles. The fiberglass rods were all broken, the rain fly was torn and patched with duct tape, and the door was laced in with fish line. I was lucky it had lasted that long.

When I left the island at about 6:30, it was still dark. I didn't have charts for the Atlantic ICW but I had talked to a yachtsman the day before who told me not to worry, all I had to do was follow the navigation markers and I couldn't get lost. It was so dark that I couldn't see the proper heading and I followed the wrong markers, which lead me right out to sea. I didn't realize it until I was being hit with five-foot breaking seas. I turned around and found my way back in. I hailed a guy in a fishing boat and he pointed out the proper markers, then I was alright.

I paddled throughout the day, right up until seven that evening, at which time I reached the city of Deerfield. I found the Hilbroa Marina and pulled the *Wind Dancer* up on the seawall, and took a piece of chain and a lock and locked it to a tree. I walked across the street to a motel. I got a room for the night for twenty-five dollars. After I took a shower and put on some dry clothes, I walked to a Howard Johnson restaurant because all of my store-bought food was gone. The restaurant was running a special: all the fish you could eat for $4.95.

When I got back to the motel, I called Rick. He told me that the news media in Miami wanted me to stop at the Marriott Hotel on the waterway by a Phillips 66 refueling station in Fort Lauderdale. They said it would be easy for me to find. He also gave me Ruth's phone number at the hotel where she was staying so I could call her. When I called Ruth, she wasn't in so I left a message for her to meet me at the Marriott in Fort Lauderdale. With that accomplished, I turned in for the night.

The journey was about to end.

Thursday, October 15

My body was programmed to awake at 4:30 every morning, plus or minus fifteen minutes. However, I was in no hurry to get started, even though I was pretty excited about finishing my journey. I took my time. According to my calculations, I only had to travel fifteen miles. The last few days on the ICW I had been averaging four miles an hour without really trying. I called Ruth's hotel and left a message for her that I would be arriving at two o'clock, and then I walked across the street to the restaurant for breakfast.

With breakfast out of the way, I returned to the *Wind Dancer* and pulled it over to the seawall to launch. Before launching, I emptied all my equipment and inspected it for serviceability. I trashed everything except my clothes and sleeping bag. Even my air mattress wouldn't hold air anymore. Then I launched, slipped into the cockpit, and began paddling. I was running about a hundred pounds lighter and the *Wind Dancer* was moving easily.

It was like she knew she was on the homestretch.

I had paddled a little over three hours and felt that I was getting close to my destination when I came upon a young man on a jet ski. I hailed him. He came over to see what I wanted. I asked him where the Marriott Hotel was. He informed me that it was only a mile away. The time was 1:45 pm. I asked him if he would go to it and see if there was a short blonde woman standing on the dock with a camera. If there was, he should tell her I would be there in fifteen minutes. Then I explained what the occasion was. He took off with a roar. In a few minutes he was back.

Ruth was there with a news photographer from the *Miami Herald* and a television crew. By that time, I had them in sight. While Ruth took a picture of me coming in, I took one of her waiting on the dock. We greeted each other. The long journey was completed.

The two news teams got their story and left. Ruth and I didn't have much to say to one another.

At that time there were still a couple of items that needed to be taken care of. We went to our room. I called Rick and told him it was finished. He said that he was picking up the cost of my trip back to Portland. That was a terrific break for me. Next, I had to arrange to get the *Wind Dancer* shipped back to Portland, Oregon.

I went to the yellow pages and let my fingers do the walking. I called a trucking firm. They would come the next morning and pick it up. Then Ruth and I went to dinner. I had not eaten since early morning. During dinner we talked. Ruth decided that she would stay married to me one more day. That was an ongoing joke with us. Each morning Ruth would decide to stay married to me for just one more day. I could relax; nothing had changed between us.

We only had a one-day stay at the Marriott so we would have to move to a less expensive motel. Ruth had rented a car at the airport. Our plan was to go back to the motel in Deerfield; it was in our budget and was a nice place with a beach. We would have a ten-day vacation.

That night when I undressed to go to bed, Ruth took one look at me and cried, "Karl, you look like a skeleton." My ribs stuck out like bars on a xylophone. I had lost forty pounds. My body fat must have been less than five percent, but I felt spry as could be. Except for the badly blistered feet going over the mountains and lapsing into a trance on Lake Fort Peck, I had suffered no medical problems on my entire trip. Not a sneeze, cough, or a headache.

To summarize my journey, I had risen from sea level to an elevation of 6,325 feet, traveled from north to south from Williston, North Dakota, to the Gulf of Mexico, and from west to east from sea to shining sea; a distance of 5,111 miles in 201 days and seven hours, averaging thirty miles a day on actual travel days. I saw scenery that most Americans have only heard about in the words of a song. I observed the purple mountains' majesty, gazed across the fruited plains, and paddled the wild and scenic Missouri River. I watched the sun rise over the Gulf of Mexico and visited the bayous and swamps of the Deep South.

To date, the *Wind Dancer* is the only boat to follow the trail blazed by the seven earliest explorers across what is now the continental United States, in its near five hundred years of history—propelled by one old man over sixty-one years old.

Journeys End

Journeys End 5111 miles traveled

CHAPTER 14
THE RIPPLES ON THE POND

In my youth, I had a deep respect for my teachers, and I still do. However, I didn't always learn as much as they would have liked me to. But I always considered what they had to say. I had my own unique of way of programming into my mind the information they gave me. I filed it away in four compartments: probable, possible, possible but improbable, and highly improbable.

I avoided both ends of absolute positive and negative, except two items. These concepts were carved in stone.

- Number one: nothing could be created or destroyed, only the form changed. Like energy to matter and matter to energy.

- Number two: every occurrence in the universe was brought about by two factors of cause and effect.

In a high school science class in 1943, it was explained to me that the energy from even a whisper would propagate out through the cosmos to be added to other forces there to be the cause of some future effect. This information was filed away in my mind in the possible but improbable basket, but I kept it in my mind for further study.

When spring came after that class, I went for a hike in a wilderness area in central Idaho. As I walked along the trail and emerged from the forest into a meadow about the size of a football field, the center of the clearing contained a pool of water fed by a spring from the side of the mountain. It was midday. I sat down on a log and proceeded to eat the lunch I had with me. It was a pleasant day in April 1943. I was just three weeks away from joining the navy. The whole world was in chaos with wars on nearly every continent.

But here in the meadow, it was like a paradise. The field was full of wild flowers, birds flitted from tree to tree, and a chipmunk or two scampered about. The pond was still. Not a bubble disturbed it surface. Sitting on the log, I bent forward and picked up a small stone about the size of a quarter. Balancing it on my thumb, I flipped it, lofting it up in an arc over the pool and it fell with a plop in the center of the pond. Immediately, the surface sprang into action. Ring after ring, the wavelets traveled outward to lap repeatedly on the bank. As I watched the action, the amplitude of the waves got less and less and the period between the ripple got wider and wider until within a short time the pond was once again still. However, the ripples continued in my mind.

If it was true what my science teacher told me, the lapping of the ripples would add their weight to the energy present in the cosmos to be the cause to some future event. I tumbled this idea in my head for a while and came to the same conclusion as I did before—possible but improbable. Then, I continued on my way. That event occurred over sixty years ago. Why that thought logged itself in my memory, I don't know. That sometimes happens to me. An odd thought will continue to bother me, especially when I can't resolve it.

It is now April 16, 2003. It has been sixteen years since I made my journey across the continental United States. In that period, I have watched the effect that the wake of the *Wind Dancer* has made on the events of the world.

When I arrived back in Portland from Miami, Rick, my partner in this adventure, arranged a news conference for me on the west bank of the Willamette River near the athletic club where I worked. Two or three television crews showed up and a couple of newspaper reporters. One of them was Barnes C. Ellis, a staff reporter for the *Oregonian*. He wrote a very good, comprehensive account of my journey. His story was picked up by the Associated Press and published worldwide, even as far away as Shanghai, China, where a retired teacher, Mr. Zuo Bang Peng, from the Shanghai Senior High School, seized upon it.

Zuo Bang Peng wrote me a letter inviting me to come to China and bicycle with him across China. What amazed me about his letter was the address he had put together from the article. The letter was addressed to: Mr. C Adams, an old famous hero who just traveled over America by boat, managerial of a car park, Portland U.S.A. No state, no zip code, and no street address, but that letter reached me in two weeks.

I accepted his invitation and wrote him back. Zuo Bang Peng then sent me a formal invitation written in Chinese that I could use to petition the Chinese government for a visa. No matter whom I wrote to at the embassy, the consulate, or the Ministry of Foreign Affairs, the results were the same: *NOTHING*. Sending a letter to the Chinese government was like sending a letter to a black hole; nothing emerges, not even a ray of light.

Out of shear desperation, I sent my petition to Mr. Peng to see what he could do from his end. He got on his bicycle in the dead of winter and peddled to Beijing carrying my request for a visa. He carried it from office to office only to be told there was no precedent for it, and therefore, it couldn't be done.

During this time, Charley and I would discuss these proceedings in the club hot tub just as we had done in planning my journey. I gave Mr. Peng Charley's address and the three of us then formed what we jokingly called the Three Musketeers. One for all and all for one, and that became the cause of the next effect.

In December 1990, Nichols D. Kristof, a *New York Times* foreign correspondent, wrote an article about the problems China was having with their education program. Featured in that story was a twelve-year-old peasant girl. She was the top student in her class but she was about to drop out of school. The article stated that, "Tuition at the school is the equivalent of thirteen dollars a year, including room and board. In this village of a few dozen mud brick homes, that is a large sum—especially to spend on a daughter." The average income for the village was only about sixty dollars a year.

The young girl was about to be swallowed by the dragon of poverty. I could not let that happen. I gathered a little money together and sent it to her to keep her in school. Other people read the article. They too sent money to China to keep her in school, but the money they sent was stopped by the Chinese bureaucrats and was supposedly portioned out to all the students. Very little, if any, went of the money donated went to benefit little Dai Manju. However, I had an advantage over the other donors. I had made my money order payable to Mr. Zuo Bang Peng and cut the article out of the paper and sent it to him. I had instructed him to find the girl and see to it she got to go to school.

When Mr. Peng got the money order and the article, cashed it, put the money in his pocket, and went down to the Shanghai harbor. He jumped on a riverboat and traveled up the Yangtze River to Hubei Province. He then hiked back into the mountains and found Yejuao, Dai Manju's village. He went to her school and paid her tuition for the rest of the time she would remain there. He stayed a few days with Dai Manju's family and became her mentor.

Meanwhile, back in the hot tub at the Willamette Athletic Club, I explained to my friend Charley what I was doing. He volunteered to help me. We formed a syndicate; we would keep the dragon of poverty from getting Dai Manju.

In 1991, Dai Manju won an award for an essay she had written. She went to Beijing to receive her award but she didn't get a scholarship. As the years went by, Mr. Peng would make periodic trips to tutor her for her final exams. She became the first in her family to graduate from elementary school.

Dia's

Beijing essay award 91

In 1995, the dragon of poverty raised his ugly head again. Dai Manju had passed her entrance exams for the university, but neither she nor her extended family could raise the tuition fee. She got in touch with her mentor and informed him of her problem. He immediately wrote us explaining the situation.

In our next hot tub meeting, Charley and I decided to split the tuition and we would join Mr. Peng in sharing her monthly living expenses. We quickly informed Mr. Peng of our decision and left it up to him to work out the numbers with Mr. Hu, the university president.

Miss Dai Manju entered the university in 1995, taking a three-year program in computer science.

Ms. Manju

Enters university in 95

Shortly after that, another disaster struck Dai Manju's family; a severe mountain storm destroyed their mud brick home. Mr. Peng and Charley joined forces and help them financially to rebuild their home out of concrete blocks instead of mud. I was out wondering the world and didn't get involved in this undertaking. During those years, Ruth and I were sailing the Caribbean, the Sea of Cortez, and exploring the Yucatan Peninsula. We had also bicycled for seven months on six of the South Pacific's major islands; for I am a born wanderer.

Daxon

Mr. Zuo Bang Peng on his bicycle trek across China

In 1997 it became clear that China was never going to grant me a visa, and Mr. Peng and I were not getting any younger. We were now in our seventies. If he was to do his journey, he should do it then, and he did. Mr. Zuo Bang Peng, following or closely paralleling the ancient silk route, pedaled his bicycle across China, realizing his dream.

In 1998 Dai Manju graduated from the university with a certificate of completion in computer science. Dai Manju is now a computer programmer for a firm in southern China, realizing her dream. In 1999 Charley brought Mr. Peng to America for a three-month visit.

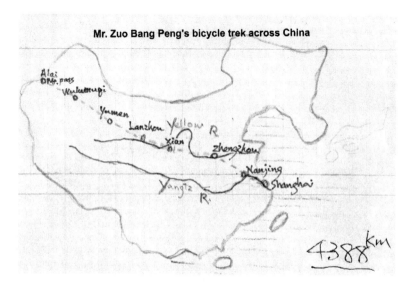

Mr. Zuo Bang Peng's bicycle trek across China

Is that then the end of the *Wake of the Wind Dancer?* Nope! While we, the participants that brought about the wake, will eventually loose our identity, the *Wake of the Wind Dancer* has caused a minute shift in the space–time continuum which will continue radiating out through the cosmos to become the cause for future events like the ripples on the pond.

Now, if I gather enough coins to purchase another sailboat—I had to sell my beloved Sea Venture—I will go sailing, which is what I wanted to do since I was ten years old.

Wake of the Wind Dancer

Charles, Daxon, & Karl

The three Muskateers in America

THE CONTINUUM

269

ABOUT THE AUTHOR

Karl Adams was born in Idaho, but now lives in Oregon. He served five years in the U.S. Navy during WWII and eighteen years in the U.S. Army during the Korean War. At eighty-three, his travels and this unique life-long adventure still continues, often with his wife of forty-seven years by his side.

CPSIA information can be obtained at www.ICGtesting.com
Printed in the USA
BVOW072318120412

287561BV00001B/55/P